D. A. Pennebaker: Interviews

Conversations with Filmmakers Series
Gerald Peary, General Editor

D. A. Pennebaker

INTERVIEWS

Edited by Keith Beattie and Trent Griffiths

University Press of Mississippi / Jackson

www.upress.state.ms.us

The University Press of Mississippi is a member
of the Association of American University Presses.

First printing 2014
∞
Library of Congress Cataloging-in-Publication Data

Pennebaker, D. A.
 D. A. Pennebaker: interviews / edited by Keith Beattie and Trent Griffiths.
   pages cm. — (Conversations with filmmakers series)
 Includes index.
 Includes filmography.
  ISBN 978-1-62846-202-9 (cloth : alk. paper) — ISBN 978-1-62674-510-0 (ebook)
 1. Pennebaker, D. A.—Interviews. 2. Motion picture producers and directors
 ISBN 978-1-4968-5792-7 (paperback)
—United States—Interviews. 3. Cinematographers—United States—Interviews.
I. Beattie Keith, 1954– editor. II. Griffiths, Trent, editor. III. Title.
 PN1998.3.P45255A3 2015
 791.4302'33092—dc23
                        2014042292

British Library Cataloging-in-Publication Data available

Contents

The Filmmaking of D. A. Pennebaker

D. A. (Donn Alan) Pennebaker began making films more than fifty years ago. This period has seen seismic changes in the ways in which reality is represented through documentary—changes that Pennebaker's own innovative and compelling work has helped to mediate. He was instrumental in establishing so-called direct cinema, an observational style of filmmaking that avoids didactic narration and talking heads interviews in favor of a desire to record situations as they unfold. In 1959 Pennebaker joined Robert Drew in the company Drew Associates (which, during Pennebaker's tenure, also included Richard Leacock, Albert Maysles, Hope Ryden, Gregory Shuker, and other pivotal documentary filmmakers). Drew sought to replicate the visual format of *Life* magazine within television's approach to newsworthy issues. With financial backing from the Broadcast Division of Time-Life, Drew and a number of his colleagues—in particular Pennebaker and Leacock—developed a portable camera synchronized to a sound recorder that enabled the kind of intimate and mobile filming that their approach to documentation demanded. Among numerous other groundbreaking documentaries Drew Associates produced using the new technology were the influential works *Primary* (1960) and *Crisis: Behind a Presidential Commitment* (1963). Pennebaker contributed in significant ways to both films.

Despite Pennebaker's key involvement in the early stages of his career with the direct cinema movement, there is a paucity of interviews with the filmmaker from those formative years. In part this situation is explained by the fact that Robert Drew adopted the mantle of public relations for Drew Associates, becoming the central spokesperson advocating their new approach to nonfiction filmmaking. (In many cases, too, it seems that Pennebaker was also content for his collaborator Richard Leacock to meet with interviewers.) Another key to the relative scarcity of early interviews is the broader historical context of Pennebaker's career, one that has coincided with the rise of critical and popular interest in the director as auteur, a notion that emphasizes the director as the primary creative and visionary presence in the realization of a work. The approach to a critical analysis of, and engagement with, cinema through the figure of the director was still taking hold as Pennebaker was hitting his stride as an independent filmmaker in the 1960s. Around this time, promoted by writings in various film journals, and extended within and through the emergence of film studies as an academic discipline, the ruminations by filmmakers on their art began to circulate more widely than previously. The shift toward an increased critical and popular focus on a director's insights into the filmmaking process is, in the case of Pennebaker, reflected in two major interviews included here from 1970 and 1971 (by Alan Rosenthal and G. Roy Levin). These are the first significant interviews in print with Pennebaker.

Through a reliance on the newly developed form of observationalism, documentary on television moved away from didacticism, and Pennebaker was convinced that the new approach to filming could be deployed in the production of films made for theatrical release. The outcome of these steps was realized in *Dont Look Back* (1967), a portrait of Bob Dylan that would eventually receive wide theatrical exposure. This milestone film signaled a move by observational filmmaking away from its recent application to journalistic reportage toward the documentation of a variety of forms of experience. Attesting to and extending its status as a breakthrough film, many of the interviews collected in this volume make prominent reference to *Dont Look Back*.

Following the filming of *Dont Look Back*, Pennebaker's film *Monterey Pop* (1968) inaugurated the prominent and popular form now known as rockumentary. He solidified the form with the films *Sweet Toronto* (1970) and *Ziggy Stardust and the Spiders from Mars* (1973). The shared basis of *Monterey Pop*—the film includes photography by Pennebaker, Leacock, Albert Maysles, Jim Desmond, Barry Feinstein, Roger Murphy, and Nick Proferes—continued in 1971 when Pennebaker and Leacock worked with Jean-Luc Godard on the film *One A.M.* The following year Pennebaker and Leacock compiled *One P.M.*, a reworked version of footage shot for Godard's film. These examples point to the fact that a central feature attending Pennebaker's filmmaking is collaboration. Pennebaker's career began in the collaborative environment of Drew Associates and continued in his long and productive relationship with Leacock. Pennebaker also collaborated with Norman Mailer on three films, and more recently he has worked on several films with Nick Doob, among others. In 1976 Chris Hegedus joined Pennebaker's production company as an assistant editor and quickly became a prominent collaborator (and in

1982 Hegedus also became his third wife). Together they have produced critically acclaimed films such as *Town Bloody Hall* (1979), *Depeche Mode 101* (1989), *The War Room* (1993), *Moon Over Broadway* (1998), *Down from the Mountain* (2001), *Startup.com* (2001), *Elaine Stritch at Liberty* (2004), and *Kings of Pastry* (2009). The close working relationship between Pennebaker and Hegedus is reflected in this volume in the form of the inclusion of a number of interviews conducted with both Pennebaker and Hegedus.

In December 2012, The Board of Governors of the Academy of Motion Picture Arts and Sciences recognized Pennebaker's exceptional career with the award of an Honorary Oscar, the first such award for a documentary filmmaker. When asked by Harvey Kubernik how he felt about the award, Pennebaker replied, "it's a little complicated." This response perhaps reflects Pennebaker's relationship, as a documentary filmmaker, with the film industry at large. In his 2011 interview with Sam Adams, Pennebaker characterized Hollywood films as "a side view of things," and he laments the kind of films that receive financial backing from the studios while projects such as his receive little in the way of external investment.

In the interviews collected here Pennebaker discusses an impressive array of topics, among them the differences between documentary filmmaking and Hollywood productions, what constitutes an "entertaining" documentary, emergent film technologies, the financing of documentary production, working with producers, access to subjects, and filmic and literary influences on his filmmaking (among the former, he mentions Flaherty in particular; and with reference to the latter he refers to Byron, Proust, and Ezra Pound, among others). In terms of his filmmaking practice, Pennebaker emphasizes that his kind of filmmaking is reliant on a combination of intuition and luck. Articulating this connection, he told David Dalton in 1999 that the "one thing I've figured out about film is that it's of the moment, intuitive," and in his interview with Dan Lybarger (2010) he asserted that "making these films is a game of chance; the [. . .] more you do it, the luckier you get." Deploying an approach to filmmaking that recognizes the role of luck and intuition, Pennebaker also rejects the imposition of stylistic rules or determinations: "there are no written rules that I know of. I don't have any myself. [. . .] I wait and see what happens in the lens of the camera and then I kind of go with it if I can" (Kubernik 2012).

The idea of not following rules might seem contradictory for a filmmaker so closely associated with direct cinema, which, in certain critical

circles, is defined through reference to a set of rigid rules that supposedly determine the character of the direct cinema observational style.
Pennebaker has consistently flouted the assumed central tenets of direct
cinema, particularly the notion that the filmmaker—in an attempt to
capture the "truth" of a moment—is an unobtrusive presence on the
profilmic scene (a condition that is reflected in references to the direct
cinema filmmaker as a "fly on the wall"). Talking with Alan Rosenthal
in 1971 about the people he filmed in *Dont Look Back* Pennebaker noted
that "they knew the camera was recording them in a way in which they
elected to be recorded." Speaking with Marc Savlov more than a quarter
of a century later and with many more film credits to his name, Pennebaker's response to the notion of the camera affecting the situation
remained the same: "I never try to pretend we're not there. . . . I don't
care if people know I'm there and most of the time they understand very
quickly what we want to film and what we want the film to do."

In a number of the interviews collected here, Pennebaker mentions
the effort required of a filmmaker in the practice of filming, especially
when surrounded by the chaotic entourage of musicians or actors. In
particular, speaking with Shelly Livson about filming Dylan's 1966 tour
with the Band (the footage that would eventually become the unreleased
but much bootlegged film, *Eat the Document*), Pennebaker admitted, "it's
hard to be part of [such a scene], because you can't totally sit there and
stare at everybody soberly . . . while they're jumping around, so you kind
of go along with it to some degree, but you can't get into it or you'll never
film it. It's one of the problems with filming: it requires an enormous
kind of concentration that most people never have to do in their lives."
Counterbalancing such an effort of concentration, Pennebaker mentions, in the interview with Martha Ansara, his willful surrender to the
moment of filming.

Pennebaker also alludes in the interviews collected here to the fact
that trusting subjects and being honest with subjects is a key to the success of his films. In 2010 he told Dan Lybarger that if subjects "think you
take what you're doing seriously, they'll take you into their lives." Pennebaker also recognizes something relevant in his filmmaking approach
for the subjects he films: a chance for them to see their own performance
from the outside. Speaking about the subjects depicted by his camera
over the years, Pennebaker told Dan Lybarger that "you're holding up a
mirror to them, and they are interested in kind of seeing how well they're
pulling it off." He was even more candid in his 1990 interview with John
Bauldie: "My sense is that the reason that they let us make films—Jane

Fonda, Kennedy, all of 'em—was that they figured that they'd find out something interesting by looking at the film."

The reference here to "interesting" situations and topics is echoed in a number of the conversations collected in this volume. Pennebaker repeatedly returns to the assertion that his best films have been produced by filming the people that interest him, and, judging by his filmography, the most interesting subjects for Pennebaker are performers like Bob Dylan. In his 1998 interview with Marc Savlov, Pennebaker explained his fascination with filming musicians in terms of a tension between celebrity, everyday life, and performance: "musicians are interesting to me because they're different from normal people and yet they are expected to have the same reactions, and so there's a constant struggle going on there. . . . I think that they lend themselves to performance, and as a filmmaker that's something you look for." The acute sensibility such performers possess of how to behave in front of a camera seems to marry well with Pennebaker's own attitude towards his films—his subjects know how to be "interesting," and as such his films will be of interest to audiences. In a related way, Pennebaker believes that the theatrics of performing on some kind of stage (be it the stage of theater, film, music, or politics) highlight the theatrics of documentary filmmaking—following someone with a camera and becoming a part of the script of their lives.

Allusions by Pennebaker to the place of performance within his films—and references to theater in his descriptions of filmmaking—run throughout many of the conversations collected here. "We're trying to make a piece of theatre," he told John Berra in 2008, "which means we're thinking about people sitting in the fifth row and what is going to keep their attention." The idea of filmmaking as theater is perhaps best summarized in the response by Pennebaker and Hegedus to a specific question posed by Kevin Macdonald and Mark Cousins in 1996. In answering the question "what is the future of documentary?" the filmmakers replied: "why can't we have a true theatre of documentary (nonfiction) filmmaking that entertains and excites rather than explains. . . . We could, by turning a few filmmakers loose in the world, create a new and different sort of theatre that searches for its plots and characters among the real streets and jungles of our times." Not coincidentally, the project outlined in these comments implicitly refers to central features of Pennebaker's filmmaking practice, and the ways in which it has invigorated documentary representation.

This volume includes a selection of the most significant and insightful interviews conducted with the documentary filmmaker D. A. Pennebaker. The conversations collected here are supplemented by a list of additional interviews. (The list of further sources includes only interviews that have appeared in print. The Internet provides a considerable archive of links to interviews with Pennebaker, and Pennebaker and Hegedus, which have been filmed or voice recorded.) Considering the centrality of collaboration to Pennebaker's filmmaking, the filmography included here lists all films Pennebaker has contributed to, including films he has directed, produced, those on which he has served as cinematographer, and other films that have involved his input.

We would like to sincerely thank the interviewers and rights holders, who each responded to our enquiries promptly and enthusiastically and kindly granted us permission to reprint the published interviews that appear here. In particular we would like to thank Harvey Kubernik who generously alerted us to his extended interview with Pennebaker from 2012. Thanks are also extended to my family, friends, and many colleagues at Deakin University who continue to provide committed support and encouragement (TG), and to Julie Ann Smith—for the roses, and everything else (KB).

KB
TG

Chronology

1970   *Original Cast Album: Company*; with Richard Leacock films Norman Mailer's *Maidstone*.

1972   Makes *One P.M.* with Richard Leacock, from footage shot in association with Jean-Luc Godard; marries Cynthia "Kate" Taylor; Leacock-Pennebaker, Inc. dissolved.

1973   *Ziggy Stardust and the Spiders from Mars*, a record of a David Bowie concert in London. The making of the film inaugurates a long and productive collaboration with Nick Doob.

1976   Chris Hegedus joins Pennebaker's independent filmmaking company.

1978   *The Energy War.*

1979   *Town Bloody Hall* edited by Hegedus from footage shot by Pennebaker in 1971.

1980   Pennebaker and Kate Taylor divorce.

1982   Marries Chris Hegedus; formation of Pennebaker Hegedus Films.

1989   Makes *Depeche Mode 101* with Chris Hegedus and David Dawkins.

1990   *Primary* added to the National Film Registry maintained by the Library of Congress.

1993   With Chris Hegedus makes *The War Room*; the film receives an Academy Award nomination and wins the D.W. Griffith Award for Best Documentary.

1997   With Chris Hegedus makes *Moon Over Broadway*.

2001   Collaborates with Chris Hegedus and others to make *Down from the Mountain*; serves as a producer on *Startup.com*, which was co-directed by Chris Hegedus (with Jahane Noujaim).

2002   Makes *Only the Strong Survive* with Chris Hegedus.

2009   Makes *Kings of Pastry* with Chris Hegedus.

2012   Awarded an honorary Academy Award for achievements in documentary filmmaking.

2014   *Unlocking the Cage*, a profile of animal rights activist Steven Wise by Pennebaker and Hegedus. Forthcoming.

Filmography

Pennebaker's career spans close to sixty years of filmmaking, and across this period he has made innumerable films within a variety of production contexts. This filmography includes major and lesser-known work but, perhaps inevitably given the length and complexity of Pennebaker's career, it is not a complete list of his work.

DAYBREAK EXPRESS (1953, completed 1957)
Filmmaker: **D. A. Pennebaker**
Color, 5 minutes

BABY (1954)
Filmmaker: **D. A. Pennebaker**
Black and white, 6 minutes

GAS STOP [aka BRUSSELS FILM LOOP] (1958)
Producer: US State Department
Filmmaker: **D. A. Pennebaker**
Color, 2.5 minutes

BALLOON [aka BALLOON ASCENSION] (1958)
Producer: Robert Drew
Filmmakers: **D. A. Pennebaker**, Richard Leacock, Derek Washburn
Sponsor: Time, Inc.
Black and white, 28 minutes

OPENING IN MOSCOW (1959)
Filmmakers: **D. A. Pennebaker**, Shirley Clarke, Albert Maysles
Editor: Shirley Clarke, **D. A. Pennebaker**
Color, 45 minutes

YANKI NO! (1960)
Producer: Robert Drew
Coproduced by: Time, Inc. and Drew Associates
Filmmakers: **D. A. Pennebaker**, Richard Leacock, Albert Maysles
Reporters: William Worthy, Quinera King
Narrator: Joseph Julian
Black and white, 55 minutes

PRIMARY (1960)
Producer: Robert Drew, for Time-Life Broadcasting
Filmmakers: **D. A. Pennebaker**, Richard Leacock, Terrence
McCartney-Filgate, Albert Maysles
Writer: Robert Drew
Black and white, 52 minutes

ON THE POLE [aka EDDIE; EDDIE SACHS] (1960)
Executive Producer: Robert Drew
Coproduced by: Time, Inc. and Drew Associates
Filmmakers: **D. A. Pennebaker**, Richard Leacock, William Ray, Abbott
Mills, Albert Maysles
Correspondents: James Lipscomb, Gregory Shuker
Black and white, 52 minutes

ADVENTURES ON THE NEW FRONTIER (1961)
Executive Producer: Robert Drew
Coproduced by: Time, Inc. and Drew Associates
Filmmakers: **D. A. Pennebaker**, Richard Leacock, Albert Maysles,
Kenneth Snelson
Correspondents: Lee Hall, Gregory Shuker, David Maysles
Black and white, 51 minutes

DAVID [aka SYNANON] (1961)
Executive Producer: Robert Drew
Producer: James Lipscomb
Coproduced by: Time-Life Broadcasting and Drew Associates
Filmmakers: **D. A. Pennebaker**, Gregory Shuker, William Ray
Correspondent: Nell Cox
Black and white, 57 minutes

MOONEY VS. FOWLE [aka FOOTBALL] (1961)
Executive Producer: Robert Drew
Coproduced by: Time-Life Broadcasting and Drew Associates
Filmmakers: **D. A. Pennebaker**, James Lipscomb, William Ray, Abbott
Mills, Richard Leacock, Claude Fournier
Correspondents: Hope Ryden, Peter Powell
Black and white, 54 minutes

BLACKIE [aka AIRLINE PILOT] (1962)
Executive Producer: Robert Drew
Coproduced by: Time-Life Broadcasting and Drew Associates
Filmmakers: **D. A. Pennebaker**, William Ray
Correspondents: Gregory Shuker, Peter Powell
Black and white, 53 minutes

SUSAN STARR (1962)
Executive Producer: Robert Drew
Producers: Hope Ryden, Gregory Shuker
Coproduced by: Time-Life Broadcasting and Drew Associates
Filmmakers: **D. A. Pennebaker**, Hope Ryden, Claude Fournier, Peter
Eco, James Lipscomb, Abbott Mills, Richard Leacock
Correspondents: Hope Ryden, Patricia Isaacs, James Lencina, Sam
Adams
Black and white, 53 minutes

JANE (1962)
Executive Producer: Robert Drew
Producer: Hope Ryden
Coproduced by: Time-Life Broadcast and Drew Associates
Filmmakers: **D. A. Pennebaker**, Richard Leacock, Abbot Mills, Al
Wertheimer
Editors: **D. A. Pennebaker**, Nell Cox, Nancy Sen, Eileen Nosworthy,
Richard Leacock, Hope Ryden, Betsy Taylor
Sound: Hope Ryden
Narrator: James Lipscomb
Black and white, 51 minutes

THE CHAIR [aka PAUL] (1962)
Executive Producer: Robert Drew
Coproduced by: Time-Life Broadcasting and Drew Associates

Filmmakers: **D. A. Pennebaker**, Gregory Shuker, Richard Leacock
Correspondents: Gregory Shuker, Robert Drew, John MacDonald, Sam
Adams
Black and white, 58 minutes

ON THE ROAD TO BUTTON BAY [aka THE ROAD TO BUTTON BAY]
(1962)
Executive Producer: Robert Drew
Coproduced by: Time-Life Broadcast and Drew Associates
Filmmakers: **D. A. Pennebaker**, Stanley Fink, Abbott Mills, Hope
Ryden, James Lipscomb, Richard Leacock
Black and white, 55 minutes

THE AGA KHAN (1962)
Executive Producer: Robert Drew
Coproduced by: Time-Life Broadcast and Drew Associates
Filmmakers: **D. A. Pennebaker**, Gregory Shuker, Richard Leacock
Black and white, 57 minutes

CRISIS: BEHIND A PRESIDENTIAL COMMITMENT (1963)
Executive Producer: Robert Drew
Producer: Gregory Shuker
Produced by: ABC News in association with Drew Associates
Filmmakers: **D. A. Pennebaker**, Richard Leacock, James Lipscomb
Black and white, 52 minutes

YOU'RE NOBODY TILL SOMEBODY LOVES YOU (1964)
Producer: Leacock Pennebaker, Inc.
Filmmaker: **D. A. Pennebaker**
Photography: **D. A. Pennebaker**, Michael Blackmore, Jim Desmond,
Nick Proferes
Editor: **D. A. Pennebaker**
Black and white, 12 minutes

JINGLE BELLS (1964)
Filmmaker: **D. A. Pennebaker**
Black and white, 16 minutes

LAMBERT AND CO [aka LAMBERT, HENDRICKS AND CO; RCA
AUDITION] (1964)
Producer: Leacock Pennebaker, Inc.
Filmmaker: **D. A. Pennebaker**
Black and white, 15 minutes

BREAKING IT UP AT THE MUSEUM (1964)
Producer: Leacock Pennebaker, Inc.
Filmmakers: **D. A. Pennebaker**, Richard Leacock
Black and white, 6 minutes

ELIZABETH AND MARY (1965)
Producer: Leacock Pennebaker, Inc.
Filmmaker: **D. A. Pennebaker**
Black and white, 60 minutes

HERR STRAUSS (1966)
Producer: Leacock Pennebaker, Inc.
Filmmaker: **D. A. Pennebaker**
Black and white, 30 minutes

ROOKIE (1966)
Producer: Leacock Pennebaker, Inc. for CBS
Filmmakers: **D. A. Pennebaker**, Jim Desmond
Color, 20 minutes

DONT LOOK BACK (1967)
Producers: Albert Grossman, John Court, Leacock Pennebaker, Inc.
Filmmaker: **D. A. Pennebaker**
Photography: **D. A. Pennebaker**
Assistant Photography: Howard Alk
Sound: Jones Alk
Concert Sound: Robert Van Dyke
Editor: **D. A. Pennebaker**
Footage of Dylan in Greenwood, Mississippi, shot by: Ed Emshwiller
Black and white, 96 minutes

MONTEREY POP (1968)
Producer: Leacock Pennebaker, Inc.
Filmmaker: **D. A. Pennebaker**

Photography: **D. A. Pennebaker**, Barry Feinstein, Richard Leacock, Jim Desmond, Albert Maysles, Roger Murphy, Nick Proferes
Music Director: Bob Neuwirth
Editor: Nina Schulman
Stage Sound: John Cooke
Local Sound: Tim Cunningham, Baird Hersey, Robert Leacock, John Maddox, Nina Schulman
Concert Recording: Wally Heider, Robert Van Dyke
Production Assistants: Pauline Baez, Peyton Fong, Brice Marden
Unit Manager: Peter Hansen
Color, 98 minutes

RAINFOREST [aka MERCE CUNNINGHAM'S RAINFOREST] (1968)
Producer: David Oppenheim
Filmmakers: **D. A. Pennebaker**, Richard Leacock
Photography: **D. A. Pennebaker**, Richard Leacock, Roger Murphy
Editor: Patricia Jaffe
Sound: Robert Leacock, Nina Schulman, Robert Van Dyke
Color, 27 minutes

ALICE COOPER (1970)
Producer: Leacock Pennebaker, Inc.
Filmmaker: **D. A. Pennebaker**
Color, 15 minutes

ORIGINAL CAST ALBUM: COMPANY [aka COMPANY: ORIGINAL CAST ALBUM; COMPANY] (1970)
Executive Producer: Daniel Melnick
Producer: Chester Feldman
Associate Producer: Judy Crichton
Produced by: Leacock Pennebaker, Inc.
Filmmaker: **D. A. Pennebaker**
Photography: **D. A. Pennebaker**, Richard Leacock, Jim Desmond
Sound: Robert Van Dyke, Robert Leacock, Kate Taylor, Mark Woodcock
Color, 68 minutes

SWEET TORONTO (1970)
Producers: David McMullin, Mark Woodcock, Peter Hansen, Chris Dalrymple
Filmmaker: **D. A. Pennebaker**

Photography: **D. A. Pennebaker**, Richard Leacock, Roger Murphy, Jim Desmond, Barry Bergthorson, Randy Franklin, Richard Leiterman, Bob Neuwirth
Editor: **D. A. Pennebaker**
Sound: Robert Leacock, Bob Van Dyke, Kate Taylor, Wally Heider
Color, 135 minutes

ONE A.M. [aka ONE AMERICAN MOVIE] (1971)
Producer: **D. A. Pennebaker**
Director: Jean-Luc Godard
Photography: **D. A. Pennebaker**, Richard Leacock
Editor: **D. A. Pennebaker**
Unfinished
Color

ONE P.M. [aka 1 P.M; ONE PARALLEL MOVIE; ONE PERFECT MOVIE] (1972)
Producers: **D. A. Pennebaker** and Richard Leacock for Leacock Pennebaker, Inc.
Filmmakers: **D. A. Pennebaker** (with Richard Leacock and Jean-Luc Godard)
Color, 95 minutes

THE CHILDREN'S THEATER OF JOHN DONAHUE (1972)
Filmmaker: **D. A. Pennebaker**
Photography: **D. A. Pennebaker**, Jim Desmond
Color, 28 minutes

KEEP ON ROCKIN' (1972)
Producers: David McMullin, Mark Woodcock, Peter Hansen, Chris Dalrymple
Filmmaker: **D. A. Pennebaker**
Photography: **D. A. Pennebaker**, Richard Leacock, Roger Murphy, Jim Desmond, Barry Bergthorson, Randy Franklin, Richard Leiterman, Bob Neuwirth
Editor: **D. A. Pennebaker**
Sound: Robert Leacock, Bob Van Dyke, Kate Taylor, Wally Heider
Color, 102 minutes

ZIGGY STARDUST AND THE SPIDERS FROM MARS (1973)
Executive Producer: Tony Defries
Associate Producer: Edith Van Slyck
Filmmaker: **D. A. Pennebaker**
Photography: **D. A. Pennebaker**, Nick Doob, Jim Desmond, Mike
Davis, Randy Franken
Editor: Larry Whitehead
Unit Manager: Stacy Pennebaker
Concert Sound: Ground Control
Concert Recording: Trident Studios
Color, 100 minutes

THE ENERGY WAR (1978)
Executive Producer: Edith Van Slyck
Producer: Pat Lowell
Filmmakers: **D. A. Pennebaker**, Chris Hegedus, Pat Lowell
Color, 292 minutes (3 parts; part 1, 88 minutes; part 2, 87 minutes; part
3, 118 minutes)

TOWN BLOODY HALL (1979)
Producers: Shirley Broughton, Edith Van Slyck
Filmmakers: **D. A. Pennebaker**, Chris Hegedus
Photography: **D. A. Pennebaker**, Marl Woodcock, Jim Desmond
Sound: Robert Van Dyke, Kathy Desmond, Mary Lampson, Kate Taylor
Editor: Chris Hegedus
Color, 88 minutes

ELLIOT CARTER AT BUFFALO (1980)
Producers: Pennebaker Hegedus Films, New York University
Filmmakers: **D. A. Pennebaker**, Chris Hegedus
Color, 45 minutes

DeLOREAN (1981)
Producer: **D. A. Pennebaker**
Associate Producers: Shirley Broughton, Gayle Austin, Bernice Sherry,
Judy Freed
Filmmakers: **D. A. Pennebaker**, Chris Hegedus
Color, 53 minutes

ROCKABY [aka BILLIE WHITELAW IN ROCKABY; THE MAKING OF ROCKABY] (1981)
Executive Producers: Daniel Labeille, Patricia Kerr Ross
Associate Producer: Saul Elkin
Produced by: BBC
Filmmakers: **D. A. Pennebaker**, Chris Hegedus
Editors: **D. A. Pennebaker**, Chris Hegedus, David Dawkins
Color, 60 minutes

DANCE BLACK AMERICA (1981)
Producer: Frazer Pennebaker
Filmmakers: **D. A. Pennebaker**, Chris Hegedus
Commentary: **D. A. Pennebaker**
Color, 90 minutes

JIMI PLAYS MONTEREY (1986)
Executive Producer: Frazer Pennebaker
Producer: Alan Douglas
Coproduced by: Are You Experienced, Ltd., Pennebaker Associates, Inc.
Filmmakers: **D. A. Pennebaker**, Chris Hegedus, David Dawkins
Editors: **D. A. Pennebaker**, Chris Hegedus, David Dawkins, Alan Douglas
Opening Sequence Directed by: Peter Rosenthal
Color, 48 minutes

SHAKE! OTIS AT MONTEREY (1987)
Executive Producer: Frazer Pennebaker
Producer: Alan Douglas
Filmmakers: **D. A. Pennebaker**, Chris Hegedus, David Dawkins
Photography: **D. A. Pennebaker**, Jim Desmond, Barry Feinstein, Richard Leacock, Albert Maysles, Nick Proferes
Editor: Nina Schulman
Color, 30 minutes

SUZANNE VEGA [aka OPEN HAND] (1987)
Filmmakers: **D. A. Pennebaker**, Chris Hegedus
Color, 30 minutes

DEPECHE MODE 101 [aka 101] (1989)
Executive Producers: Bruce Kirkland, Daniel Miller

Producer: Frazer Pennebaker
Filmmakers: **D. A. Pennebaker**, Chris Hegedus, David Dawkins
Color, 120 minutes

JERRY LEE LEWIS: THE STORY OF ROCK AND ROLL [aka JERRY LEE LEWIS] (1990)
Filmmakers: **D. A. Pennebaker**, Chris Hegedus
Color, 52 minutes

COMIN' HOME (1991)
Filmmakers: **D. A. Pennebaker**, Chris Hegedus
Color, 28 minutes

LITTLE RICHARD (1991)
Producers: Mark Woodcock, Peter Hansen
Filmmakers: **D. A. Pennebaker**, Chris Hegedus
Photography: **D. A. Pennebaker**, Jim Desmond, Richard Leacock, Roger Murphy
Sound: Robert Leacock
Color, 30 minutes

BRANFORD MARSALIS: THE MUSIC TELLS YOU [aka THE MUSIC TELLS YOU] (1992)
Producer: Frazer Pennebaker
Filmmakers: **D. A. Pennebaker**, Chris Hegedus
Photography: **D. A. Pennebaker**, Chris Hegedus, Nick Doob, Ronald Gray, Crystal Griffiths
Color, 60 minutes

THE WAR ROOM (1993)
Executive Producers: Wendy Ettinger, Frazer Pennebaker
Producers: R. J. Cutler, Wendy Ettinger, Frazer Pennebaker
Associate Producer: Cyclone Films
Filmmakers: **D. A. Pennebaker**, Chris Hegedus
Photography: **D. A. Pennebaker**, Nick Doob
Sound: Chris Hegedus, David Dawkins
Assistant Editor: Rebecca Baron
Associate Editor: Erez Laufer
Color, 96 minutes

WOODSTOCK DIARY [aka WOODSTOCK DIARIES] (1994)
Filmmakers: **D. A. Pennebaker**, Chris Hegedus, Erez Laufer
Editor: Erez Laufer
Color, 180 minutes

KEINE ZEIT (1996)
Filmmakers: **D. A. Pennebaker**, Chris Hegedus
Color, 92 minutes

VICTORIA WILLIAMS: HAPPY COME HOME (1997)
Filmmakers: **D. A. Pennebaker**, Chris Hegedus
Color, 28 minutes

MOON OVER BROADWAY (1997)
Producers: Wendy Ettinger, Frazer Pennebaker
Filmmakers: **D. A. Pennebaker**, Chris Hegedus
Photography: **D. A. Pennebaker**, Jim Desmond, Nick Doob
Sound: Chris Hegedus, John McCormick
Associate Editors: David Dawkins, Erez Laufer, John Paul Pennebaker
Color, 97 minutes

BESSIE: A PORTRAIT OF BESSIE SCHONBERG (1998)
Filmmakers: **D. A. Pennebaker**, Chris Hegedus
Color, 58 minutes

SEARCHING FOR JIMI HENDRIX (1999)
Producers: Alan Douglas, Frazer Pennebaker
Filmmakers: **D. A. Pennebaker**, Chris Hegedus
Color, 60 minutes

DOWN FROM THE MOUNTAIN (2001)
Executive Producers: T Bone Burnett, Ethan Coen, Joel Coen
Producers: Bob Neuwirth, Frazer Pennebaker
Associate Producer: Rebecca Marshall
Filmmakers: **D. A. Pennebaker**, Chris Hegedus, Nick Doob, Jim
Desmond, Joan Churchill, Bob Neuwirth, Jehane Noujaim, John Paul
Pennebaker
Editors: **D. A. Pennebaker**, Nick Doob
Color, 94 minutes

ONLY THE STRONG SURVIVE (2002)
Executive Producers: Bob Weinstein, Harvey Weinstein
Producers: Roger Friedman, Frazer Pennebaker
Associate Producer: Rebecca Marshall
Filmmakers: **D. A. Pennebaker**, Chris Hegedus
Photography: **D. A. Pennebaker**, Chris Hegedus, Nick Doob, Jim
Desmond, Erez Laufer, Jehane Noujaim
Editors: **D. A. Pennebaker**, Chris Hegedus, Erez Laufer
Sound: Chris Hegedus, John Paul Pennebaker, Kit Pennebaker
Color, 98 minutes

NATIONAL ANTHEM: INSIDE THE VOTE FOR CHANGE CONCERT
TOUR (2004)
Producers: Frazer Pennebaker, Joel Gallen, Maureen Ryan
Associate Producers: Walker Lamond, Rebecca Marshall
Filmmakers: **D. A. Pennebaker**, Albert Maysles, Chris Hegedus, Anto-
nio Ferrera, Nick Doob
Photography: **D. A. Pennebaker**, Albert Maysles
Editor: David Dawkins
Assistant Editor: Sabine Kertscher
Associate Editor: Christine Park
Production Assistants: Rod McDonald, Aronya Waller
Color, 315 minutes

ELAINE STRITCH AT LIBERTY (2004)
Producer: Frazer Pennebaker
Filmmakers: **D. A. Pennebaker**, Chris Hegedus, Nick Doob
Color, 94 minutes

ASSUME THE POSITION WITH MR. WUHL (2006)
Executive Producer: Robert Wuhl
Producer: Frazer Pennebaker
Filmmakers: **D. A. Pennebaker**, Chris Hegedus, Nick Doob
Screenwriters: Allan Stephan, Rebecca Reynolds, Robert Wuhl
Color, 30 minutes

65 REVISITED (2006)
Producer: Frazer Pennebaker
Filmmaker: **D. A. Pennebaker**

Photography: **D. A. Pennebaker**, Howard Alk
Editors: **D. A. Pennebaker**, Walker Lamond
Black and white, 65 minutes

MONTEREY POP: THE SUMMER OF LOVE [aka MONTEREY 40] (2007)
Produced by: Pennebaker Hegedus Films
Executive Producers: Brad Abramson, Shelley Tatro, Michael Hirschorn
Producer: Erik Himmelsbach
Supervising Producer: Mark Anstendig
Associate Producers: Ken Shapiro, Abigail Parsons
Filmmakers: **D. A. Pennebaker**, Erik Himmelsbach
Color, 60 minutes

ADDICTION: THE SUPPLEMENTARY SERIES: OPIATE ADDICTION:
UNDERSTANDING REPLACEMENT THERAPY (2007)
Produced by: Home Box Office
Executive Producer: Sheila Nevins
Producers: Frazer Pennebaker, John Hoffman, Susan Froemke
Co-producer: Micah Cormier
Filmmakers: **D. A. Pennebaker**, Chris Hegedus
Color, 19 minutes

THE RETURN OF THE WAR ROOM (2008)
Producers: Pennebaker Hegedus Films, McEttinger Films
Filmmakers: **D. A. Pennebaker**, Chris Hegedus
Color, 82 minutes

KINGS OF PASTRY (2009)
Executive Producer: Frazer Pennebaker
Producers: Flora Lazar, Frazer Pennebaker
Associate Producers: Rebecca Lando, Patricia Soussloff
Produced by: Pennebaker Hegedus Films in coproduction with BBC,
VPRO, Danish TV, SBS Australia, YLE Finland
Filmmakers: Chris Hegdus, **D. A. Pennebaker**
Additional Photography: Nick Doob
Editors: Chris Hegedus, **D. A. Pennebaker**
Color, 84 minutes

THE NATIONAL (live concert webcast) (2010)
Produced by: Vevo

Filmmakers: Chris Hegedus, **D. A. Pennebaker**
Color, 67 minutes

Other Projects

WIDENING CIRCLE (1956)
Writer: **D. A. Pennebaker**
Sponsor: YWCA

WIDER WORLD (1956)
Writer: **D. A. Pennebaker**
Sponsor: Girl Scouts of America

SUEZ (1956)
Producer, Writer: **D. A. Pennebaker**
Sponsor: Julien Bryan
Color, 14 minutes

YOUR SHARE IN TOMORROW (1957)
Assistant Director, Camera: **D. A. Pennebaker**
Sponsor: New York Stock Exchange

HIGHLANDER (1958)
Editor: **D. A. Pennebaker**
Sponsor: Highlander School

SKYSCRAPER (1958)
Filmmakers: Shirley Clarke, Willard Van Dyke
Photography: Shirley Clarke, Willard Van Dyke, Wheaton Galentine,
D. A. Pennebaker
Sponsor: Tishman Realty

CHRISTOPHER AND ME (1960)
Writer (song for titles): **D. A. Pennebaker**
Sponsor: Edward Foote

MARDI GRAS (1960)
Photography: **D. A. Pennebaker**
Sponsor: Walt Disney

MR. PEARSON (1962)
Photography: **D. A. Pennebaker**
Sponsor: Canadian Broadcasting Corporation

TIMMONS (1964)
Photography, Editor: **D. A. Pennebaker**
Sponsor: Granada Television

CASALS AT 88 [aka CASALS AT EIGHTY-EIGHT] (1964)
Photography and Sound for Budapest Sequences: **D. A. Pennebaker**,
Richard Leacock
Sponsor: CBS

VAN CLIBURN (1966)
Photography: **D. A. Pennebaker**
Sponsor: AT&T

WILD 90 (1967)
Producers: Norman Mailer, Supreme Mix
Director: Norman Mailer
Photography: **D. A. Pennebaker**
Editors: Norman Mailer, Jan Pieter Welt
Black and white, 90 minutes

TWO AMERICAN AUDIENCES (1968)
Filmmaker: Mark Woodcock
Photography: **D. A. Pennebaker**, Mark Woodcock
Black and white, 40 minutes

BEYOND THE LAW (1968)
Producers: Buzz Farber, Norman Mailer
Director: Norman Mailer
Photography: **D. A. Pennebaker**, Nick Proferes, Jan Pieter Welt
Black and white, 110 minutes

McCARTHY (1968)
Photography, Editor: **D. A. Pennebaker**
Sponsor: McCarthy Headquarters

MAIDSTONE (1970)
Producers: Buzz Farber, Norman Mailer
Director: Norman Mailer
Photography: **D. A. Pennebaker**, Richard Leacock, Jim Desmond,
Nick Proferes, Sheldon Rochlin, Diane Rochlin, Jan Pieter Welt
Editors: Jan Pieter Welt, Lana Jokel, Norman Mailer
Associate Editors: Harvey Greenstein, Lucille Rhodes, Marilyn
Frauenglass
Sound: Nell Cox, Robert Leacock, Nina Schulman, Kate Taylor, Mark
Woodcock
Color, 110 minutes

JOHN GLENN (1970)
Photography: **D. A. Pennebaker**
Sponsor: Glenn for Senator Campaign

ROBERT CASEY (1970)
Photography: **D. A. Pennebaker**
Sponsor: Casey for Governor Campaign

SESSIONS AT WEST 54th (series) (1997)
Executive Producer: Jeb Brien
Produced by: Automatic Productions for American Program Service for
PBS
Interview Segments Photographed by: **D. A. Pennebaker** and Chris
Hegedus
Color, 10 episodes; 10 minute interviews (approx.)

As Producer

STARTUP.COM (2001)
Executive Producers: Jehane Noujiam, Frazer Pennebaker, Chris
Hegedus
Producer: **D. A. Pennebaker**
Associate Producers: Rebecca Marshall, Ed Rogoff
Produced by: Pennebaker Hegedus Films/Noujaim Films
Filmmakers: Chris Hegedus, Jehane Noujaim
Photography: Jehane Noujiam
Editors: Chris Hegedus, Jehane Noujiam, Erez Laufer
Color, 103 minutes

THE CUTMAN (2003)
Executive Producer: **D. A. Pennebaker**
Producers: Yon Motskin, Michael Shemesh
Associate Producer: Christina De Haven
Director: Yon Motskin
Writer: Yon Motskin
Color, 27 minutes

FOX VS. FRANKEN (episode in *The First Amendment Project* series) (2004)
Supervising Producer: **D. A. Pennebaker**
Filmmakers: Chris Hegedus, Nick Doob
Color, 30 minutes

AL FRANKEN: GOD SPOKE (2006)
Executive Producer: **D. A. Pennebaker**
Filmmakers: Chris Hegedus, Nick Doob
Color, 90 minutes

SAINT MISBEHAVIN': THE WAVY GRAVY MOVIE (2008)
Executive Producer: **D. A. Pennebaker**
Producer: Michelle Esrick, David Becker
Director: Michelle Esrick
Photography: Daniel Gold
Editor: Karen Sim
Consulting Editor: Emma Joan Morris
Color, 86 minutes

Thank Yous

HARLAN COUNTY, U.S.A (1976)
Filmmaker: Barbara Kopple

STARTUP.COM (2001)
Filmmakers: Chris Hegedus, Jehane Noujaim

CONTROL ROOM (2004)
Filmmaker: Jehane Noujaim

NO DIRECTION HOME (2005)
Filmmaker: Martin Scorsese

Appearances

WILD 90 (1968)
Director: Norman Mailer
As the character "Al"

BEFORE THE NICKELODEON: THE CINEMA OF EDWIN S. PORTER
(1982)
Director: Charles Musser
As voice for "Film as a visual newspaper" segment

CINÉMA VÉRITÉ: DEFINING THE MOMENT (1999)
Director: Peter Wintonick
As interview subject

THE BALLARD OF RAMBLIN' JACK (2000)
Director: Aiyann Elliott
As interview subject

HOLLYWOOD ROCKS THE MOVIES: THE EARLY YEARS (1955–1970)
(2000)
Directors: Edith Becker and Kevin Burns
As interview subject, uncredited

SEE WHAT HAPPENS: THE STORY OF D. A. PENNEBAKER AND CHRIS
HEGEDUS (2002)
Director: Gerold Hofmann
As himself

D. A. Pennebaker: Interviews

D. A. Pennebaker

G. Roy Levin / 1970

Interview conducted September 2, 1970, in D. A. Pennebaker's office in New York City. From *Documentary Explorations: 15 Interviews with Film-Makers* (Anchor Press, Doubleday and Company, 1971). Reprinted with permission of Jordan Levin, Bryna Levin, Maurie Levin, and G. Roy Levin's Estate.

G. Roy Levin: On the phone you said that you don't make documentary films.

D. A. Pennebaker: Well, I try not to. I can't help it if you call it that. I mean, if somebody paid me, I'd just make anything. You know, just a working man.

GRL: You're willing to make any kind of film? You really don't care at all?

DAP: That's what I'm told by everybody else.

GRL: I don't believe that.

DAP: You do what you're told. You want to see documentary films, somebody pays you to do it, right?

GRL: There aren't any films that you want to make?

DAP: Oh sure. God, yes. But when you work here, you work. If you're a cameraman or a filmmaker, you're committed to making films people want to pay for, most of the time. I've got seven or eight films in the back room. Hour-length, hour-and-a-half, half-hour-length films that I can't sell to anybody. What does that prove? That I'm virtuous? That I know something nobody clsc does?

GRL: What kind of films are they?

DAP: Oh, they're just films about people, but they don't have any

3

particular form to them. A film of Jack Elliot and people like that. I made it in a nightclub one night with Janis and some people singing in there.

GRL: Janis Joplin?

DAP: Yeah. They're not documentaries. They weren't intended to be documentaries, but they're records of some moment. I've got a film I made in Russia, a film I made of the eclipse. They're just films that I made because something happened that interested me, but I can't make a living off these kind of films. Not for a minute. But I don't call them documentary films. When people come to me, they've already got a sense of what they want to call the film they want me to make. If they want to call it documentary film, that's their problem.

My definition of a documentary film is a film that decides you don't know enough about something, whatever it is, psychology or the tip of South America. Some guy goes there and says, "Holy shit, I know about this and nobody else does, so I'm going to make a film about it." Gives him something to do. And he usually persuades somebody to put up the money who thinks this is the thing to do. Then you have the situation where this thing is shouting on the wall about how you don't know something. Well, I think that's a drag. Right away it puts me off. There are a lot of things I don't know about, but I can't stand having someone telling me that. That's what the networks do: "Ah, you don't know about dope. We're going to tell you about dope today. Here is an interview with Mrs. Jones. She knows about dope." And Mrs. Jones, gee, she's a billion people around—I mean, how can one or ten or even five hundred people know really what's going on? Then five minutes later it's all changed anyway. So the whole basis for this kind of reporting is false. It pretends to be reporting but it isn't, most of the time.

On the other hand, it's possible to go to a situation and simply film what you see there, what happens there, what goes on, and let everybody decide whether it tells them about any of these things. But you don't have to label them, you don't have to have the narration to instruct you so you can be sure and understand that it's good for you to learn. You don't need any of that shit. When you take off the narration, people say, "Well, it's not documentary anymore." That's all right, that's their problem. That's why I say that films that interest me to do, I wouldn't consider documentaries.

If I was going to make a film on dope, let's say, if I made one this week, it might say one thing. If I made it next week, it might be quite different. But you couldn't call that documentary film. It's not very analytical. I don't know what it is, but I've got to be absolutely prepared that that's the way it's going to go, that there isn't a thing to say about dope that's going to be universal and I'm the one that's got the message to do it. So you pay me a little money and you tap me on the shoulder and I'm blessed. And I get to do it. Ah, that's bullshit. I don't trust people just because they have a camera. I don't even trust people who write books, and that's a lot harder than shooting a camera.

GRL: You spent a long time working with [Robert] Drew. How long?
DAP: Two or three years. That's not a long time. A long time just getting into the camera.

GRL: In that time, were the films you made what most people would call documentary?
DAP: They are half and half. They are kind of half soap opera, half documentary. The part that interests me, that I like about them, is the soap opera, I suspect. The parts where they failed are probably as documentaries. They probably weren't quite objective. I don't know, they were different. Which ones have you seen?

GRL: *The Chair, Susan Starr, Football*, the one—
DAP: *Football* is, I'd say, one of the good documentaries. *Yanki No!* is a good documentary. They were good documentaries in that they had a measure of unpredictability and life that made them interesting, just as I guess *Target for Tonight* [Harry Watt, 1941] was documentary and so was *Night Mail* [Basil Wright and Harry Watt, 1936]. But there was a kind of freshness and excitement in them that pulled them out of that, so you remember them. You don't remember them for their marvelous insights into the mail service or anything; you remember them for their poetry, or whatever it is. I think that *The Chair* is abominably edited, that it was reduced to a kind of straight-line plot analysis when in fact what is most interesting about the story in the film was the people involved, the characters, and the problem was they kept shifting their positions; these were people who were supposedly guided by the majesty of the law, who supposedly proceeded straightforward, but they didn't, they jumped around. Well, we ended up with just a rinky-dink plot, and in the end nobody remembers a thing—but Drew was always persuaded that the plot carried. He edited it, actually. Ricky [Leacock] and I shot it, but we were out on something else when it got edited; when we saw it later, we were both quite shocked.

As for *Crisis*, I think part of it was badly edited and part of it was marvelously edited. And it makes a difference; the halfway point in that film is fantastic. The first half is sort of a paean to Kennedy—it has a statue of Lincoln; it was just filled with the worst kind of prosaic, predictable bullshit. The second half was marvelous. Ricky sat down—I'd quit by then, kind of over that film—and found both ends of the telephone conversations. It really opened up. So in fact there is a great deal to be learned by looking at it. There's nothing to be learned from the first half, it simply summarized your position.

I just glanced at something on television the other day. CBS is doing something on Africa. First the cat goes down there, he gets off the plane, he's in Africa, right? He's going to dig black faces and bizarre things. He's got his camera out and there's a guy doing traffic. In any English place or most of the East, traffic is a marvelous thing. Well, the cat gets carried away, so for the first four minutes some cute editor in New York decides this is a wonderful insight, and it's bullshit. So we're all treated to what some editor and some cameraman—neither of whom know anything really, about Africa or about anything, other than to get the film into a bag—take a cute shot. Well, in the end, you just have to think, if they're looking at the wrong things, where are the right things? How do you see the right things? And who is doing that? You never see it in documentaries, so I don't know. I'm actually more interested in somebody's bullshit Hollywood film. At least when I go see it, nobody's bullshitting me. They're doing what they know how to do, and most of the time it's boring too, in a sense, except if the story happens to be good or if it's just the animal, simple thing, at last you see something that's alive. I can't stand dead films, I guess. And my sense is that most documentaries, by their very nature, the minute they're conceived, become dead.

GRL: Are there any documentary filmmakers that you like?
DAP: I don't know what you call documentary filmmakers. I was quite surprised, in fact I was knocked out when I saw *Warrendale*, because I'd seen some films that Al [King] had done before, and I thought they were terrible. They used to be dead alligators lying there, perfectly exposed and set. But in *Warrendale* he had the wit to see that it was drama and to go for the drama and get that. He isn't a cameraman. I was surprised, because normally I can hardly conceive of anybody making a film without a camera. I mean, what is it you do? It's an easy thing to say, but it means that later he just picks up and kind of summarizes somebody else's intuitions. It's like two people painting a picture. I'm sure you could do it

if that's the way it had to be done, but it seems a strange and incredible way to do it, and it's hard for me to imagine it coming out. Well, he did it. *Warrendale* is an honest film. It's not the greatest film ever made.

In a way it doesn't have anything like the excitement of *Target for Tonight*, which I'm sure is fake. It was all shot in a studio, though some of it in planes, but everybody doing lines. They're all actors. But it had a kind of excitement, because at the time everybody was going to war, or because the people who did it, Grierson, or whoever was pushing the buttons on the thing, they had a kind of excitement. I don't care whether it comes from real people reciting lines or actors reciting lines. Lines are lines.

GRL: Have you ever seen *The Battle of San Pietro*?
DAP: Sure. A Huston film. It's a good film, although if you see it a lot of times you realize what a total amount of fakery went on in the editing of it. He's using shots from all over the place, so it isn't really . . . It looks on first viewing, or second viewing, to be just some cat with a camera watching everything go to pieces, but in fact it's incredibly put together, and after you've looked at it a lot of times, and I have, you begin to see the cheating that took place in the editing. But you accept that because you know that Huston came out of that kind of filmmaking, and to him that wasn't cheating. Only cheating let's say to Al Maysles, who thinks it's cheating—but that doesn't make it cheating. Of course, the film is going to be here a hell of a lot longer than Al Maysles is, so in the end, cheating is a misnomer. But if I was going to make a battle film, I wouldn't do those things. I'd be afraid to. That's because everybody is smarter now, but it took that film to get us smarter, so it doesn't take anything away from the film. In fact, it gives something to it because the evolution had to be toward more truth, not less. And if that was true, how do you get more truth? Well, you find out what in it could be more true, and that takes looking and thinking, so that it does a lot of work. Just as another Huston film did, *Let There Be Light*, the one about shell-shocked soldiers. That's probably got less contrived editing.

GRL: I've seen both of them only once, and on first viewing it seemed to me to be the opposite, that *Let There Be Light* is more gimmicked up.
DAP: Maybe it is. I've only seen *Let There Be Light* once, a long time ago, and it's fuzzy in my mind. *San Pietro* I looked at a lot because it has a lot of vitality to it, a lot of excitement, and he throws away a lot of form— and that passes for excitement too. If that film were made now, it would

create a lot of excitement. That's as up to date a film as is being shot around now. There's nothing around now that's as well done as that.

GRL: I've looked at a good number of the wartime documentaries, and a lot of them were really well made, exciting in the editing, but they were often offensive, infuriating, because they were so chauvinistic.

DAP: Actually I have a lot of Signal Corps films. They didn't even bother to do that. They just show endless landings. Of course, the great final travesty on all war films is the film that wasn't about any war at all, which was *Victory at Sea*. It was just stock shots, it was the thing that NBC did on television. A thirty-two-hour show with that mellifluous voice of what's-his-name? The guy, the announcer. Well, you know, he's got the terrible, very English accent, and he's announcing all these battle scenes. Then there's a shot, there's just long, black cannons shooting at each other. Everything could be anything. It gives you a terrible feeling that there was no war at all. It's all somehow out-takes, and edited versions. I never sensed I was in a place when they told me I was in a place. I'm sure somebody tried to—they must have. There are some pictures from Kwajalein, but in the end it didn't matter. That's what's fearful. You could have taken Kwajalein and put it with Tinian and nobody would have cared. It was just people doing the same thing in the same shot to the same music. It was just an endless kind of tapestry of no place, no time.

GRL: That kind of thing seems most dangerous to me in television documentaries where it's done in part by the voiceover commentary that changes the sense of what you see.

DAP: Scourby. Did you know Alexander Scourby? He does some Band-Aid commercial now. I can just hear him saying, "Three hundred fifty thousand were killed at Tarawa Beach," you know, but with this kind of meticulous accent like a man selling you a brooch at Tiffany's. Terrifying. So out of sorts with what he's talking about. But it didn't bother anybody. People just accepted it—"That's nice." Somehow it upgrades war. Sort of makes it a noble enterprise, I guess.

GRL: What I liked about *San Pietro*, contrary to all those others that were so harsh and chauvinistic and shrill, is that there's a humanity there.

DAP: Yeah, that's true, but the thing about *San Pietro*—and this is my personal feeling—is that all those things are his style. He's one of the great stylists. People, I think, make the wrong assumptions about

Huston. Most of the time I don't think he is a very good storyteller. He has the reputation for being a good storyteller because he's gotten some good writers, but he really was a great stylist. He put the mood of a place marvelously down, very toughly, very ruthlessly. *San Pietro* was a terrific story and I think his style is the thing that made it real. But the story is what it's about. It's just like *Breaking the Sound Barrier* [David Lean, 1952], it was about something. It was about a lot of people trying to take a place and finally saying, "Fuck it," and it didn't matter. It still ends in hopeless, impossible slaughter. I mean that incredible thing where the tanks go down the road, each one at a time, and get blown up. But they have to keep doing it. There's a fantastic story there about what people have never shown in a war film, because it has taken itself away from Rock Hudson going down in a tank. It was just some slob you'd never seen before—you're never going to see again—so you had to put it together: what is this about? Are they going to take the town? That was the story. And in terms of that, it was hopeless, because in the end it didn't matter if they took it or not. The Germans just left finally. Well, that's a fantastic story, and I think it was so subtle that in the end you went away still working on it.

If he'd applied the same style, the same kind of compassion, whatever else, to a bad story, you would have hated it, because it had to have that underlying corridor. The opening thing with Clark—wasn't it Mark Clark?—saying, "We have this problem," and he goes on and he sounds just like your school instructor telling you there are too many bikes being stolen, he wants you all to smarten up and no more bikes be stolen, and in the end he says, "Well, we lost this one," he says, "but that's war for you." If you listen to what he's saying, it's horrifying. Yet he's just saying a straight thing that he didn't see as horrifying, and suddenly Huston translated that into a real thing: a lot of people trying to cross that river and most of them don't make it, but that's war for you. Which people don't have any sense of—that isn't war for most people. War is something removed. We win. Or, if we win, that's what war is. Not, we lose. And that film is about we lose. It's pretty important.

Breaking the Sound Barrier was the same way, was a first-rate movie in that it was a terrific story, and you were surprised. I was, anyway. You didn't think there was going to be any story. That's what documentary should be. You really care about that fucking plane. They were all actors, everything was fake—it's just fantastic the way you really care about the plane. You make an hour-and-a-half documentary on some airplane, I'm not going to look at it. I don't care about airplanes.

I don't happen to make fiction films. I might start tomorrow. If they paid me enough, I'd probably try. I'd probably make a terrible one. I'm willing to do it, but I don't make that kind of film. I'm actually drawn into a peculiar kind of genre, which is a semimusical reality thing. I don't know what it is. I know how to do it, I know how it begins and I know how to edit them pretty fast. I'm good at it, I guess, but I didn't think that's all I was going to do all my life.

GRL: What about *Dont Look Back*? How do you feel about that? Is it a documentary?
DAP: A guy acting out his life.

GRL: Weren't they real situations?
DAP. It doesn't matter. Would you care if I told you it was all fake? What if I told you it was only a script?

GRL: I'd feel cheated.
DAP: Michael Pollard wants to do it with a script. Get all the same people, have them play different roles, but all learn the lines—he learned the whole thing by heart, he knows every line in it. He can recite it. Someone performed part of it onstage. Like a play. He learned all the lines and just did it as a play. Does it matter? If it works, I don't think it matters. It shouldn't. But I'd agree with you, I'd probably feel cheated too.

What happens is that when you watched the film, you withheld an enormous amount of technical criticism because you felt the other had too much run; and if at the end I said, "Hah, I fooled you, it was all fake," you'd say, "Like fuck you did, because I'm going to let loose to hell with technical criticism now. I don't have reason not to anymore." Well, that's the style. That is just saying, "What's this fucking Cezanne doing?" It's just that you're used to one thing and then got used to another. We all have that problem. I'm about in the middle of it. [. . .] It shouldn't matter if it was scripted, but I agree with you, it does.

GRL: I don't think it's true that if you made a fictional film in that style it would necessarily have to be good or bad.
DAP: You couldn't fake it in a hundred years. You'd know it and you'd say, "What's this guy doing?" That's what happened to Norman [Mailer] a little bit. They're interesting in that they're kind of rough. I mean, they're rough to the cob, and they sure as hell aren't documentaries, but they're not fiction either. I don't know what they are. They're about a

guy defining himself as he goes along. The last he made, *Maidstone*, was a pretty good film. It hasn't been released yet.

The things that are interesting . . . like if you happened to really want to know what was going on in the Hollywood dope scene, fag scene, everything else, you'd go to see *Myra Breckinridge*, and you'd find out a lot of things. Whether it stands up as a story or as a drama is something else again. I can't answer that, but in a sense, if you were really interested in that world, that is documentary. In the right sense of documentary, you do find out something. If it interests you.

Information outside of what is needed to fulfill the plot. Fiction films have this problem. They have this big urn they have somehow got to fill, and as they get closer and closer to the end, you have fewer and fewer possibilities, and you know finally that it has to end a certain way, he's got to be killed, he gets the girl—whatever it is—so that filling of that urn gets less and less interesting. Then comes the problem, why do you deal with the plot? Well, it's because we're caught in a transition. Like you're frustrated if I tell you it was documentary and in the end I tell you it wasn't. There's no reason why you should be. That's what plays do all the time.

GRL: No.

DAP: Well, they try to. Let's say *The Connection* tries to. There are guys running around saying, "This is really going on, on the stage," and you know it's not going on on the stage.

GRL: But that was the part that didn't work.

DAP: Then why did they get into that bullshit? Why is there a need for it? Why not just eliminate it? Why not say, okay, if you don't need the urn, let's get rid of it. There is still some peculiar compulsion to hang on to this strange little starveling called the plot. So now you have Hollywood going through numerous tortures trying to get new and interesting plots that won't seem so draggy that people will walk out on them.

GRL: Outside of some Broadway movie houses they have small screens where they show scenes from the films being played inside, okay? Now one of the things I saw was a Western, but what you saw was a shot of the camera filming a big action sequence. You also see commercials on TV which are about the making of the commercial.

DAP: But people aren't really interested in how the play got made, how the movie got made.

GRL: But they're not interested in plot, at least not in what used to be called the "avant-garde" of the arts. No one considered a serious play-wright writes straight, realistic plays now. Nobody paints straight, realistic paintings, makes straight, realistic sculptures.
Contemporary dancers who are considered good—whatever that means—don't—
DAP: What you're talking about now is fashion. I happen to like plot, and I like realistic art and I don't like abstract art too much.

GRL: Where do you go, to Broadway?
DAP: No. I don't even go to movies, for God's sake. I don't have time to go to the movies. I have a six-month-old child. Actually, movies don't interest me that much.

GRL: Is filmmaking just a trade, the way a blacksmith would have a trade? Do you have any particular kind of feeling, for example, about *Dont Look Back*?
DAP: Yeah, I like it, it's an interesting film, it's easy to watch. I haven't looked at it for a long time, but it was interesting to me to make and to watch because I learned a lot. I learned something about Dylan, about myself, I guess. I don't think much about it now—it's left my hands. Dylan was doing his thing and we had to make something that would work theatrically. Well, that was kind of hard at the time. All experience told everyone you couldn't do it. The problem was to make that into a really working musical, not a documentary. Most people look at it and say it's documentary. It is not documentary at all by my standards. It throws away almost all its information and becomes purposely kind of abstract and tries to be musical rather than informational. Many people complained about the movie—it didn't tell about the lifestyle of the hippies or dope or something like that; that's what most complaints are. Especially the people who were in it. They felt it wasn't informational, although I broke my neck trying not to be informational. I never felt any reason to be informational because it wasn't something that I should tell you about. What I want to tell you about is the mood, I guess, not the information.

GRL: The documentaries I like best are ones that have a very personal point of view, that are subjective—documentaries that don't pretend to be objective.
DAP: Yes, but it can't be done obviously. The trouble with a documentary

is it really requires a lot of artfulness, and most people making documentaries, for one reason or another, feel embarrassed at being artful. Or else they're artful in a totally obvious way, which is not artful. You know, like they shoot their reflections. I'd like to see a good documentary on Nasser. That really interests me a lot. And I'd like to see a good documentary on Cuba.

GRL: Have you see Marker's film *Cuba Si!*?

DAP: Yeah. I thought it was kind of bullshit—he was so caught up with that French love of the liberal. I know that's not right from my own first-hand information. I'm not looking for somebody to give me a cause to follow. That's not the purpose of film, although that's what it seems to be used for. It's such a fantastic flag, it's so persuasive. There you are, your eyes glued to one end of a room, you can't look anywhere else—anyway it's all dark everywhere else—and the music is crashing around you. My God, it's like a moonbeam. So whatever it says to do, for a minute you feel like doing it; but at the end, the more it turns you on, the more you flip the other way later. It kind of sets up its own battle. I wouldn't mind seeing a film about Nasser in Egyptian. It doesn't have to be English. And I can tell a lot.

I would have loved to have made a film when Donovan Avis went down with his kid to give Castro those Red Cross trucks. Castro demanded a whole lot of Red Cross stuff in return, and Donovan went down, and he was kind of the in-between guy. He took his son along, just to take him along. And the son just went out and stayed and hung out with Castro for a week. I think he said they fished a lot. That was a great makings of a film. It wouldn't have to have a personal point of view. Just have it so that he was there and interested in everybody who was interesting. You don't have to be slanted toward or against it. Either way, it doesn't matter. It's no help. The mood of that moment, in that man's time, in the young American kid's time, would have been a fantastic thing just to be on film. I don't know what you would have learned from it, but I'm sure you'd know more about something you need to know than you knew. But that's exactly the kind of thing the networks wouldn't dream of doing. They are so terrified of a nonoriented position in a so-called documentary, they never would just let that go.

Did you ever see a film I made on Timothy Leary's wedding called *You're Nobody Till Somebody Loves You*? Well, I'm not for or against Leary, but it was just that afternoon, what happened there, the mood of that place, and it's kind of not what you would expect to see. It lasts about fifteen minutes. We ran it with *Chinoise*. In a sense that would be a documentary for me. That is about as close as I come to it.

GRL: One reason I like documentary is that you get moments that I don't think you can get in fictional films—even though I can't think of many. Do you know *No Vietnamese Ever Called Me Nigger* [David Loeb Weiss, 1968]?

DAP: I haven't seen it, but that is true. And I think Al does it in *Salesman*. Al has some marvelous moments in that. But moments are like aesthetics, really—they're putting you off. Moments are cheap now. I'm looking for a longer line than moments. We all know moments are going to happen. You can stand out on the corner here and watch the soliciting on Broadway. You'll see marvelous moments. But you don't do it because you want something a little bit more substantial. It's like aesthetics—they're for women and children, really. You want something more coming out of it. Moments are the cop-out. It's like after the film: the people who go away and they've got nothing to lose, and they say, "Oh, what marvelous faces." There is always some line that they've got. That doesn't mean anything.

GRL: Why did you make *One Parallel Movie*?[1]
DAP: Oh? You saw it?

GRL: Yeah.
DAP: Did you like it?

GRL: Some of it I liked a lot. Some of it I didn't.
DAP: I don't know. I got dragged by shooting Jean-Luc [Godard]'s film after a while. I liked Jean-Luc, we got along fine, but I thought he was crazy. I had no business making his movie. We trusted each other about as much as Chinese pirates, for God's sake. So after Ricky and I both did just what we were told in the beginning, I started to branch out. I got more interested in the effect he had on people, in his machinations, and I just started to shoot, kind of notes. I do it all the time when I can afford it. I film notes on something that is interesting, people hanging out, going to sleep. His relationship with people, the way he maneuvered them, the way it didn't work finally, and his attempt to come to grips with what he considered to be the American Revolution, which I don't think he has the foggiest notion about. None. Particularly the Panthers. None. And there was a total lack of comprehension among all the people involved.

It intrigued me. The lack of communication by people who all got put in the same boat. They all signed the same anti–Vietnam War manifesto and they were all saying quite different things. In fact, if it really came to blows, they'd probably be on different sides.

When I got it all shot I had it hanging around awhile; I didn't know what to do with it. We'd talk a little about it. I said, "Maybe I'll shoot a film," and he said, "Okay, you shoot a film," and then, "Can I have some of the footage?" I said, "Yeah, you can have everything. We'll just use each other's footage if you want, or whatever," and then he went away, and I got kind of dragged because there was this fucking film we had, just sitting there, gathering dust. So I said, "All right, I'll put it together the way he said to put it together." I had a ten-minute reel in which he outlined the thing to us all. So I put it together to see if it worked, but instead of because you could see right away that he intended first to have the reality and then the art, and the art wasn't on par with the reality. It worked the other way around really; to see Ricky first doing the so-called art and then see the reality, it pulls you into the reality, which to me is vitally more interesting in the end. So I flipped the order a little bit, but I left them just as hunks, and when I got about halfway through . . . well, after a while it wasn't that interesting. So what I got into was making a movie, and I got through it somehow and it got finished. I still don't know what it is. Henri [Langlois][2] liked it, Jean-Luc hated it, but then he reluctantly decided it was okay. I don't know what it is, but that's documentary.

GRL: Then a lot of that footage you purposely shot for your own reasons. Not for Godard?
DAP: Right. Toward the end especially. Like the stuff with LeRoi [Jones].

GRL: But he was around when you shot it?
DAP: Yeah, he was standing there watching, but he didn't want that. He had it in his head what he was interested in and wanted. I don't see how you can find out what's going on if you have it in your head what you're really interested in. But he's that type; he says, "You're just fucking around. You're not coming to grips with anything." But I suspect I'm wronger than he is. So I said, "Sure."

GRL: In the version I saw, there were lots of shots of Ricky shooting, but I don't remember seeing any shots of you shooting.
DAP: He didn't use any of Ricky's material, which has got me shooting

too, I guess. I didn't use it either. The only one I did show was the one in the mirror. It's very easy for me to criticize Jean-Luc. Where he's listening to the interview with Eldridge,[3] and Eldridge says, "We really don't trust you fucking filmmakers around here because you're only out for yourself," it's meant to be cute, to show Jean-Luc sitting there, thumbing his cigarette, and being guilty about it.

I didn't mean to be in any way critical of Godard. . . . That's not quite honest either. I certainly meant it to be critical of him, but I wasn't trying to put him down. I mean, I don't feel in anyway superior to Godard, either as a filmmaker or a revolutionary-watcher or anything else. In fact, I feel that Godard probably knows a lot of things I don't know at all. So I didn't want it to be a putdown of him at all, and I felt it was very important at that instant that I show myself—the shot of myself in the mirror—and I remember when I shot it thinking, I'm not blameless, I'm not removed from this at all. Everybody was going over the thing about we were part of the system. So there were things that I didn't plan a lot. It just seemed to me something that fell into place, and then at the end I shot the kids in the street.

GRL: What about the Jefferson Airplane?
DAP: That he set up.

GRL: And the cops coming?[4]
DAP: No, that wasn't set up. That happened.

GRL: Does he have any intention of coming back to edit the film?
DAP: Well, he tried it. He came back, spent a couple of days here, went through it and then he sort of gave up. He's into something else. It didn't interest him anymore.

GRL: Who paid for it?
DAP: NET paid for part of it, and we paid for the rest. We're out about fifteen grand, probably.

GRL: Do you hope to release *1 P.M.* as a commercial feature?
DAP: I'm not sure that chick will ever give a release on it.

GRL: Who is that chick?
DAP: That lawyer, the lady in the film gobbling about curing the business. It comes after the Eldridge thing, where she's in an office. Well,

there's a little bit that she cut off the head of that roll that actually makes the reel more intelligible. I don't know how you could make any sense out of the whole end of the film without seeing it, but she insisted that be cut out of the film. Well, I won't cut it out. She's a lawyer, and she could sue us. She's just a sorehead. That she ever got put into the film really enrages me, because she is absolutely unnecessary to the film. We thought any business lady would have done, but we had to have this one, and somebody gave her a contract which allowed her to censor the whole film if she doesn't like any part. I mean it's a really bullshit, dumb story—I feel ashamed to tell you about it. So I said, "Okay, we're going to run the film up there,[5] and you can stand in front of the projector and what you don't want in, you can hold your hand in front of the projector." If the chick has the balls, with a room full of people, to blot out a part of the film, that takes a lot of something. Well, she went and did it, and the opening of the second reel is very important, and should never have been cut. I'm not going to cut it out, so at this point we're at a standstill. I'm not going to have anyone tell me how to edit a film—it's crazy. Even Godard was outraged when he knew about it.

GRL: Has *Dont Look Back* made money for you?
DAP: Yes. Not really very much. Mostly because we're so little. Like there are about ten thousand theaters in this country, and a reasonably good Hollywood movie is going to get into half of them, a third of them, without too much trouble, but we're lucky to get into five hundred. It's very hard; we're very inefficient. We don't have too many movies, we don't have too much muscle, we don't have an operation that's able to put together a selling operation that can hustle a film into the last nickel and dime, so we're probably operating at about 5 percent efficiency where everyone else is operating at about 75 percent. The theaters and a lot of people make money out of the film, but we don't make much money. Our total profit right at this point is probably about a hundred thousand dollars, of which we owe Dylan maybe half.

GRL: How do you keep going?
DAP: It's tough. In the end, what's going to keep us in existence is 16mm distribution of films that we release theatrically.

GRL: In the college market?
DAP: In the colleges, and probably that is going to expand. Those theaters out there are going to run *Tom and Dick and Alice and Bill* till their

roofs fall in. And the other films, like *Chinoise*, have no chance unless some alert person says, "Okay, let's do it a different way." At that point you might as well do 16. You can get really good 16 projectors now, and 16 sound. There's no need for 35 in that market. So it means we can compete a little bit. It's hard for us to compete with 35. We're doing the same thing everybody else is, but maybe dumber, a little slower, a little more expensively, probably. So the fact that we're small should help, but it doesn't really.

GRL: The films that are being released to the colleges, is that through other distributors?
DAP: No, no. We do it. We have this great big room in there and letters come in and come out. We may have half a dozen films that other people have done that we're distributing, but not too many. I'd like to end up with films that I've made that aren't readily distributed. I've got maybe a dozen films like that.

GRL: Mainly feature-length films?
DAP: Well, maybe not feature films. Some of them are only an hour, some of them thirty-five minutes, some of them are like short stories, but you could band them together in programs. I haven't got a prayer for any of these theatrically. It just doesn't pay. The cost of opening a film theatrically in the city is between thirty and fifty thousand dollars. That's quite an investment, to me anyway, and it hasn't got much chance of making it back in New York. You don't start to make it until you get into those other ten thousand theaters, and we aren't going to get in anyway, so our best bet is to go right into that 16 market. Forget the 35. And if you want to show it in New York, get a theater and put a good 16 projector in there and just run it for a while, in 16. I wouldn't even blow up those things.

   The only reason to blow them up is if you're going to really go for a wide distribution, then it pays you, because the prints hold up longer and the system is geared to 35 and maybe it looks better in most theaters. But any film we've made we could have opened in 16. *Dont Look Back* played for six months in San Francisco with the answer prints.[6] Never had a 35 print—they were all 16. Nobody ever knew it.

GRL: Have you ever shot any films in 35, or have they all been in 16?
DAP: I did one—a dumb film called *Skyscraper*. That's "documentary."

That's a dumb, dumb picture. It's a bullshit documentary. It's just pretty
pictures.

GRL: One could say the same thing about most features, that they're really just bullshit, that they're not about anything.
DAP: No, no. I'll tell you why. You know why? I mean, sometimes I feel
this way. I might not tomorrow. There's a difference, because a feature
film is like a major job, like building a ship, a boat for a fisherman. Every
decision, everything you do is made with one intent, that somebody is
going to make a living out of it, that a whole system is going to be sup-
ported by it. Now a little thing like *Skyscraper* was made as a kind of dig
at that system, so we're trying to show off a little bit, show that we can
be cute too. But in fact nobody gets any benefit out of that film, except
Tishman, who owns the building, gets the publicity. We don't make any
money for doing it; the distributors don't make any money distributing
it. It's a gas. It has no real purpose in life. It's floating around pretending
it's ready for the party, but doesn't even know where the party is.

Take the dumbest film you can think of coming out of Hollywood, the
worst film you can think of. That thing was made fantastically, right? I
mean those guys hammered every nail in there in perfect style and fashion. When it's all together, a lot of people live off it for a long time, even
if it's not very good. They support their families, they buy cars. That's
not unimportant. Maybe it's not artistic, maybe it's not a lot of things,
but it isn't unimportant. A lot of people, that's what they know how to
do, and they're not going to stop. Just like building a boat to go out fishing with, what's that to fish? Who needs the fish anymore? They're all
loaded with strontium 90 anyway, and yet every fishing boat that is built
in Japan, it takes those cats one day to get down a forty-foot plank and
saw it lengthwise. You can't tell them that's not important. That's the
only thing they know how to do and they're doing it.

So I don't put down any of that Hollywood thing on an artistic level
because I don't feel strong enough on that. It's because we're in business
too, just like everybody else. We have to make a living, keep it all alive
and pay the rent, and if I can do anything else that interests me on the
side or in addition, that's great. If I can do it and have it succeed, it's
fantastic. But I don't care if I don't. I'd like to get feedback, but on the
other hand I've got to survive. I mean survival, keeping my family alive,
my kids fed, that's as important as making a movie. I don't knock that.
Even what the mailman does isn't less than what I do. Mailmen, really,

they're very talented, and they're very good at what they do. But there's nobody guiding it most of the time. It's like missing the moon with a ship full of people. It's a terrible thing, but that's the way most things go. In the United States there's nobody to help. Floating endlessly around. Everybody wants to blame somebody for the horror show.

There is nobody to blame, because nobody knows how to stop it or control it or do anything with it. It's just floating, knocking people down in the streets. What do you do with it? And Hollywood is just the same syndrome, just this great machine going berserk, but it is marvelously attended. It's really fantastically mad, what it's about.

GRL: People do what they do. I come here and I talk to you and I do this book. I don't know how worthwhile it is, okay? It started somehow, and I'm doing it, and that's nice, but finally it doesn't matter to me terribly. I think it's worthwhile in that there's some information that people will be interested in, some—
DAP: Hey, you'd like some feedback, even if it's only your wife.

GRL: There's some information that I think will be useful to people, so I'm going to do it, I'm—
DAP: Mostly to you. I mean you'll find out something.

GRL: I'm finding out more than anybody.
DAP: That's right. That's the thing you dig most or you wouldn't do it.

GRL: Right, and that's one of the nicest parts.
DAP: You'd hate to do five of these books.

GRL: I would.
DAP: Right. You see? What's wrong with the fifth one that is not wrong with the first one?

GRL: I guess it would just bore me.
DAP: Yeah, so you wouldn't be finding out anything, and maybe by then your audience will be finding out more, because you'd have the whole thing all down pat, so in fact your audience really doesn't preoccupy you very much at all. It can't.

GRL: But let me try to go ahead. Perhaps there is nothing wrong with

the guys in Hollywood doing what they do. They're earning a living, and it's a trade, but they monopolize things, the whole system—
DAP: They don't. That's the thing. You say "they." Who's "they"? Gulf and Western? Kinney? Here's this fucking Warner Bros. controlled by a parking lot company. What do you think motivates a parking lot company to make a movie? It isn't just money. They all want to go fuck the stars, they want to get in on the action, right? And they think the action has got to be with movies, and they meet all those girls and all that shit goes on. They want to get into it too. Now, somewhere in the back of the building there's a controller who says, "Profits are down. Quick!" and somebody starts to rustle papers and they all begin running in different directions. Next thing you know a supermarket, Gristede's, will be running Warner Bros. Well, what really runs it? What makes the changes? What determines what happens? I don't think it's anybody.

GRL: Well, there is a System somewhere.
DAP: Well, of course, there's a System. Everybody spends his whole life looking for it, and the System seems to be that it's devoted to going onward, crushing as it goes whoever wants to stop it. But it's not anybody. I refuse to believe that there's a creature sitting on top saying, "What else can I fuck up today? What is there I haven't got into yet to really put to the wall?" Nobody's got that control.

GRL: Obviously there's not just one cat, but don't you ever get angry or frustrated that you can't do the kind of film that you would like to do?
DAP: All the time. No, no. I don't, because I honestly don't feel that I should make films all the time. I'd like to go a year without making a film. Does that sound terrible? I don't care. I don't mind going sailing on my boat for a whole fucking year. That's as interesting and amusing as making a film. It could be. I happen to know how to make films. I can earn a living making films. I even like making films, and when I finally reluctantly get dragged into starting a film, I usually end up getting interested in finding out something about it that I didn't expect to. But if I could avoid it I wouldn't pick up a camera. It's funny, but I don't feel that my whole purpose in life is turning out films. I don't feel indispensable to the film industry at all.

GRL: The Maysles, for example, would probably say that they—
DAP: The Maysles are quite different. They do what they have to do,

but they're interested in something different. I'm not interested in that. They've got a kind of artistry of their own that they're fabricating, and in a sense—not in a depreciatory way—it's a kind of Hollywood artisan concept in that they want to be the best in their field, making a certain kind of film. They want to put their stamp on it, they want to get into whatever is hip, whatever is going on, and somehow we'll all get it, you know? To depict it, film it in their way. Well, I don't feel any particular compulsion to go make a film about the Vietnam War. I don't think I can bring anything to the Vietnam War that just knowing that it's going on doesn't bring to most people. I don't have any philosophic insights into the war. I don't know anything about it. I wouldn't mind making a film with General Giap if I could, because I think he's an interesting man. I wouldn't mind watching Westmoreland during the Tet offensive—that was an interesting time. Those are instances when it occurred to me that I might have been able to do something that nobody else was going to bother to do. But most of the time everybody is doing it ten times over, and I don't feel any need to just do it again. And I don't. Proliferating films isn't a big deal. I mean what are you going to do with them? I've got these films in there. You should see them. Racks of them.

GRL: They're cut?

DAP: Some of them are, in a way. I've got a whole color film, a feature film of Dylan in there going to waste. Fantastic. I've got the most fantastic music performances that you've ever seen in your life. There's nothing ever that even comes close to them.

GRL: That obviously has commercial value. Why is it not released?

DAP: I don't know. I haven't quite finished it yet.

GRL: And Dylan has the right to say yes or no?

DAP: Oh, yeah.

GRL: Did he pay for it?

DAP: Yeah.

GRL: Is he interested in seeing it?

DAP: I don't know.

GRL: He doesn't call you on the phone?

DAP: No, I haven't seen him in a long time. I'm still working on it actually, a little bit, but I don't think that if it's not out this month or this year we're in trouble. In about ten years it'll be just as interesting, Dylan will be just as interesting as he is now. I don't mean to seem like a dilettante about it, because the films do mean something to me once they're born; then they're real people. But I've got a lot of just raw material, and I just don't see any point in manipulating it in some momentarily fashionable form, copping it together and trying to get it into a theater. We have films in theaters. That doesn't bring any money. It doesn't bring any instant change or karma or fame or anything else. It's just like doing anything else.

The filming of the thing is the least important. It's knowing where the thing is happening and having some access to it. Whether you film it or not is your own problem, my own problem. Sometimes I can't stand it, I have to film it; sometimes I just let it go by. That's what you're doing with your life. You try to be where you want to be. If you feel the need to have that camera proceed every place you want to be, there's something very bizarre about that.

GRL: Gets to be a way of life.

DAP: Well, in a way, but that's not the way I want to live. I don't take the camera on picnics with me. And the trouble with documentaries is that they presuppose that the filmmaker is really recording his life. And in most instances he's not. He's recording some kind of venture. He's probably using somebody else's venture, like *Salesman* was a venture for Al. He thought about it for a long time before it appealed to him.

GRL: Do you worry much about or get involved much in the business structure of Leacock-Pennebaker?

DAP: I have to sometimes, but I try not to. It doesn't interest me much. I ran it for many years. I ran it before Ricky came in. I ran it by myself. It was just like shaving a lot. In the end it was just a drag to have to do. I find no excitement consummating a business deal or making money out of a deal. I just like to get paid regularly, and I'd like to be able to get films out of the labs. I never expect to get rich making films.

GRL: There seems to be a kind of ambivalence or self-deprecation about your work, because sometimes when you talk about it you sound genuinely interested and concerned, and other times—

DAP: Obviously there are things that interest me. The film is just a little piece of shit that you end up with, and if it's 10 percent of what happened it's a lot more than most things get. If you just see what is going on all around you all the time on every level . . . it's lethal what's happening in the world. The feedback is so incredible now. Just generally through various media, the rate of increment of energy output is staggering. And what's a film? It's just a little window someone peeps through. The fact is that what really film could do and should interest me to do, is try to break through that increasing area of what's going on and try to get involved in that feedback. I mean now it's so delayed.

GRL: What about TV? Does that interest you?
DAP: TV is pretty much closed off to us. Sure TV is very interesting. I haven't got many ideas about TV. I don't see how to make it more interesting than it is. I know that it's pretty lame most of the time, just because it's so dead. I don't think *Sweet Toronto*, for instance, would be a big hit on TV.

GRL: *Sweet Toronto*, is that *Toronto Pop*?
DAP: Yeah, it never was *Toronto Pop*. I don't know where that name popped up. That's a fantastic film.

GRL: You talked about feedback. You said that the increment of the knowledge that we're gaining is so enormous that really one can't comprehend it or cope with it.
DAP: Well, look. At the very moment that you, let's say, are putting on your hard hat and are running out screaming, "Up the war, down with students," at that very moment, if something gets through to you or not, you just see something you didn't expect to see that would snap your head. I don't know what it would be. That would be interesting, not because it's going to change either one of us, but because it's going to entertain you. That is what art should do. It should snap your head, suddenly. You're all set, and you knew you had it all figured out and there was no problem. Now all the people on this side of the wall go down with the tide, and suddenly, bang! It isn't that way. That's entertaining. That's tremendous. That's what people's heads are for, maybe. That's what they go out and hope will happen. Only they are so protected, it's hard to make it happen. Well, that's what I'm trying to do, except I don't see it as making the world better for anything. I can't make that judgment or take that responsibility. But the problem of being able to do that, that interests me, I have to admit. How would I be able to do it? I'd persist.

GRL: What about the possibility of going into video cassette or cable TV?

DAP: I don't know. These are just disseminations. I don't care about that. Like *Sweet Toronto*, I don't know how we're going to get it out. We can't even get John Lennon to look at it. He's closeted out there in Los Angeles, and I don't want to do anything until he's seen it. I only want him to look at it, then we can talk. There's no money problem at this point on releases or anything. It's just that I want him to see the film and see his old lady⁷ perform, and if he digs what she does as I do, that's good. If he doesn't, then I don't know what we'll do. But I know that it's a fantastic film. Those guys in there will never do it better. In a sense, it's the definitive performance of certain extraordinary rock 'n' roll guys, and I wouldn't even try to do it again.

I just have to be persuaded that sooner or later that news is going to get out one way or another and that film is going to get released. That's what happened to all the others, to *Dont Look Back* and *Monterey*. They sat on the shelf, no way of getting them released. That finally gets through to the mechanism that gets things released and oils the wheels; whether it's money or pressure or power, it happens. And I don't do it. It does it. If the film is a dog—and I can be persuaded that it's great, but in fact it could be old fashioned. And the fact is, if a film doesn't have any news, then nobody is going to carry it. If it has news, it'll get out. I may be dead before it gets out, but it'll get out. I'm persuaded of that. So I don't worry about it. I've done all I can do, I'm not a hustler, really.

We set out to do something in *Sweet Toronto* five days before it happened. I didn't care about shooting a lot of that. I didn't even shoot the Doors, I didn't even put a camera up. I was just interested in the first four people on that poster. I didn't even know John was coming. I went up there to film those guys because they knock me out, and nobody had ever done it and I really wanted to do it. I just felt that was just right, and I don't regret an instant. The film is fantastic.

GRL: Let me read these four names from the poster: Bo Diddley, Jerry Lee Lewis, Chuck Berry, Little Richard. That's it. You didn't care particularly about Eric Clapton?

DAP: No, no. I didn't even care about Lennon. I didn't go to film Lennon. Lennon and Clapton and Yoko showed up, and did this ending, and the ending is fantastic, and I wasn't prepared for it. It's beyond anything that the first four guys do. The first four guys are going to be a movie, a perfectly transforming movie. What John does is extraordinary, him and Yoko. You can't believe that. In the end it really puts you through a change you didn't expect. So that's a great movie. That's really what movies should do. You go in one way and come out another. People would go in who hate rock 'n' roll and come out just knocked out. That's good.

GRL: You do the editing of all these films yourself?
DAP: Yes.

GRL: Are you politically concerned?
DAP: I'd say I'm politically naive. I hear it all and I can return it all to you, but I'm not too smart about it. It's like anything else, it's a business, and I'm not in that business, so whatever I hear is already old. It's like I can't read *Variety*. It's like Greek. It would drive me crazy to have my life contained by that newspaper. And in politics it's the same way.

I've been to Russia a couple of times. It always makes me laugh, because people I know in Russia are about as concerned about their politics as I am about ours. They don't know what's going on in Moscow. They don't know who's running, or why, or how. Somebody says, "Jesus, you just invaded Czechoslovakia." "Czecholowhat?" It's just like me. I don't know what we're doing in Watts. And I'm damned if I'm going to let anybody put the whole weight of America's political ventures on my back. I just say, "Yeah, I just can't carry that." So it's ridiculous for me to be half-assed into it, but I do get into it. You read the papers, like everybody else; you get into the ball game sooner or later, but that doesn't guide what I film, particularly, I'm not into political films. Look, I was not interested in shooting Johnson in the last two months in the White House.

GRL: Are you interested in making features?
DAP: Yeah, I'm interested in feature length because it's just sort of a good length. People have adjusted their time spans to get into that, whereas in fifteen or twenty minutes, they're not. Fifteen or twenty minutes is like reading an article at the bottom of *Reader's Digest*. You get about that much interest. A feature-length film merits a certain kind of attention, a certain kind of interest, and I think it's a good length.

GRL: And fiction?
DAP: It just never happened.

GRL: You're not pushing to make it happen?

DAP: Not particularly. I think people are pushing me to do it, but I'd rather not. I'd rather make films about things that really happened, if I had my choice.

GRL: In working with Drew, are there any stories about how the network censored things that you did?

DAP: We weren't into the networks very much. Most of our stuff got syndicated, never went on network. But in the final cutting of the film, it was Drew. Drew was the hand that guided the way those films looked. Like *David*, which was one of the most interesting films I did. About the dope addict. *Jane* was maybe the most competent, most professional, but that really wasn't much of a film, it wasn't about much, in a way. *David* was the most interesting film, the first whole film I did really. The film that I'd like to have made was quite different from the one that was cut. The film that was cut reduces something that is actually very complicated to a rather prosaic, dull story. And the story in fact was false as it was finally made.

GRL: Things were set up in it?

DAP: No, but in the way it was edited—not the way it was shot. The narration and scenes were put together, were constructed with false voices and this bullshit stuff. Looking at it now, that stuff there just screams of its wrongness. And it isn't just me. I show it to people who wince at some of the things that were stuck in there, which at the time everyone thought were very well concealed within the fabric of the film. But the film itself still contains an interesting dramatic idea: a place where you can go, stay as long as you want to and leave any time you want; but once you leave, you can't come back.

GRL: When you shoot now, are you concerned with getting some kind of truthful reality and using it that way in the editing, or do you not mind juggling?

DAP: I see what you mean, but I don't think of it quite that way. Usually the first cut of anything, the first thing I do is assemble, which is in time order. I would never violate time unless there was a good reason to, but I wouldn't feel constrained not to if I wanted to. I have no rules about it at all. I think the main thing that keeps me honest is the absolute conviction that I'll get caught out. It's very hard to fool people's eyes.

They're smart. Even people like your old grandmother who you think, "Gee, she's so dumb, she really doesn't know the commercials from the program," they see everything. They're just trained all their lives to seeing what the bullshit is and what isn't. And most people are like that, so I think you give it up. They may not be able to explain it, never quite be able to tell you why, or they may tell you the wrong thing. But if you fuck around, and you say this is real and then it isn't, people find out, they lose interest. If you say this isn't real, this is all pretend, this is the Forest of Arden, people will go along with that too. You have to be consistent, then people will accept it.

GRL: You have no particular moral compunctions about using footage however you think it will work best?

DAP: I sort of do, but I'd probably violate them if I felt strongly enough that the results justified it. I think in the end the film justifies it.

On the other hand, I feel very strongly about what Guggenheim did. I didn't see it, but he did a film on Kennedy,[8] and he took some footage that I shot in *Crisis* of Bob Kennedy who was on the phone trying to deal with that Tuscaloosa problem, those kids in the middle of the university, and he just happily lumped it into the film and said, "Cuba crisis." He had a narrator saying what was going on in the Cuban crisis over this silent picture. Okay, it's just Kennedy on the telephone, but I do feel morally it is wrong, and for this reason: you have a situation where you've got entree to a politician in a hard situation, where he's giving you a kind of license—he may be giving it to you for the wrong reasons, to get a little publicity, but if he's an interesting person, he's not. This is the way I felt always with Kennedy, both Kennedys, and particularly with John Kennedy, that in the back of his head was the idea that someday, somebody who understood better than I did what was going on, who understood the whole problem that he was facing, was going to look at that and find out something, and it wasn't for me to get too smart with what was important, what meant something and what didn't.

Actually, I find that films that I make for myself I edit very little, I only edit them if something goes wrong with the camera or I make some terrible mistake that you can't stand to look at, but generally, if the thing is at all well shot, I feel no need to edit at all. Only reason to edit is if something has to be an hour and it happens to run two. In which case, you've got to edit. And that requires a whole different set of skills. But most of the films shot which are lying back there as just things, I don't feel any compulsion to edit them at all.

GRL: Let's say that completed they're an hour and a half. Presumably you shot much more than an hour and a half of film.

DAP: No, no. I shoot films one to one, just the way they come out of the camera.

GRL: Which ones?

DAP: I did a film long ago in Russia.[9] I spent three months on it, it was a long, hard film, one of the first films I ever did. Well, it's a lame, little child. It's a beautiful film, but it's just lame. It's got fake synch-sound, stuff like that. So I went back and Henri was there—Henri Langlois. He's one of the people I knew, and I said, "Okay, this time I'm going to do it the easy way. We'll just shoot for one day." I had synch-sound, a rig and somebody to do sound, and we shot one day. It's an hour-and-a-half film that's not cut.[10] How can I cut it? It's like a journal, and how do you cut a journal? Who's to say what's the most or least interesting? And filmmaking for me really has that kind of journalistic quality.

Now later there may be reasons to cut it. Like I had a lot of footage on Dylan, and you don't want to look at all the concerts. And I'm stuck with a different discipline, which is the theatrical discipline. Probably two hours would have been just too much. Even though, who's to say? If you were really interested in Dylan, two and a half hours wouldn't be too much. If you were interested in pop, two hours of *Monterey Pop* wouldn't have been too much. But my feeling was that two hours was too long. It was just a feeling. I could have been wrong, and I felt when it came down to an hour and a half, it was right. It could work and the theatrical audience went away still a little hungry. Which is right. So you just make those decisions. That involved editing, but if you don't have those decisions to make, there's no editing.

GRL: Are most of those dozen unreleased films journals shot at a one-to-one ratio?

DAP: Some of the early ones are more experiments, like a little short story I did with a girl in Ottawa,[11] and that might have to be edited, although I don't know how. I never knew how to quite finish that, but that's about an hour film. I took a situation where I knew something about the girl—I knew that she'd been through an extraordinary tragedy and that she was about to have a child. I tried to film one day with her—there were several of us involved—in which I was never going to explain what the tragedy was. But it just didn't come out. I felt that everybody involved understood without having it explained to them what I wanted to do, that in some way or other it would come out that this girl had been through some enormous tragedy. And it sort of did come out, but I've never been sure because I've never quite finished the film. It was just an idea to see if you could do something like that. I let people enact their own tiling of what they wanted you to know. It's the same in *Dont Look Back*. I never gave Dylan any kind of directions as to what I thought was right or wrong. I never asked any questions. It was entirely up to him the way he wanted to present himself.

GRL: Are you concerned about what influence the camera has on a person?
DAP: I kind of like to deal with people who are actors and performers because they are sort of protected. Sometimes I'm concerned with people who aren't protected against the camera, but in the end I guess I've never tried to make a film about anybody that I really felt hostile to. It would be hard to do. Some people could probably do it and do it well. It's hard for me because I have this terrible feeling that afterward, having observed somebody going through that vulnerability, and then to come back with a film that really hit on them, the first question anybody asks is, "What the fuck's this cameraman doing? What kind of a thing is that to do?" You don't know if you're going, to put down more of yourself than the guy you're after. But I'm not certain. That's just the way it seems to me. I'm sure there are people who will come along with a very acid camera and be able to really make it, make everybody be happy about it too.

GRL: I was also thinking of, say, somebody like Dylan, who is a performer. If one is concerned with getting some sort of reality about the person, the essence of the person, are you concerned then that he might perform for the camera, hide himself from the camera?
DAP: No, because I'm in no better position to judge Dylan than anybody else. I'm not a psychologist or anything. I don't have any particular qualifications for making any judgments of any interest, of any value. All the judgments I make about Dylan are based on my reactions to his music, like everybody else, so when I film Dylan, if he chooses to put on an act for the camera, I assume everyone looking at it can instantly tell as well as I can that it's an act. I don't hold any special abilities to determine valid action from invalid action, and I'd just assume that everybody is looking for him to make a break, and if he makes a break, some people will see it, some people won't. I don't feel that because I'm there with a camera I have any special privileges, and I don't feel I should exert any. I

don't feel that I particularly have any right to ask him any questions, to have him explain anything. What's an explanation? If I need an explanation, you can only assume that I think the audience does, and then what am I doing? I'm just making a rinky-dink film to get ahead, make a little money.

GRL: But if the film gives us—and I think it does—certain perceptions about Dylan, some sort of feeling about him, why shouldn't I think that you had something to do with that?
DAP: Well, I would think it's Dylan.

GRL: Do you believe any cameraman could have gone there and shot that and got what you got?
DAP: It's like . . . how can you imagine somebody in bed with your wife? [. . .] If you sent me out to film some cat that's really not interesting, all I'd show you is a modestly well-done bit—but zap! It's nothing. A lot of people really resist wanting to know about Dylan—he's hard work. The first problem they have is, is he valid, is he a poet, is this young Byron on the loose? And most people want to say no. They want them dead. They don't want to have them alive and around, troubling them. So a lot of people are going to resist, and I can break through that. That's just a thing I know how to do—construct a dramatic thing in which I'll find a way to make Dylan break through. But it's Dylan that breaks through, not me. I just do the thing to make it work. Now maybe the thing needs both, because everything Dylan is about is right there in his music, which he's written. It's not easy to read it. Maybe I've made the mood a little more real, make people want to read and think about it; but I haven't brought any great truth about Dylan to the stage. I just haven't done it—Dylan does that. So if there is any artistry in what I do, it is deciding who to turn this fearsome machinery on.

GRL: That's a great deal of it.
DAP: If Al Maysles had been there he would have shot a totally different film, but I think a lot of Dylan would have come through, and it still would have been fantastic, see? I can believe that.
   Happy Mother's Day. Extraordinary, fantastic insight by an Englishman into America, and it's horrifying. It's an extraordinary film. I could never make a film like that.

GRL: But Ricky Leacock might not have been able to do *Dont Look Back*.

DAP: Because Dylan didn't interest him. Sure. But if he had made a film of Dylan, it would have been interesting because Dylan is interesting. Now that's the thing. If I had made *Happy Mother's Day*, it probably wouldn't have been a good film, because the situation really wasn't that interesting. It took a different kind of art to make that film work. It took a kind of introspection, it took that irony that Ricky has, the way of making a thing seem slightly ridiculous when in fact it's quite real. The guy climbing a ladder to take a picture of the prizes. Beautifully done. It's so understated. You have to decide in advance that you're going to deal with irony, and irony is hard for me to deal with. I don't shoot that way. So it would have been hard for me to make that film, you see? If Ricky made *Dont Look Back*, he certainly wouldn't do the same film, but it would have been carried through since Ricky would have been open to all the emanations and the things that were going on. Dylan would have come through some way, differently, but in some way. And probably it would have been fantastic. I don't know that it would have quite the chemistry that's in it, but *Dont Look Back* has a kind of responsiveness that I have to Dylan, born of Dylan's coming very close to things that I've been thinking about for a long time. It's sort of an epiphany that took place. And I think that some of that probably does come through in the film.

I've gotten so I'm wary. Someone comes and says, "I've got a great idea for a marvelous film about the marshes in New Jersey." I'd be very quick to say, "No, I'm not going to do it. Don't talk any more about it, I'm going to eat," because you'll get drawn into things and you get persuaded.

I really have to be very tough with myself. I just have to know what it is, where I can go and where I shouldn't go—and I'll make a lot of mistakes. Actually, I'm probably more willing to go into left field than Ricky is, or than most people, because often the best things I've ever gotten into have come that way. But it's very tough, not so much with the situation as the kind of emanations from it, the overtones of a situation, the people involved, and if I feel that it's just not right, it's murder—I've just got to avoid it like the plague. So I don't try to fool myself about it.

I don't think I could make a film about anything. I used to, but . . . The first film I ever made, a thing called *Daybreak Express*, is a very pretty film, a musical film. It's like a five-minute version of *Monterey Pop*. To see it would make you laugh.

GRL: You're not concerned with things like trying to make documentaries that will be on TV and reach a much larger audience and perhaps influence more people?

DAP: The audience doesn't attract me that much. I like the feedback, but not necessarily from the audience. I don't know what that audience is. I have no real affiliation with a TV audience. I've never been exposed to it very much. There are a couple of things on television, but they fall like stones into a well. You never hear a word. God, you work for four months on something, for some prime time, nothing! Wanda Hale says, "The other night . . ." and that's it. Nothing. You can't. Your mind protects you against getting too involved in that emotion. The most feedback I get is actually from people who just walk in here. They see mostly *Dont Look Back* or something that they dug, and they just kind of want to see if there's something else here, if they can get into anything here, you know? That's the most interesting feedback. Occasionally we get some critical feedback. Most of the time they're not too interesting. You'd like them to say real good things, but only a couple of people ever wrote anything particularly perceptive about *Dont Look Back*. I was sort of surprised.

GRL: Who were they?
DAP: I thought Penelope Gilliatt got into something that I hadn't thought about, but I think she was right on: that one of the things that comes through in *Dont Look Back* is the quality of hanging out, the friendship involved with the people, a quality I guess I've never seen in the movie. In fact, the more I thought about it, the more I guessed that was one of the most compelling reasons for me to do it. And she caught that. And a couple of people out West. Most of the New York critics, they just saw this Dylan Unmasked or something, here's a documentary film.

GRL: So the documentary is a dead genre? And you make films to make a living and that's it?
DAP: Well, it may not be dead. It may be resurrecting. Maybe it'll get interesting. Television is killing it. It's murder now. I can't get my children to watch a documentary—they go to sleep. "There's a very exciting documentary on tonight's show." Wow, I mean, whew, they don't want to see it no matter what it is. "It's about Black Panthers." That's not the way you want to find out about the Black Panthers. You'd rather see a movie with . . . I don't know who . . . yeah, with Cassius Clay playing the part of a Black Panther, yeah, playing the part of Fred Hampton. The whole plot, you know? And it's documentary, but . . . that's the trouble now. It's not that it's better, it's just that people have been so put off by the bullshit that they get in the documentary.

GRL: But with Cassius Clay we'd think about the Black Panthers the same thing we think about war. We'd think it was Brian Donlevy again. That's one of the real dangers.

DAP: Sure. That's true. I agree, I agree. There's no answer to this, it jumps back and forth. But what you really are looking for is somebody somewhere along the road that knows something. Now the trouble is the road in films is such a peculiar one. Like the editor that knows something, he hasn't got too much access to make use of it. All he can know about it is how to make a cut work, or how to do this or that. His political knowledge isn't called for. Nobody has a chance. The only person who really has got any chance to put out what he knows is the writer, and then that's very tough too. That gets so butchered up by the time it gets through, that that's lost, so that there isn't really much of a place for a person who knows anything really of interest to get it out as there is in, let's say, a book. That's the only interest you really have in any artist, in how much he knows. Or anybody. That's the basis. They find ways of concealing it, dressing it up and filming it, making it come at you a different way, but in the end that's really it. If Jackson Pollock hadn't known something, then nobody would be looking at his pictures at all. It wasn't the colors or the way he jumped around; it was because he knew something was happening and he was there a little bit before everybody else. And if you wanted to know what was happening, which people do have the need to know, you could find out from him, if you knew how to do it. Same with film. That's why the personal film does have a possibility now. Imagine if you could get Johnson interested in making films, if he made a documentary film about the presidency. That would have to be an interesting film.

GRL: I'm not sure of that.

DAP: Because you're convinced as I am that he is never going to deal with film, that he is just going to sit there and say, "All right, turn the lights on, I'll talk now." But if he could really get into film the way he's going to try to get into writing . . . Like he's going to sit down and write journals, right? He's got a secretary there, and at first maybe he figures somebody's going to do the work for him, but ultimately he's going to get interested and say, "God damn it, I do want the truth of what happened that day to come out. I want everybody to know what Kennedy said and what I said." So he's going to write it the way he remembers it happening. He may lie, but probably he won't. Probably, in the end, whatever it is that got him will force him to make those journals true.

Truth does have some compelling quality about it that makes you want to try to adhere to it. If, instead of doing journals, he would make a film. . . . You can't film things after the fact, but if he could figure out how to tell what it is he knows about it—that man knows something that not many people know. But to have Walter Cronkite tell me about what Johnson knows is bullshit. Walter Cronkite doesn't know any more than I do really, and I like Cronkite. He is better than most of them, but he doesn't know. He doesn't know anything about film either. They just run some pictures and he talks. That's not film. That's not movies. That's bullshit.

GRL: Have you ever heard of the Videofreex?
DAP: No.

GRL: They're into television and they're sort of freaks. Among other things, they want to make these informational videotapes to send around to a kind of underground or alternate network. Like they made one on the pouring of a particular kind of concrete.
DAP: What do they use them for? Just look at them?

GRL: Right, so if you wanted to know how to do this kind of concrete, you can look at the tape and find out. There's a commune in northern Vermont building this big dome with parts of cars, right? So one of the Freex, a guy named David Cort, has been going up there all summer taping this dome going up. And he's doing one on growing herbs, right? You want to know about herbs, you look at the tape. And Ricky has a similar idea, but using Super 8 cameras. He wants to give it to people who know about specific things—not necessarily filmmakers—give them cameras and let them make films about the things they know about.
DAP: The people who know about the thing already know two things: how the thing works and also how it doesn't work, and they'll be less susceptible to the kind of easy bullshit that will find its way into most films on how something works. People find it obviously easy or they try to find the excitement because they are afraid to lose their audience. It's all always premised around some hoked-up thing. But if you took scientists, my God!

Like for instance, there was a guy who went down to Mexico to study meteorites. And suppose he chopped one open and he found evidence of a life molecule. Supposing you were going to make a documentary about that. The thing is to make a film about this guy who is interested in this and see it over his shoulder. The fact of finding the thing and the life form is the way *Argosy* magazine would play it up, right? He's just a cat whose name they use, and they say, "There's life on Mars!" and it's that bullshit. But here's a guy who knows as much about meteorites, as much about life forms as anybody alive and you're going to be there the instant he first decides that it's happening. That's a fantastic moment.

How about being in the room when [Harold] Urie watched, on television, watched the guys landing on the moon? Or [Thomas] Gold? Both of them had said opposite things. Gold had said, "You're going to fall into sixty feet of graphite," and Urie said, "Bullshit, it's hard as a rock." One of them was going to have to revise his whole concept of physics in about two seconds—and these are the two most eminent physicists in the world. What a thing to watch on film. There's nothing like that. Nobody is going to write about that. That's something just unbelievable. That's film. We went to NET, we went to about ten people trying to get the film. Nobody is interested. I almost wanted to do it anyway, just to see, because the idea just struck me. I don't even care about the fucking machine on the moon or anything else. What I finally did is I filmed a bunch of Russians watching it on television. That's in the Russian film. A whole roomful of them, laughing, having the best time, saying, "This will show our fuckers, this will really put their noses out of joint. Now they're going to get to work and get something up there." They were just having the best time, they just loved the idea that the Americans were getting on the moon. Something like that is fantastic.

What you get now on film is bottled and long digested. It's like the guy said, "The trouble with movies is by the time you see them, they're old-fashioned," and that's absolutely true. That's truer in my head than anything McLuhan says. Anything on television is now. Movies, the minute you see them, they're old-fashioned. They're about something that went on yesterday, and the end is calculable. You know where they're going to end. But it doesn't have to be that way. Movies could be the other way, open-ended. I don't know how. That's going to take real playwriting to figure out how to do it, and that of all things interests me now in films, this trying to get past that problem, because that's what movies need.

Right about now there is no movie playing in New York that having seen halfway through you don't know how it's going to end. And it's sad. It should be the opposite. The movies should open up. I've seen only two or three in my life that ever did. A movie made in France called *La Vie commence demain* [*Life Begins Tomorrow*, Nicole Védérès, 1950].[12] That film really knocked me out. When I saw that film, God, I just felt sooner or later that is what television should be, because you never forget it. Gide sits there and smokes a cigarette, and you can't take your eyes off the cigarette. It just disappears. He just sits there, and he's marvelous. He really talks about things. Up to then they were just names, suddenly they're absolutely real. I have the feeling I know them, that I've spent weekends with them. That's incredible that somebody could do that.

The film that would have really interested me to do as much as anything, and I'd still love to do it if I could find a way, was that period in Italy when Byron and Shelley went down and hung out in Pisa which was just fantastic. That was a turning point, that was a center, this enormous maelstrom, and Italian people worked off of what took place that summer for the next hundred years. Hemingway was still working off the Byronic legend. It's a fantastic story even in the ending. The carabinieri threw them out—they were firing through the windows of the house. It was a crazy thing. But at that point Byron suddenly decided and realized that the play wasn't the thing. The act was the thing. He wrote maybe two or three lines of any interest, but in fact the real thing was the gesture. That's fantastic. When a man who has had that incredible effect on the world, you watch him go around the corner, find out something . . . that would have been the most marvelous movie. You could look at that movie for all time. And you couldn't do a documentary about that. You'd do it just like *Dont Look Back*. You just hang out.

GRL: How would you do it?
DAP: My idea always was to do it with Dylan. To me Dylan is the Byron legend. There's pretty good documentation of a lot of the things that Byron really thought about, then there are the things that nobody quite knows about. Get people in those parts and let that take place. Enact what you know, and let the rest be filled in, let it happen, and see if one part doesn't make the other part.

GRL: They would improvise?
DAP: No, I don't think improvisation is it. I think you get too much bullshit in improvisation. I wouldn't do it with actors. I'd do it with real people. I'd do it with people that have been there. Most actors haven't been there.

GRL: But it would still be improvisation even if they weren't—
DAP: Oh no. It would be like this. Let's say that Dylan had a script and was acting, pretending that he was, let's say John Barrymore on tour, or

somebody. In other words, that he had a role that he "was consciously playing, with words that identified him, kind of a little play within the story. Now you filmed it and he did that. Now let's say that would have been a fatuous exercise in something, it might have been interesting, but only because Dylan was interesting. But let's say that your purpose in the thing is you want to know first of all what happened to Byron, what made him go to Greece, when did he come to the realization that he wasn't the world's greatest writer?

But let's say you assign those roles to people. It could have been Brando in his prime, it could have been anybody that really has been there—you have to have someone that's been there, who has been on the top of that thing and assessed himself in terms of being on the top. And that's a hard thing. You know right away who has it and who hasn't. You can smell it. That's what Hollywood actors, who stars are. Some of them have been there. Well, you put these people into it, and you work out a story line, work out a plot of what you know happened. Trelawny arrives, and Caroline Lamb comes through and throws a scene—whatever it is. You have the situations, you have four or five people who have each written their view of them, so you can pretty much put it down on paper and have people say the lines. But there are a lot of things you don't know about, so you just let it happen—if it's going to happen. They all know. You don't have to explain. Everybody knows what the problem is without your even telling them, because if they're interesting, the same thoughts have gone through their heads.

I don't quite know how to do it yet, but that would be worth doing because what you're after is interesting. Putting together what happens when an atom bomb hits a town, it's not interesting to me. I don't know why; maybe it should be. But I've already seen it, I've seen the bomb go off, I've seen the pictures of the houses burned, I've seen the pictures of Hiroshima, I've seen all of that and he's not doing anything except somehow martyring himself. He's making himself the precursor of the cause.

GRL: You mean Peter Watkins's *The War Game*?
DAP: Yeah. And it's bullshit. You know what I mean? He's not making me more antiwar. His ideas are all bullshit ideas. The fact is if you really wanted interest in the bomb, the story to make is the one about Stinky Groves and Oppenheimer. Now that's a fantastic story, and it's never really been done.

In terms of playwriting, in terms of filmmaking, you can't just go for the effect. That's like a little thing they do out at UCLA, for their film theses. They're little impressionisms or something. Filmmakers aren't immune to the pressures on playwrights or authors. They've got to think, do their homework, and decide what matters, what they should put their efforts to, and why. They can't just create a little reality, a little subcosmos that is so real that for a moment people will be totally affected by it and be persuaded of film's power. The film's power is vastly overrated that way. It may have a very overwhelming effect on you at the time, but its persistence is very low. Much less, let's say, than a good play. Or even a good book. You don't agree with that?

GRL: No, I don't.
DAP: I think the persistence of the film is very overrated. I think it tends to fade very fast, except for some extraordinary filmmakers who understand imagery.

GRL: But our whole conception, image of the West, for example, of war, of—
DAP: It's drummed into you a million times, but that's not through any art, any artistry. That's because you never see it any other way. The cowboy, he's just endless. You don't have any alternative. But how many movies have given you one tenth of the work for your head to do—let's say, that *Man and Superman* does?

GRL: I used to feel that way. I wrote plays for a long time, I went to the Yale Drama School for three years. I saw and read hundreds of plays, literally. But I don't believe it any more.
DAP: I agree that's not all there is. I dig Shaw—he just knocks me out. To see *Man and Superman* played, it's like a marvelous machine with everything working. It's just beautiful when it's well done, but it's old, it has nothing to do with what's going on now. The theater is gone. It's just the economics of theater. There can't be enough people to see the play so it's got to be film, or it's got to be television. The thing that interests me in film is mood, see? Which is what dreams are. The reality of dreams always fades, but what you do remember—but you never put words to it—is mood. You remember very definitely what the mood of the dream was, usually. If you were happy or unhappy or lost or something. You describe events and the things you saw, but the thing that really holds you was that mood. Well, that's what film has—and people very seldom describe mood in a film. But the mood is what really compels people,

what they really love about a film. The thing you loved about *San Pietro* was that strange mood of that terrible range of violence and then those children. The mood is what interests me solely in film. I'd throw away all information. But I don't see it as a turning away from Shaw, I see it as kind of coming out of Shaw. And I still love Shaw.

GRL: It's really contrary to Shaw.
DAP: But it isn't really, because I don't have either the kind of mind or the abilities Shaw had. I couldn't create that kind of play in a million years, but I feel that if I make a good movie, it's just as valid as his play. I don't think it's as good as his plays, but it's just as valid in terms of the work it does. I don't feel frustrated. I know that I'm a different kind of person—all my reactions are visceral.

GRL: Do you like Godard's films?
DAP: Yeah, I do. Godard's films are not mood. Godard's films are closer to Shaw, because he's burning with that religious conviction, and they have a very tough logic working through them. But again, my favorite film of Godard's is *Chinoise*, which is just the mood. I guess that's the thing that persuaded me most about it. The early films I don't like much. I like them, but they're not . . .

Godard wants his films to be really hardline. He's like Shaw. He's got that message, and he wants you to get it because it's a hard message, and he knows most people don't listen to it. I don't listen to it. I don't even know when it's coming on and I know it makes him so furious. . . . The idea of being able to work on a film purely non-pragmatically really intrigued him. But he said he'd never be able to do it as long as he lived.

GRL: You're not really interested in just shooting somebody else's film?
DAP: No, not particularly, but I don't preclude that at all. I might if it were interesting. You know when you're interested in something, you don't have to really sell yourself. A film could follow out of that. It doesn't have to. I don't feel bereft if it doesn't, but if I'm going to go anywhere, that's where I'd like to go. I can't stand the idea of making a film that I'm not interested in.

Notes

1. "In early 1969 Jean-Luc Godard approached Pennebaker and Leacock about making a film called *One A.M.* This film was never finished. According to Pennebaker, shooting was completed but the material was never edited. Pennebaker says, 'I assembled the rushes trying not to edit them too much and added a few other scenes—notes I filmed during [Godard's] shooting. LeRoi Jones's street Mass just happened. It was not part of the script. This is not the film Jean-Luc intended as *One American Movie* (*One A.M.*) nor is it a substitute. It's a parallel movie, *One P.M.*'" (From program notes, Cinémathèque at the Metropolitan Museum, 1970)

2. The film was shown for the first time publicly on July 30, 1970, as part of the Cinémathèque at the Metropolitan Museum, "An exhibition of films presented by the City Center of Music and Drama and The Metropolitan Museum of Art, conceived by Henri Langlois, Director, Cinémathèque Française."

3. An interview with Eldridge Cleaver in Oakland, California.

4. There is a sequence in the film where the Jefferson Airplane plays on the roof of a building, in Manhattan, and the police arrive, stop their playing and make them leave.

5. At the Cinémathèque at the Metropolitan premiere.

6. The first print made for projection from a finished film. From examination of this print, changes in black and white gradation or color balance are made for subsequent prints.

7. Yoko Ono.

8. *Robert Kennedy Remembered*, 1968.

9. *Opening in Moscow*, 1959.

10. *Moscow—Ten Years After*, 1969; not released.

11. *Michèle et Michèle*, 1964; not released.

12. With the actor Gérard Philipe, and includes interviews with Sartre, Gide, Picasso, and Le Corbusier.

Dont Look Back and Monterey Pop: Donn Alan Pennebaker

Alan Rosenthal / 1971

From *The New Documentary in Action: A Casebook in Film Making* (Berkeley: University of California Press, 1971). Reprinted with permission of Alan Rosenthal.

The film *Dont Look Back* is the most effective presentation of the reality of contemporary youth attitudes that I've ever seen.
—Ralph J. Gleason, *San Francisco Chronicle*, 1967

Pennebaker's *Dont Look Back* was shot in 1965 and covered that year's triumphant tour of England by Bob Dylan. *Monterey Pop* was shot two years later. Both films give vivid insights into the youth generation of the mid-sixties, the one by concentrating on the folk idol, the other by looking at the generation en masse at a pop festival.

In *Dont Look Back* Pennebaker uses cinéma vérité techniques to get into the flesh of Dylan just when, as one critic put it, "he was feeling around the edge of fame." One sees Dylan confronting audiences, blasting out "Hattie Carroll," putting down interviewers and matching his style against that of Donovan. Occasionally, however, Pennebaker's camera leaves Dylan to capture the lyricism of Joan Baez or to record Dylan's manager Grossman making a deal with the BBC.

But at the center there is always Dylan, looking at the camera, commenting, pacing up and down, and working at a song. What emerges is a brilliant portrait of a nervous, talented, and sensitive artist. The portrait may be a shade too flattering, but I suspect it's fairly near the truth.

Monterey Pop covers the international pop festival held in 1967 in Monterey, California. The performances of the late Janis Joplin, the Mamas and the Papas, the Who, and nine other groups or individuals are well shot, but the depth of penetration varies. Thus, the earlier performances seem to be two dimensional, with the real spirit of the artists as individuals only being captured in the performances of Otis Redding and Ravi Shankar. However, the real achievement of the film is that it breaks down the barriers between audience and artist, to reveal the flow between the two.

Monterey Pop inevitably suffers comparison with Mike Wadleigh's *Woodstock* (1970). The latter is more of a technical tour-de-force, but becomes weak at the edges when it attempts to become a documentary of ideas. *Monterey Pop* hardly goes into documentary coverage; yet I find it much more subtle in conveying the mood and feelings of the masses of beautiful youth, intellectuals, Hells Angels, and hippies who wander around with flowers and decorate the festival.

Along with the Maysles, Leacock, Terry Filgate, and a few others, Pennebaker can be considered one of the founding fathers of American cinéma vérité; he has constructed a style and approach to film which has influenced a whole generation of filmmakers. According to Pennebaker, film must show something that no one ever doubts. The audience must believe what it sees, even if this conflicts with the ability of a filmmaker to express his own point of view. Truth is all important.

Pennebaker was trained as an engineer; he got his first film experience with Francis Thompson making re-enacted documentaries. In the late fifties he teamed up with Ricky Leacock, then a young cameraman who had shot Flaherty's *Louisiana Story*.

A few years later Leacock and Pennebaker, sometimes individually and sometimes together, were responsible for shooting a large number of films for Time Inc.'s "Living Camera" series. The aim of most of the films was to follow an individual or a number of individuals for a few months through the resolution of a crisis or critical situation, varying from a Broadway debut (*Jane*) to John Kennedy fighting an election primary. My own choice among these films is *On the Pole*, a film about racing driver Eddie Sachs, and *The Chair*, a study of Paul Crump waiting for commutation of his death sentence. Since *Dont Look Back*, Pennebaker has worked with Norman Mailer on *Wild 90* and has also done some shooting for Godard. As to the future, he sees himself being pushed more and more into fictional films.

Alan Rosenthal: Who first suggested the idea of a film about Bob Dylan?

D. A. Pennebaker: Dylan's manager, Albert Grossman, came to see us and said he wanted to make a film about Dylan's trip to England. Dylan also wanted to get into filmmaking himself and wanted somebody to show him the ropes and give him a sense of the thing.

AR: Were you required to present an outline? How did you settle on the budget?
DAP: We just shook hands; there was no formal contract. There was no outline, no script—in fact I've never ever used a script on any of the films I've done so far. As for money, I was paying for the film, so the money was my problem.

AR: What attracted you about doing a film on Dylan?
DAP: Dylan was important—that was the first thing I was convinced of. I wanted to find out more about him, and I didn't know any other way. Asking questions was no good; I wanted to watch Dylan in as intimate a way as possible. Of course, there were limitations to this. I knew I wasn't going to find out everything about him and nobody could expect me to. What was important in this case was that the pictures themselves were secondary. What really concerned me was the ongoingness of the mood. To me films are like dreams.

AR: Did Dylan put any restrictions on you?
DAP: No. No more than I would impose.

AR: Was there any discussion about the audience for whom the film was intended?
DAP: I always assume that there is a wide audience for a good film. I believe that, if a film is any good, people will want to see it, and you charge the best fee you can get.

AR: In approaching this, were you conscious of any sort of influence from other films like *Lonely Boy*?
DAP: No. Frankly I think that *Lonely Boy* wasn't a very good film. Certainly Paul Anka didn't seem to me to be a very interesting guy; but on the other hand, I think he was more interesting than was shown by the people filming him.

AR: You've said or written somewhere that in many ways the Dylan film presented some of the most difficult problems you've ever come across. Can you outline some of these problems?

DAP: Dylan wanted to make a movie alright, but he wasn't particularly interested in having people understand *him*. Sometimes a guy wants a film, but he's not going to help you at all. You can't even state the rules. So you're three-quarters through the film and it's marvelous, and then suddenly for some reason you breach unspoken or understood rules, and he says, "I don't want you to film anymore." It's a game in which no rules are ever stated, but you must understand what are rules of nature.

AR: What were these unspoken rules which you say were gradually developed between you and Dylan?
DAP: They are hard to put into words because, as I say, they are not word rules. You don't violate certain things. You don't oppose the standards of the person you're filming, or if you do you must suffer the consequences. You also have to listen the whole time—and let the person being filmed know that you're listening and giving him your 100 percent undivided attention. At the same time you have to realize that he is not necessarily interested in what you have to go through. If you have to bring in a lot of lights and have him go through things twice, he's likely to say, "This is a drag. I don't have time, and I'm not interested."

AR: Could you be more specific about breaching unspoken rules?
DAP: Well, at one point, Joan Baez was with us when we were driving near Liverpool. We stopped at a gasoline station, and a bunch of gypsies drove up. Joan then began talking to the gypsies, and I just happened to be filming, for no particular reason; I wasn't particularly interested in what was going on. Joan then went over and got a couple of little kids, and when one of them recognized Dylan she asked if they wanted to go and meet him. They said "Yes," and she brought the kids over to the car. Dylan was mad at Joan; he said, "You just don't treat kids like that; they're not toys. I lived in a truck like that once, and I know what it's like. You just don't do that kind of thing." He was furious with her, and he was mad at me for filming it because he assumed somehow that my filming it had made it happen. He thought Joan had fallen into the trap of the camera. He saw it all as a kind of camera game, and it annoyed him because it was neither true nor real. That got him so mad at me that I knew in his mind the whole of my filming had become slightly suspect.

AR: You mention "falling into the trap of the camera." This brings up the old question of the camera itself altering or creating the situation.

Were you aware of people playing the camera game? Did you ever stop shooting because of people's acting?

DAP: It happened very seldom, because all the people involved had a very good understanding of what the camera was doing. They knew that the camera was recording them in a way in which they elected to be recorded. They were enacting their roles—Dylan as well as anybody else—but they were enacting them very accurately. In this instance, I don't think I ever elected to decide whether or not I thought they were acting well or not well. If Dylan wanted to come in and look solemnly at the camera, I had no business telling him not to do that. He understood what a camera was. What determined my turning on and turning off, in most instances, was whether I thought the situation was interesting or not. What you are kind of asking is, did I ever knowingly censor? And I don't think so.

AR: How do you sense an interesting situation developing? Can you give me any instances of beginning to shoot and then cutting off, or others where you suddenly realized that you were onto great material?

DAP: Once Johnny Mayall came in and sang some of his Irish folk music. I knew it didn't really interest Dylan and it didn't interest me much, yet it would have been impolite to stop shooting. So I continued but I knew that I would never use it. Now, when Donovan walked in the place and began to sing, it didn't matter whether he sang well or not. Dylan was so interested in Donovan, and in finding out what was going on in Donovan's head, that every instant was interesting; I just kept shooting because I had no idea what was going to happen.

AR: What was your biggest actual technical problem?

DAP: By and large, the calisthenics involved and keeping up with a story in rain or snow; carrying the equipment; not having any crew. The crew was just myself and a girl—Jones Alk—who did the sound.

AR: What were the difficulties in editing?

DAP: It was just a matter of timing. You start at one end and you go through to the other end. It's like writing a book. You try to disabuse yourself of all your preconceptions of what it should be; and as soon as you get your mind cleared, then it's very easy. It took me three weeks to edit that film. I did it on a viewer—I did not even use a Moviola.

AR: Let's move on to *Monterey Pop*. How did you get involved with the film?

DAP: John Phillips and Lou Adler were going to do the festival and wanted to film it. At the time, there was a lot of nonsense going on which I wasn't fully aware of; they were to sell the film rights to ABC in return for which ABC would underwrite the major part of the festival. I think the sum being talked of was $400,000 of which $100,000 would have paid for the film; the rest was underwriting the festival. In the end ABC chose not to do it, and we had to get a release from them and pay back the $400,000 out of our net. So it started off as a theatrical film with a fairly high chunk on its head as opposed to what it really cost to make.

AR: What do you reckon was the total cost of the production?

DAP: $125,000 to $150,000.

AR: With these kinds of big events, festivals and so on, there is quite often a problem of releases. How was that covered?

DAP: It was quite complicated. I know that initially the foundation that set up the festival was supposed to cover releases. That is to say, the releases were the responsibility of John Phillips and Lou Adler. It later developed that they hadn't gotten complete releases, and some people even contested the ones they had. As a result we had to spend maybe nine months hunting for releases, and it became a big hassle. If you have the money up front to pay for a release from a guy at the time, that's the best, because that is when everybody is most anxious to settle. If you don't do it then, you might as well leave it until the film is complete and you can see who exactly you have in.

I don't think in the end it really matters. I don't think anybody is going to hold you up in the end because of the lack of a release. For instance, we had Ravi Shankar running much longer in the film than was permitted by his verbal commitment; but when he saw the film, and the way he was used, it was alright. We had to pay, but he wasn't unreasonable. I have never had anybody be unreasonable, either in releases in general or in terms of money. Of course, you have to pay performers, but people in general you don't.

AR: You were producer-director of this. How did you put together your crew?

DAP: This is probably the first film I have made where a lot of other cameramen were involved. Two or three people had worked for us previously, and one guy was a still photographer from California and I had a sense of his being hip to the California scene. Altogether, we had six cameramen. Barry Feinstein was one of them. Then there were Nick Proferes, Jim Desmond, my partner Ricky Leacock, Roger Murphy, and myself. I went out to Monterey a couple of days in advance, got a sense of the place, and as far as the filming went gave each person a certain area to shoot in. I also set up a way of indicating which songs we were going to shoot, so we wouldn't all shoot different songs.

AR: What kind of cameras did you use?
DAP: They were our own cameras, the cameras that I designed for this kind of thing. They sit on your shoulder and the magazine tilts back. Two cameras front stage had twelve-hundred-foot magazines which I felt was essential; if they both started at roughly the same time, they could carry us through a major hunk of music and the reloading wouldn't be a problem. All the other cameras were running on four-hundred-foot loads.

AR: How did you have your cameras set up?
DAP: There was no backstage camera—it was onstage and was my camera. We never set up any specific play positions—the cameras could move as they wanted—nor did I indicate types of shots. I let everybody decide what they wanted to do—close ups, wide-angle, what have you. What we did eliminate was the wide-angle covering shot from the back—the old protection shot. It is useless, particularly for television.

AR: In a musical festival such as this, the sound recording setup must have been fairly complex.
DAP: Yes. What we did was set up the sound on eight tracks. Even though it was for television, I was hoping to go stereo. We just set the volume level on each track and stopped worrying about mixing trumpets with drums or voices with other voices. Everybody had their own track, and as long as they didn't overload the track I could mix them later as I wanted.

AR: You had six cameras working, and with every camera you had crystal control?
DAP: We had a recorder working with each camera, which was

cue-sound, from the position of that camera; but the actual sound of the music was recorded from stage mikes into a big Ampex eight-track recorder. One of the tracks carried a sync signal, which later enabled us to sync it up to the cameras. All the cameras were crystal controlled and in sync with each other, and as I've said also synchronized to the cue track. I could always find where I was on the main track.

AR: You had six cameramen around. There were also cameramen from the various TV stations. Did you get in each other's way at all? Did you try to define areas for shooting color?

DAP: We weren't worried about that. When we weren't shooting the musical performances, everybody was out shooting anything constructive and interesting, and I made no effort to find out whether people were covering the same thing. It never occurred to me they would. I wasn't after one person covering the main gate and somebody else covering the Hells Angels. I was after what interested them; and if a guy found himself covering the Hells Angels and wanted to stay there, that was his business. In the end, I think everybody got into some aspect of the thing that I could never have anticipated; and in a most surprising way, it all pulled together.

AR: Can you say a word about the color stock you used and any problems in processing.

DAP: I used 7242 reversal Ektachrome, and most of the film was shot with a film speed of 500 ASA. The idea of using the 500 ASA enabled us to have only one type of film in the camera and shoot under very dark conditions, or go out in daylight with either a neutral density filter or stopped way down. This way we managed to get the widest possible latitude for shooting and avoided that ridiculous changing of magazines from one kind of film to another.

AR: Did you play around with the color when it went to the labs?

DAP: You mean to get special effects? No.

AR: Where artificial lighting is concerned you normally have to be very careful about the color temperature of your film. You were shooting under all sorts of strange lighting conditions. Did this question of color balance worry you at all?

DAP: Not really. Color balance is something that has come out of the super-elegance of the Hollywood film concept and is furthered by industrial and advertising films. If the faces don't match or the colors don't match, everybody gets offended. They say that if the pictures don't look real, people will be offended. You know Cezanne put an end of all that a hundred years ago. I am not particularly offended by slight excess of blue light or a slight excess of red light. It depends on how you use it. Color is just like sound—it's like musical sounds that a band makes. There are no laws that say you can or cannot use any color, or have to worry about color match in film—that is not the point of it. One has to understand what a film can do under certain conditions and use it the way you want it.

AR: What were the main things that went wrong?
DAP: My camera. At one point I think somebody gave me something strong. I think Chip Monck gave me something and my legs became wobbly, and I put my camera down and forgot I was using a battery belt. As I walked away I pulled the camera off the table, and broke the lens on the cement floor. This was just before Hendrix. The camera was a mess, but I managed to put it all together again and to finish shooting with it. I had no idea whether or not it would work. Things like this always seemed to happen.

AR: Were there any other mishaps like that?
DAP: We had camera and focusing problems; batteries would wear out, and I wondered whether we would have enough equipment to survive. The logistical problem is with you all the time, and the problem is that the equipment is not that well manufactured and designed. Our equipment is better than existing standard equipment, but it isn't good enough for a war.

AR: You couldn't have done the film with an Eclair or a BL?
DAP: At the time the Eclair wasn't crystal controlled, and you can see what the problem would have been of going to a master track. If you wanted to cut from one camera to another, you would have had to do something with the speed of your sound and nothing would have been in sync.

AR: What sequences did you drop in editing?
DAP: Certain long things didn't go in, like the Grateful Dead. It was the first time I had ever seen them in person, and I was really knocked out by them; but they ran so long—maybe three-quarters of an hour—and

knocked things off balance. We dropped certain obviously bad performances, and there were other groups that I just didn't think were musically interesting. We dropped Mike Bloomfield's band although they were in the first two-hour version of the film. Then a lot of people were really turned on by the Electric Flag, so leaving them out was a distortion in a way.

A lot of people perhaps saw the movie as being a kind of an award—all the winning bands—but it wasn't meant to be that because obviously I don't think of Simon and Garfunkel as a winning band; but I think that the song they did and the work it did in the film was essential. I didn't think you could just start off with the Jefferson Airplane. I don't have any rules about it, but it seemed that if you took Simon and Garfunkel out you just didn't have a beginning.

AR: Did you use the sequences chronologically?
DAP: In a way, yes. The film has a chronology in my head, but I don't think it's the actual chronological sequence of events.

AR: You mentioned the dropping of certain groups. I believe you also cut out Paul Butterfield?
DAP: Originally the film seemed to me to swing out when it came to Paul's group and that of Mike Bloomfield. I happened to like those groups, and I wanted them there. But when we played in Paris with those groups, I felt the film came to a stop. The audience survived the stop, and it was okay; but when I did the same thing with a very long sequence with Ravi Shankar, the film became unbalanced. You can ask people to sit and listen to something they are not totally interested in once, but it's very hard to do it twice. My reason for including Ravi Shankar and excluding Paul and Mike was that Ravi was something new. Most of the people who saw that film never imagined that they would have to sit and listen to a raga for twenty minutes; but having done that, they were different people.

AR: When you're shooting verite style, do you find you are also thinking in editing terms?
DAP: No. I just can't think that far ahead. Your first problem is to get as much of it onto film. In editing you try to find out what you've finally got, but in the shooting the problem is to try not to miss anything.

AR: How did you handle the distribution?

DAP: We went to a couple of major companies and asked if they would distribute it, and they said it didn't interest them. They didn't think it would go, or maybe they thought they couldn't make enough money, or they had their own things to hassle. So then we decided to distribute it ourselves, which sounds like a nice, simple, brave answer, but it's really hard. It's hard work because we don't do it very well, we are not very efficient at it—how can we be? We don't have the access to theatres, we don't have the sales, we don't have the muscle that a big major has, we can't put out half a million dollars in advertising. We do very little advertising.

When Allan King came down with *Warrendale* I tried to persuade him to release it theatrically, but also said to him, "You really have to understand you will never make any money out of it, whether we do it or anybody else, but it will give you some access to money, or at least to action, and perhaps your next film you can get the money to do it out front." Well, he finally went with somebody else, but I don't think he made much money out of it. That's the most difficult thing—nobody really wants to distribute a hard film like *Dont Look Back* or *Monterey Pop*. They're too "amateurish," too "unprofessional." In fact, the nicest compliment I ever got on the Dylan film was from a kid in Texas who said, "I didn't even realize it was a movie; I just thought kids went along and shot home movies." That was exactly right.

Donn Looks Back:
Cinéma Vérité with Dylan, Bowie

Merrill Shindler / 1976

Spend five minutes with D. A. Pennebaker and he's got you calling him "Penny." After ten minutes you're an old friend, and the fifty-one-year-old New York–based filmmaker is telling you about the two families he's raised—one grown up and flown the coop, the other ranging in age from two to six. Penny is open and ingenuous, a large-boned hulk of a Welshman in baggy corduroys and a torn rugby shirt; and his ease is infectious; indeed; Penny's casualness forms the heart of his documentary film style.

Donn Alan Pennebaker was recently in town for a retrospective of his works: presented as part of the Pacific Film Archive's "Music and the Movies" series, which featured showings of *Dont Look Back* (1967); *Monterey Pop* (1968); and, the premiere screening of *Bowie*, his 1973 film of David Bowie's last performance with the Spiders from Mars, at London's Hammersmith Odeon (which garnered a standing ovation from the Halloween Eve crowd and raves in the local press). Between films, Pennebaker bantered with the crowd and the press, speaking of his belief in the hard grind of independent filmmaking; his current project of filming a trip down the Mississippi on a raft with an Antioch theater group; and of the endless insights and experiences gathered on the visual fringe of folk rock as it evolved from the sixties into the seventies.

Pennebaker first surfaced in 1967, when he released his extraordinary cinéma vérité documentary *Dont Look Back*, an almost random chronicle of Bob Dylan's prophetically chaotic 1965 English tour. After six years of running "a little company" that made films for Time-Life, he made his first independent film, *Daybreak Express*, in 1964.

It's an abstract meditation on a jazz riff by Duke Ellington, filmed totally on New York's subways. The film relies heavily on visual distortion, a technique Pennebaker has since dumped for the most stringent of "what-the-camera-sees-is-what-the-film-is" techniques. "I don't know how to direct," he says. "I just trust in God or whoever takes care of documentary films."

After watching a dozen Pennebaker films, interspersed with a half-dozen Pennebaker appearances, the line between the man and his works begins to blur. He's a living documentary, his own film of himself. And, like his other works, Pennebaker is disjointed, disorganized, and irreverently original.

Opening scene: How Pennebaker got together with Dylan.

"Dylan had seen a couple of my films, I don't know where. I guess his wife Sara had got ahold of them—I knew Sara before she married Bob. And, uh, Albert [Grossman, Dylan's manager] came in and asked me if I'd like to go on a tour. It was just as simple as that. I went down and met Bob and I said, 'Yeah!' It was gonna be a film that we paid for, 'cause we were risks. There was no indication of what we were gonna do with it. Albert probably wanted shots that he could use as publicity for other tours. Nobody thought there was a feature film in it. I mean, we went to Columbia and said, 'I really need money badly for this. I'll give you 50 percent interest in it for five grand,' and they laughed me out of the office."

Flashback: Why Dylan withdrew Dont Look Back *from circulation.*

"Dylan was breaking up with Albert and I think that was one of the problems. Dylan asked that we not distribute it for a while. The film is jointly owned by Dylan and I. I paid for it, but the arrangement was . . . people go see it because of Dylan, not because I made it. So his role in it is extremely valuable."

Slow pan across a littered landscape: The true story of the other film Pennebaker did with Dylan, an hour-long, 1966 color project entitled Eat the Document.

"It was done, in Paris, Denmark, Sweden, and England, again with the Band, It was done for ABC-TV, but it never ran because Dylan had his accident and it was very late in being delivered. The arrangement was that this was his film and I was gonna help him do it. It's not even a good or bad film, but it's unique in that we don't have too many people like Dylan jumping in and making films." (It's also almost impossible to describe—in *Rolling Stone* no. 77, Jonathan Cott said that "The quasi-methedrine logic [. . .] suggests a self-consciously disintegrating structure, an antidocumentary that uses the 'star' image in order to demystify and decompose it. [. . .] The film's structure corresponds to what Dylan must have experienced on this mixed-up confusion tour.")

A brief aside: 'Hard Rain' viewed in soft focus.

"I dug the music, but I got the feeling Dylan wasn't having a good time. At least it was news. . . ."

Close-up: Why people in Pennebaker's documentaries act as if there's nobody in the room.

"It's simply, 'Don't look at the camera'—once you condition them to look away from the camera, they'll do anything. They decide I'm some sort of idiot who doesn't know what he's doing, so they just do whatever they're doing. . . . And I keep the camera low, shooting from my chest."

Long shot: Monterey Pop, *Pennebaker's most successful film.*

"It was California and everybody is interested in California. It was just the right thing to do and I really dug doing it. My fee on that whole thing was fourteen grand. . . . At that point it was gonna be a ninety-minute TV special and the TV people looked at it and said, 'No sir, not on my network.' So we were stuck with having to get our money back out of this pile of film. It was lucky—we did it right and it came off. It's like shooting from the hip and putting the bullet through the bottle. [. . .] We survived off that film for a long time."

CH-CH-CHANGE OF FOCUS: The story of why 'Bowie' has never been released.

"Well, the grisly story is . . . it's not grisly! It was made originally as a video disc for RCA television, and I said, 'Listen, this is a really extraordinary concert and should be done as a feature.' And RCA said, 'Okay, y'know, if it won't cost too much.' I did it all myself, mixed the sound and blew it up to 35 and at that point Bowie separated from [Tony] De-fries, his manager at MainMan. I think he wanted to put all that behind him, I think he associates this film with Tony, and the whole feeling that that was part of his life he wants to forget. In a way, he's been bothered by the film chasing him. We were given a moral commitment that we'd eventually be able to distribute the film in some areas. . . . RCA would like to see it distributed, if only because they agree with me it's a good film. If David sees people like it, he'll probably go along with that."

Tight close-up: Pennebaker's long history of working with temperamental art-ists who hold on to their films.

"That's always the case when you get up where the stakes are high. You make a film of your block party, or your grandmother, and nobody cares what you do with it. But the minute you get major media heroes and attempt to, in a sense, ride what's somebody else's pool game, you get drawn up very short. It's not surprising—you're just off the street like anybody else and suddenly you want to get a ride on what everybody else has been paying rent on, enormous quantities, for a long time."

Closing scene: What Pennebaker thinks of musicians and rock & roll, tossed off as he rides into a technicolor sunset.

"I love making rock & roll films but I really don't want to be a rock & roll filmmaker. I just like the whole idea of it. You got two seconds to do it right and we did it right, and we got away with it. Anyway, I'm a frustrated musician myself; I think musicians are a strange type of clergy among us. They're the closest we have to saints these days."

Speaking of Samuel

Martyn Auty / 1982

From *Time Out*, December 10–16, 1982. Reprinted with permission of *Time Out*.

Samuel Beckett is one of the world's greatest living playwrights. He is also one of the world's most private and mysterious writers, rarely appearing in public and never allowing interviews. That, at least, is the myth. We greet BBC2's bold week-long Beckett season by investigating the reality behind the myth. [. . .] Martyn Auty talks to film director D. A. Pennebaker about "hunting Beckett with a movie camera. . . ."

You can tell Alan Schneider is a stage director who's earned Beckett's confidence. He calls him Sam, and not many people get close enough to the great man to do that. Schneider has specialized in Beckett ever since he first saw *Waitin' for G'dough*. He also directed the little-seen but legendary *Film*, which Beckett wrote expressly for Buster Keaton in 1965, a year before the great tragi-comedian died. Schneider's first Beckett production—*Godot* in Miami—was a disaster. The audience got so confused and frustrated they rioted in the stalls. D. A. Pennebaker, director of the recently revived Dylan movie *Dont Look Back*, was there and remembers the seat-slashing orgy. He's admired Beckett and been friendly with Schneider ever since. When Schneider was offered the world premiere of Beckett's *Rockaby* for a festival in Buffalo, New York, he invited Pennebaker and Chris Hegedus to make a film around the rehearsals and first night performance. "I didn't really know much about Beckett," says Pennebaker, "but I always reckon making a film is a good way to find out about something. Chris and I conceived the notion of a pursuit—with hunters and quarries. In *Rockaby* Billie Whitelaw's character is the quarry and death is the hunter, but in the preparations for the performance there are similar relationships: Alan Schneider is the hunter and

Billie the quarry. The academics we interviewed at Reading University are hunting for Beckett and so are we as filmmakers."

Pennebaker's familiar, freewheeling, hand-held shooting unobtrusively documents the early stages of rehearsal in Whitelaw's London flat. Schneider and Whitelaw drink coffee, exchange anecdotes about Sam, and work through the script intensively. Whitelaw finds her unconscious hand gestures help her to pace the monologue evenly. Schneider encourages and enthuses. You warm to him as the film goes on and he emerges refreshingly unpretentious. Whitelaw, of course, is engagingly frank on the subject of Beckett in particular and acting in general: "I never read books. The only thing I read is the script I'm working on," she confides. And later, in her dressing room she remarks to Pennebaker (behind the camera), "What a stupid way to earn a living, for God's sake, dressing up in funny clothes and going on stage. . . ."

Pennebaker finds Whitelaw's approach echoes his own search for context and for some outside relevance beyond the words on the page. "When Billie talks about the recent death of her mother, for example, it provides a cue as to how to relate the play to personal experience. For the same reason we chose to show Alan making his way to Billie's flat and the incidental details that preceded and followed the rehearsals. All my films work in this way. *Dont Look Back* operates on the principle of a journey or exploration. I don't make documentaries in the sense that Grierson defined them. I prefer to tell stories about real life, the way Robert Flaharty did with *Moana* and *Nanook of the North*."

Filming the actual performance of *Rockaby* presented Pennebaker and Hegedus with unfamiliar problems: "Theatricality is not our usual style but although Alan Schneider didn't tell us how he wanted it filmed at all, we were determined to get a sense of live performance." The fourteen-minute piece divides into four sections signaled by Whitelaw's reprise of the word "More." At each break the camera position changes, shooting from her left or right profile. For the last section the camera takes her head-on. Pennebaker explains the formal structure: "If death is the hunter, then the drama equals death. It zooms slowly on Whitelaw's body and face until she 'pushes it back' with a gesture of the eyes. The final time she is no longer able to push it back and she dies before the camera, but as she does so her head turns slightly and finds release from the eye of the camerahunter. So the zoom helps us to get to know her and the one 'intercut' close-up we use—her arms on the arms of the rocking chair—seemed essential to indicate something of the tactile reality she's about to leave behind."

The film offers a keener insight into the dramatic function of Beckett's work than anything in the string of critical-biographical documentaries made to date. But academic questions are not ignored: "We wanted to raise some of the intellectual questions about Beckett in a real-time context," says Pennebaker, "that's why we took a trip to the Beckett Archive at Reading University and filmed Martin Esslin speaking at a seminar before the premiere in Buffalo. Esslin is there as a balance to Billie and to ourselves who confess we can't 'explain' Beckett's work. The film, if you like, is our adventure to Beckett-land."

D. A. Pennebaker on the Filming of *Dont Look Back*

Barbara Hogenson / 1984

From *Film Library Quarterly* 17, 1984. Reprinted with permission of Barbara Hogenson.

> Grossman: "They've started calling you an anarchist."
> Dylan: "Anarchist. You're kidding. . . ."
> Grossman: ". . . Just 'cause you don't offer any solution."

Dont Look Back (1967)

In making *Dont Look Back*, D. A. Pennebaker did not intend "to extol or denounce or even explain Dylan." His goal was simply to record Bob Dylan's 1965 concert tour of England. However, in the documenting of Dylan, he also made a record of himself as an innovative filmmaker working in a new documentary form. Now that the film is back in distribution, after years of legal entanglements, we can look at it as a historical document that records pivotal moments in the careers of two artists.

For both, the time was one of youth and transition. It was early in Dylan's career and yet far enough along that he was nearing the turning point from folk to rock. Dylan, who was approached by reporters and fans alike as a new Messiah, was changing.

For Pennebaker, *Dont Look Back* was his first full-length film since the break with Drew Associates, where he worked on the films, *Primary*, *On the Pole*, *Jane*, *David*, and others. At Drew, he was instrumental in the technical development of the lightweight camera and the synchronized sound recorder, both of which decreased the amount of technical interference in the action being filmed. In *Dont Look Back*, he was able to adapt the ideas developed at Drew, where he was one of many filmmakers on any given project, to his own individual style.

In 1967, the year *Dont Look Back* was first released, the reactions ranged from one extreme to the other. *Variety* praised it as a "relentlessly honest, brilliantly edited documentary" while the *Cleveland Plain Dealer* called it "a cheap, in part, a dirty movie, if it is a movie at all. . . ." Those who came hoping that the film would solve the riddle that was Dylan did not walk away with a neatly wrapped answer. Pennebaker, unlike many of the reporters filmed in *Dont Look Back*, did not hope to interpret Dylan in two minutes or even in ninety minutes. Although he shot the film in black and white, he realized that Dylan could not be portrayed in black and white. Neither of the men offers any easy solutions.

The following interview is excerpted from an oral history of Mr. Pennebaker. The project was sponsored by the Oral History Research Office at Columbia University.

Barbara Hogensen: How did you come to make the film *Dont Look Back*?

D. A. Pennebaker: Albert Grossman, Dylan's manager, first came to see Ricky Leacock. I wasn't in the office. He wanted to know if we were interested in making a film about Bob Dylan. Ricky said, "Who's Bob Dylan?" Albert was a little taken aback.

When I came back, Albert asked me about Dylan, and I said, sure, I knew about him. He asked, "Are you interested in making a film with him?" And I said, "Yes." I arranged to go down and meet Bob at the Cedar Tavern. He was very interested in seeing some films of mine. I think he'd seen the Casals film on television, and he'd gotten a hold of some other films through Sara Lownds, who had worked for us at Drew Associates as a secretary.

Dylan was very interested in getting into a lot of things, and he decided he wanted to get into filmmaking. The assumption was that by making a film, or having me make a film about him, he would somehow find out about filmmaking. He and Albert felt this was a good cheap way of getting into the business. I didn't know how we were going to fund it. What I gathered from Albert was that it would be up to us to put up all the money, that they were just going to allow it to be filmed. I went to CBS and Columbia Records looking for people to invest in the film. When the guy from Columbia Records said "no," I realized that I was never going to raise the money. So I got from Albert some travel money for myself and other crew members, and we put up everything else—the stock and the processing, all the money for it.

BH: Had Dylan been approached to make a film before?

DAP: I think he'd been approached by Warners and a few other people to make serious films and had turned them down because he's that kind of person—and films, particularly the way they were presented to him, were all establishment. You had to have a script. You had to put yourself in the hands of a producer and a director, all things that didn't interest him.

BH: He eventually acted in *Pat Garrett and Billy the Kid.*
DAP: That was much later, when he'd gone out to California and he'd gotten "greened" a little bit in that world, but initially he turned his back automatically on anything that was system—that was establishment.

BH: Was he as interested in the making of the film once you started shooting?
DAP: Not particularly. He just got busy doing other things, and was under terrible pressure. I was hanging around the edge. Occasionally it interested him, when some scene would take place. He'd say, "Hope you got all of that." After a while he just lost interest. He didn't see it as moviemaking. He saw it as just me fooling around with my camera.

BH: Why did you choose to film a tour in London rather than in the U.S.?
DAP: It was the next tour, and he was very well known in England; much better known there than here. In a way he was imitating himself. It was a drag and he didn't like to do it. He wanted to be doing rock 'n' roll. He didn't want to be doing folk. He was getting tired of it, but he'd created it, and he had to do it. That's one thing that made it hard for him. In this country, he didn't try to do rock 'n' roll. I don't think he'd have done it in this country. He went up to Newport and he sang "Maggie's Farm," and it blew all their minds away. The folkies never forgave him for that.

    At the time of the filming, it seemed to me that he had to face a very heavy decision in his life. I could sense it coming. So I wanted to make the film.

BH: Dylan gave his interviewers in the film a lot or trouble. Did he give you the same kind of trouble?
DAP: No. No, no, he didn't. That was all just a kind of game that he played, but he did it specifically because he knew we were filming. It was showing off. He liked the idea of being an intellectual youth. It intrigued him, because most newspaper reporters of the ilk that he would run into

were really buffoons to some degree. It wasn't a very heavy victory for anybody, to show that one of them was a buffoon. And occasionally, they weren't buffoons. Occasionally, they were a little smarter than that. But it was part of the picture he wanted to create of himself, as a kind of young Tartar. He was very much influenced by both Jack Kerouac and Allen Ginsberg. He was interested in the idea of being a writer, and the idea of being a jail kid. I mean, he would like to have actually done time, I think. That whole idea of a jail kid writer really intrigued him.

BH: What was your working relationship like with him?
DAP: He was a very easy guy to get along with. We got along very well. I liked him quite well. I think we were very good friends. But I didn't try to become a part of his scene. Dylan was under terrible strain, and I knew that there were probably drugs going down, around, and I wasn't interested in getting into that at all. So I kept a kind of distance.

BH: What did he think of the film after you had edited it?
DAP: We had this screening and a lot of people turned up. Most of them seemed to be very hostile to me. I felt very paranoid. They were prepared to love Dylan and hate the movie. And Dylan was hanging out there, and he was a really "heavy" celebrity among Californians. After the movie was over, I just felt it was the worst screening of a film I'd ever been present at, mine or anyone else's. It was a disaster.

There were a few things that were surprises to Dylan. He had never seen that little scene of himself down in Greenwood, Mississippi. (Dylan sings "Only a Pawn in Their Game" to a group of blacks and civil rights workers in Greenwood.) Ed Emshwiller and Jack Willis had gone down there to make a film on civil rights. They shot this stuff with Dylan and didn't know what to do with it. Dylan, which is to say Albert, was not going to give them rights to use it. Jack Willis sent it over, and I just put it up on a shelf. It sat there until there was one moment when I was putting the film together, and I came to that point where the BBC interrogator asked him, "How did it all begin, Bob?," and I looked up and there was this piece of film. I thought I might as well look at it now and fastened it on, in order to see it, and it stayed in the film.

Dylan then said, "Well, you're going to have to do a lot of work on this film. We'll have another screening tomorrow and I'll make a list." I was very depressed because I was finished with it and I didn't want to change anything. So with despair I brought it in the next day and this time there were even more people, and the screening was even worse than the one before. Screening facilities for 16mm in California are planned to be bad. It's partly the equipment and partly the people who run it all. Their commitment to Hollywood means that they'll ruin 16mm films. This was a relatively well-thought-of screening room, but the film kept going out of sync; the equipment didn't work; the projector was horrible. At the end I was ready to commit suicide. The lights went on and Dylan had a big pad, and he jumped up and said, "Well, it's perfect; can't change a thing."

It was then two hours long, and I finally got it down to ninety minutes. I sent him a print and he had only two objections: I'd cut out a piece where he was writing a song. He said, "I bet you never shot a picture of anyone writing a song before." I said, no I hadn't. I didn't want to cut it out, but I was afraid it was just too long. I looked at it again, and I stuck the whole thing back in—about five minutes of film. The second thing was the fight. He said, "I don't like that fight. I don't want people to see me like that." I said that I understood, and I didn't like to use that, but on the other hand, it was really important to the film, and I'd thought about it a lot. Albert agreed with me that it was very crucial.

BH: Didn't you start to make another film with Dylan?

DAP: The next year, I went over to England again with him. Dylan called me and said, "Well, now you've made your film," which he called *Dylan by Pennebaker*. He said, "I want to make *my* film, but I want you to help me. Come along and be the camera." I could see it was going to be difficult, because—I don't know, he had the Band then. I wanted to go because this was what he wanted to be doing now, and he'd found a way finally to make it work. You could see the difference. At the last Albert Hall concert, God, everybody was there. The Beatles were there. The Stones. Everybody. He was excited, but he felt very frustrated. When you saw him with the Band, he was like a little kid out there, jumping around. It was this wonderful jump from one film to the other, and that interested me. I realized it was going to be his film, that I had to lay back. I didn't want to get into a film competition with him. I had to try to help him make a film of his own.

And I did. I tried for a while. I stood it as long as I could. That year, with the Band, there were a lot of problems. Dylan would never sleep; he'd drive everybody nuts, and he was going a little crazier every day. The filming had no logic. Whatever he filmed, he would take long hours and we would set up scenes with people, and acting, and he would pretend to be directing. Things were just so goofy that finally I couldn't stand it.

Henri Langlois had invited me to come down to Cannes to show *Dont Look Back*. I said to Dylan, "Listen, I'm going to split," and Dylan was furious. I said, "I've left the camera equipment." I flew to Cannes with a print of *Dont Look Back*, which by the way I had shown to the Beatles earlier in the hotel room in London. They all came one night to see it. It was sort of a crazy thing because they didn't know what the film was about. Had no idea what it was about.

I was at Cannes for two days, and by the end of the second day, I went to Henri and said, "I'm not going to show the film." He said, "Well, I've got the screens up." I said, "Just tell them the print has broken or something. I can't do it." That festival is so hard that I didn't think it would interest me to try to take it on. It's the ultimate in the business. So I left. Never showed the film.

BH: Did you try to find a major distributor before you started distributing it?

DAP: Before we distributed it, I'd gone around to all the majors, Seven Arts and Warners. I remember at one point going to Screen Gems with the goddamn film, and I'd set it up in the screening room, and a guy came in and looked at it about ten minutes—and about four people came in, sat down. Then one of them got up and another one got up, and finally, by the end of the first reel, the last guy got up and left. The projectionist said, "Do you want me to put the second reel on?" I said, "Well, I've seen it, don't put it on for me. But if you want to see it, go ahead." Nobody would look at it. I was showing it at various places and people were going crazy to see it. I knew it was going to be a hit. Yet I thought I was in some dream world, where the guys running these companies just didn't know what was going on out there.

We found these guys who had this chain of porno theaters out West. There were two guys, and it was called Art Theater Guild. Until then they'd had these slightly soft-core porn films that they made. One of these guys had a kid, a young kid who was a Dylan freak. So the kid ran it at the Presidio, and we didn't even have a 35mm print. We gave him one 16mm print. He only had one print. They ran it for six months out there and never told anybody it wasn't 35mm. If it had been destroyed, we'd have been out of business.

BH: What was the critical response to the film?

DAP: *Variety* reviewed it. Everybody reviewed it as a regular theater film. I was surprised by the level of criticism. People whom I knew really sat down and looked at that movie and thought about it in a way that nobody had ever done with anything I'd done before, and put down on paper things that I hadn't bothered to think through, but I could see were right. It was like double-checking something, and it came out right. That was the first time I ever got any kind of critical feedback that was interesting to me.

BH: Did you think that young people would be more accepting of your filmmaking style?

DAP: I didn't think about that at all. I guess I assumed that people who were interested in Dylan wouldn't worry about the form. I didn't think that they'd accept one form better than another necessarily. I just assumed that the Hollywood form was here to stay. I didn't really think I was fighting it. Later I refused to enter the film in the Academy Awards. An actress, I can't remember her name, became outraged with me about the film. She said, why are you doing this so badly? It's like you're trying to rub it in our noses. You know it looks bad. I'd never thought of it that way before, but she saw it as If I were trying to somehow assault them. I really hadn't thought it through. The fact is I did it the only way I could do it.

BH: Do you think the sixties as an era affected your filmmaking?

DAP: Oh, I'm sure they did. Everything seemed possible for a while for us. I'm sure that it provided a lot of impetus for things that I don't fully understand. Everything was getting overturned, and suddenly you could put a film in a theater and make money out of it. It seemed to me to go with the times. Nobody had any idea that they were the sixties, don't you see.

1966 and All That:
D. A. Pennebaker, Filmmaker

Shelly Livson / 1984

Interview in New York City, Spring 1984. From *All Across the Telegraph: A Bob Dylan Handbook*, edited by Michael Gray and John Bauldie (London: Sidgwick and Jackson, 1987). Reprinted with permission of Michael Gray.

Shelly Livson: How did filming Dylan's 1966 tour come about, after you'd already made your film of his '65 tour, *Dont Look Back*?
D. A. Pennebaker: Dylan wanted to make a film of his tour with the band [later the Band], and he wanted to direct it and he asked me if I would help him film it.

SL: Making the film was his idea?
DAP: Yeah. . . . It was to be a TV show, that's what I was told, and later on I did have some talks with ABC about it. I wasn't supposed to be the producer, and I wasn't supposed to be the editor necessarily, though it was unclear. We were going to do it as we went along.
[In the event, the ABC-TV deadline was one of the things blown out by Dylan's motorcycle crash. When it came to editing, the film material effectively split into two potential projects. Dylan worked on editing the mainly non-concert footage with Howard Alk, who had been Pennebaker's assistant on *Dont Look Back* the year before. The resulting film, never widely shown, was *Eat the Document*. The other potential project, the film Pennebaker might like to have made, using mostly the still-unshown concert footage, never was put together, since this time around, unlike with *Dont Look Back*, Pennebaker had merely been hired to help shoot whatever film Dylan wanted.]

SL: When did you join the tour? You didn't go on the Australian leg?

DAP: I was doing something else. I don't remember what it was now. I met him in Stockholm.

SL: And then from Stockholm [April 29–30, 1966] you stayed with the tour till London [May 26–27]?
DAP: Yeah. Through the Albert Hall.

SL: How many cameramen were there?
DAP: Just Howard Alk and myself.

SL: And did you have a sound man?
DAP: Yeah. We had a sound man. And Dylan had a sound man, Bob Alderman, who was supposed to be recording all the concerts on a sync tape. We later found out that for some reason it was breaking down— that it hadn't worked and that none of the concerts had any sync track on them; so one of the problems we had was trying to sync those concerts up. I had one sound person with me—well, I guess I used Jones Alk, Howard's wife . . . my recollection is that it was Howard and I and Jones. Pretty much the three of us were doing it.

SL: Were all the concerts recorded?
DAP: We recorded every concert from beginning to end, on audio tape.

SL: And did you film all the concerts as well?
DAP: Parts of concerts. Some concerts were filmed. Some concerts Howard Alk filmed and I wasn't even there. I went to Cannes for two or three days and so there is some material that I never saw that Howard shot. But most of the stuff, I shot. As I recall, most of the filming, I did. [. . .]

Again, it was Bob's film, and he wasn't really interested in making a concert film. He was interested in making a film for television. He wasn't even interested in a theatrical film. He was interested primarily in directing material off the stage. Stage material did not interest him, and in fact I shot a lot of it kind of on my own . . . The time that I got on the stage with him, I filmed the whole concert from on-stage—he didn't know that I was going to do that. He was kind of surprised to see me there.

SL: Which concert was that?
DAP: I think it was Glasgow. But it might have been Edinburgh. . . . My recollection is that it was in Scotland. I filmed two or three concerts very hard and then I filmed in France and [at the] Albert Hall. I missed three

concerts. I missed Cardiff, Birmingham, and Liverpool. Or maybe it was Cardiff, Bristol, and Birmingham.

SL: Did Howard Alk film those?
DAP: Yeah. But again, I've never actually seen what he filmed.

SL: He gave it to Bob?
DAP: Bob has all that footage as far as I know.

SL: The press reports at the time indicated that the audience reaction was pretty negative to the electric half of the concerts. Was that your impression?
DAP: No. Some places it was, some places it wasn't. It varied. It didn't bother him that much. . . . In general he was having so much better a time with the band than he was by himself that you could see right away that the difference was night and day in terms of his performance.

SL: So he actually enjoyed the tour?
DAP: Well, he liked playing with the band a lot.

SL: We were led to believe he was on some kind of death trip.
DAP: Oh, there was a lot of weird behavior on the trip. I don't think it was a death trip. The pressures were enormous. . . . He did behave weirdly sometimes, but the one thing that I was really sure of was that he really liked playing with Robbie and having that electric music all around him. It was a really big incentive to him musically and I saw him do a lot of work. He wrote a lot of music on that trip, some of which we filmed. I think there's snatches of it in the film that he made.

SL: About Paris: the reports were that there was particularly negative reaction by the audience there, and that Dylan was supposedly tuning up for ten minutes between each song, and that he said if you don't like it, go read a newspaper, or something like that . . .
DAP: Yeah, he did long tune-ups. . . . Well, the French were very freaked out by Dylan. I think he couldn't be too outrageous for the French. I think no matter how outrageous he was, they were ready to—despite the screaming and yelling I think they took it as some kind of monumental manifestation of some sort. There were people who were outraged in the audience but I never got the feeling that any audience was really totally hostile.

But that may be just my memory. You gotta understand, when you're making a film, you're really underwater. And you don't have time for a lot of the niceties of social gatherings, and you tend to be really preoccupied with what you're doing, and sometimes it's backstage and sometimes it's onstage and sometimes it's audience. Sometimes you miss what later everybody remembers as the same occasion. You were just somewhere else, or else you're just absolutely out of it.

It's a really hard process to follow a concert-tour, because you're unlike anybody else. They can knock off at five in the morning and sleep for eight hours. You're processing film and getting your batteries charged practically round the clock. So you're never off, you're always doing something.

In this instance I felt that there would be more people helping us but the people were not much use to us. It just came down to Dylan and me, and sometimes I had somebody else doing the sound. I think he had some actress there—Zuzu was doing sound at one point and at another point I think I had [. . .] Marianne Faithfull. I mean people like that were always in very good control of themselves because they had to go out and do concerts and stuff—they didn't mess around and get drunk and stuff. So you could always count on them to be alert and capable for periods of time. A lot of the people who just hung around, who were supposed to be helpers, got really into the process of knocking themselves out and became useless. And that's a problem you get used to, but it still makes it difficult.

SL: Who were the people hanging around Dylan on that tour?
DAP: I don't remember. They used to change overnight. . . . I do remember the two Canadian girls that came in. Later, Robbie married one of them. We were looking for somebody to help us do something and we found them out on the street. They were hanging around outside the Embassy, or something. We brought them along. [. . .] They were friends, and they went to England with us and they were very helpful and Robbie fell in love with one of them and married her.

You really get cut off. You don't have access to normal—I mean, you're not going to go out and hire a union camera person. . . . They're not going to work under those conditions. So you look for people who are already there, who look like they're going to hang in and be useful to you.

There was an endless succession of people, many of whom I never knew. Some of them I did: people whose names were familiar to me appeared and disappeared. It was constantly going like a big New Year's Eve party. It's hard to be part of that, because you can't totally sit there and stare at everybody soberly, you know, while they're jumping around, so you kind of have to go along with it to some degree, but you can't get into it or you'll never film it. It's one of the problems with filming: it requires an enormous kind of concentration that most people never have to do in their lives.

SL: How many hours would you say you shot each day?
DAP: Some days I wouldn't shoot any. You don't go at it like picking potatoes . . . if you did, you'd never get anything. But in this case it was a little complicated, in that I was kind of trying to do two different films.

In the beginning I was only trying to respond to Dylan, what Dylan wanted. Dylan said, "I'm going to direct you. Get the camera and we'll decide what to do." He would direct people and say, "Can you film it this way?" "Did you get that?"

SL: Would this be on the street, in the hotel room?
DAP: Everywhere. He'd put little scenes together. I believe there was one up in my room in the hotel. We were at the Georges V [in Paris]. There was this huge mirrored clothes cabinet, and he had people going in, closing the doors and coming out. There would be a succession of people— I don't know where they came from, people would find them for him. There would be strange women and guys and I would just film these little scenes and then he would set up things. Sometimes he wouldn't do anything: he was just totally into something else and we would be sitting around. And sometimes I would film the way I felt. I would film things as I saw them, and I would decide what to film. I'd film concerts.

So really I was trying to make two different films, and I don't know why I made the last film because I never expected to release a film or anything of it. It's just that I didn't know what else to do. . . . Making home movies—well, it's simply that it doesn't interest me very much, as a rule, to make other people's home movies for them—I'm not sure how to do it. It's not that I put them down at all, I don't: [but] as soon as you're looking through a camera trying to figure out what someone else wants to get, it's very hard . . . my sense is to give them the camera, let them shoot whatever they want. And in a way we were doing that. Howard was doing some of that himself. But since I was really responsible for most of the camera-work, I felt very ambivalent as to what I should be doing: and I never did sort it out. In fact, since then I've never—I would never do a film like that again, under those conditions. It's just simply too hard.

SL: Are there any special incidents in dealing with Dylan on the tour that come to mind?

DAP: One thing I remember. We were in Stockholm, or in Denmark, I don't remember which; and Dylan wanted to do some scene. But we had been up all night, shooting all over the place, and everybody was really gone, and we were down by the docks and it was dawn. And he was shooting film at a tremendous rate, and I had only brought a certain amount of film to Stockholm; we had the rest in London.

And we were out on this dock, and there was this big American destroyer sitting alongside the dock—have you heard this story?

SL: No.

DAP: I'm surprised [this story has] never surfaced because there must have been twenty people there. We were filming in a little cluster, about fifty yards away from where the boat was, and on the boat—I had spent some time in the Navy so I knew—they had blown the whistle and everybody was coming out in the morning for assembly. So there were all these sailors assembling all over the deck, and they started to notice us, because Dylan had this huge—his hair all over the place, and we were really quite motley, and I was there with a camera, and we must have looked really peculiar.

So pretty soon all these guys began watching us, and we figured we better get out of here—we got some problems. And [Bob] Neuwirth tried to get Dylan, but Dylan wouldn't leave. So pretty soon there's a big announcement and the gangway comes down, and this guy, the captain of the ship, comes down the gangway and comes over to see us. And I don't know if they're going to arrest us or not—who knows? Maybe there's some drugs around me or something . . . just something told me that we shouldn't be there.

But there was no way to escape. The guy came over and he stood there. Dylan barely noticed him—and then suddenly caught sight of him and twitched a little bit. And the rest of us were covering our faces and everybody, five hundred sailors, were all lined up watching. And he says: "Are you Bob Dylan?"

Dylan says something just totally ridiculous. I mean, he was not responding to anybody on the same level, and so he said something like "No, I'm Mother Hubbard," or something like that. And the guy says: "Didn't you write a song called 'One Too Many Mornings'?"

And of course he was singing that song on the tour, and Dylan said yeah. And the guy said: "When I was a freshman in college, I wrote a novel, and that was the title," and he shook hands with Dylan and walked back on the ship. And Dylan was really touched. He stood there for a minute and he just—he couldn't absorb all the connections that were going together—that he was in this foreign land, thinking he was totally a stranger—like, on a battlefield on which he was walking around the edges and nobody knew who he was, and suddenly this entire destroyer comes up and—it was really an amazing moment. He was totally caught off guard, and quite caught up in it. And I never again saw him respond in that way to a peculiar situation.

SL: When the tour was over, and it came to editing the material, did you start work on the film as soon as you got back to the States after the tour?
DAP: Well, we got it processed first. Then we had to sync material up, so two or three people were put to work syncing it up. It took maybe a month to sync it up.

SL: Were you working on your film or did you turn over the footage to Dylan?
DAP: We had all the film in the studio. Dylan came in sometime in July. He drove down and we looked at stuff—he spent two or three days looking at stuff in the studio and then he said, "Well, I want you guys to go ahead and make some sort of rough edit to get an idea of what you did/ because ABC was coming after it." [. . .]
    So [Bob] Neuwirth and I started to edit something together—we did a twenty to thirty minute thing, just a rough idea. Then Dylan had his accident and [his manager] Albert [Grossman] got pissed at me because he said I wasn't helping him edit enough. And I explained to him that I was never supposed to be editing it: I had another film to make.

SL: You weren't helping Dylan edit?
DAP: Yeah, well: we started something and then Dylan didn't know what he wanted to do. Then he wanted us to come up and work up at Bearsville. I couldn't do that. So we sent an editor up there to work with him—but then Dylan and Howard Alk started editing film. . . .
    I think this was before the accident. I heard about the accident when I was in California, and then I came and I saw him a couple of days later, walking round with a brace. He didn't appear very knocked out by the accident so I never quite knew what happened or talked to him about it.
    But he was very pissed at everybody and I don't know whether it was because they were putting pressure on him to get the film ready for TV

and he didn't want to do it, or whether he felt he was in some kind of film competition with me: which I certainly never wanted to get into. And I don't know, he was just very pissed about it all, and I could see nothing positive coming out of trying to make the film.

I didn't—I certainly wasn't going to grab the film away from him: it was not my film. I had made my film [*Dont Look Back*] the year before: that's the way I felt about it. So this one was basically his, and if he didn't want to make it, that was fine too. I didn't care. So we just tucked away the film that Neuwirth and I had worked on. We just buried it, and they went on and made a film. [. . .]

It's an interesting film. I've always felt that he made it out of our outs [out-takes]: which was like he was trying to prove something.

It's interesting because he was involved and he set out to make his own film. How much of it is his film and how much was Howard Alk's film I don't know. I think that he [Dylan] was, at the time, not in his highest creative powers. That was the feeling I got, so I didn't spend a lot of time trying to coerce him or coax him to make a film. . . . But I think he was very influenced by Howard's film ideas, which didn't interest me much, frankly, at the time, and they still don't. I think they tend to be sort of intellectual ideas. But I don't think they are very interesting visual ideas, for me.

So, personally, *Eat the Document* was not that interesting. It's only interesting because he did it, because he was involved in it. It's like if Abraham Lincoln or Nixon did a film: you'd have to be interested in it.

SL: Well, the film that you made . . . ?
DAP: We didn't even make a film. You gotta understand it's a sketch: it's like a rough thing you do on a piece of paper—not a finished film. It was just a work print and the original was taken away when they cut *Eat the Document*. And they cut the original . . . so, at this point, no original even exists to make that film. That film is lost irrevocably to the process. Because when you take the film, the original roll: if you cut it up and use the original in one film, you probably can't use it for another.

SL: Are you saying that they took all the original film?
DAP: They cut a final release print of *Eat the Document*, and to do so they took the original—when they did that I asked Howard to go through and not cut that original. I said someday somebody's going to want to look at that. This is the inevitable second film to *Dont Look Back*, because it's what happens if, you know, you don't look back. . . . I said you don't have

to cut the original: go in optically and make an optical dupe and for the purposes of that film it would be fine.

But they chose not to. They actually cut. I think Howard was feeling very protective of the film and he felt that *Eat the Document* was in some sense his film, his and Dylan's, and that he wanted to make that film have some plausibility. And I can understand that, as a film-maker. It's just that it never interested me that much and I don't think the film interested the audience that much.

I think it just mystified people. This is always a question you get into with people like Dylan. Can that fantastic kind of sovereignty that surrounds a name that gets emblazoned on the public mind—can you do anything off it? And always the answer is, no you can't. Whoever's the greatest movie actor of all time can't just walk out and make a hit record. It took Barbra Streisand a long time to be able to conquer two worlds, and she had to work her way up, even though she was tops in the other. And I think that's the same with anybody.

And I think Dylan found that out with his other film, *Renaldo and Clara*. No matter how interested people were in Dylan, and the myth of Dylan, you can't just deal off of that.

I mean, I happen to think that Dylan at his best is a first-rate poet. But you know that if you take the half-dozen first-rate poets—Ezra Pound, whoever—and you put all their total incomes for their lives together, you aren't going to make one big concert date. So you have to figure that being a first-rate poet is not a very productive line of work if you're looking for a return. So he never really went at it in that way. He could do that if he wanted to. You could take fifty lines of Dylan that are as good as anybody's ever written in this century, as far as I'm concerned. But there are thousands of lines he's written that are terrible and deserve to be lost. In music that's easy to do, so that works for him fine. It doesn't mean he's less of a poet. It's the way he goes at it, that's all. So you don't try to be Lowell at the same time as you're Dylan. And there's no reason why you should be.

And the film thing. I guess I had somehow hoped, and I've always had this feeling—I had it about Dylan, I had it about Mailer. I mean, in addition to being artists, really good artists, there was some kind of sense of film and what made film work. They responded to film. But it still left them a long way from being able to turn out a film that was going to be successful—and I don't mean necessarily critically successful in the Hollywood sense of it.

SL: Did you see any of *Renaldo and Clara*'s ideas as things he wanted to do back in '66?

DAP: I have to tell you something. I haven't seen *Renaldo and Clara*. I want to see the long version—but there's lots of things you just can't get to do.

SL: That film was also called confusing by the critics.

DAP: Critics—I don't worry about critics. In any kind of interesting work, critics can sometimes help you but mostly they can't. They can really only help you with work that's right today. Anything that's got any kind of lead-time to it, they're always looking for the wrong thing. They're being dressed by last year's style. . . . That's not my business, to please critics. So I never really worry about critics and what they say.

What I do respond to is [with *Renaldo and Clara*] that there was a lot of ambivalence—not in the film itself but in the making of the film. Dylan couldn't decide whether it should be long or short. If you make a four-hour film, then that's the film you want. You don't cut it no matter what. I mean, you just finally make life come to that. If you do cut it, it means that maybe you weren't sure and you're prepared to try different ways. . . .

It's like, we had a two-hour *Dont Look Back* originally—I always have a longer version of the films—but we never released that. We made it, edited it, mixed it, had a release print, and I sat and looked at it maybe two weeks in different situations, and showed it to different audiences, and then I knew that it had to be cut and I knew where to cut it, and I knew that it had to be about ninety minutes long. . . .

People don't pay for film by the length—really what they're paying for is somebody's taste: somebody's judgment of what a film is all about; when it's told you all it's going to tell you. If it starts to go over old ground, nobody's got time for it. They've got other things to do. You can't have it cut off and say "you can leave here if you want to." It's still tied to the novel: it has the same kind of form as the novel, and you want to finish a novel, you don't want to stop wherever it's convenient. And so the dramatic sense of it is, it has to be a story—it has to be one story.

You have to plot it out, figure out what the story is, and go for it. And I sensed that all the way through [*Renaldo and Clara*], what he had was this wonderful idea happening, and the [Rolling Thunder] tour itself—full of all kinds of dramatic possibilities in his own life, and the idea of using fictional people: I think all of that is terrific. What he never had a sense of is what the story was going to be about. In other words, what he was going to settle for to release.

I don't think he should have released two lengths. Those are just as important decisions, maybe more important, than decisions made within the film of what to shoot, what kind of camera-work or anything else. What you finally put out there is just like his songs: the song is the song. But in film he's not bringing that kind of spiritual solvency, that determination of what he knows is right. He's not bringing that to the film, and it's hard on the film. People don't know whether to accept it seriously or not.

And I think that makes it hard to distribute. Film distribution in the real world, for independent filmmakers, for people who make their own films—I don't know what it is equivalent to, but it's as crucial to the life of the film as anything you do within it.

SL: Going back to the '66 material—not *Eat the Document* but what you called the inevitable *Dont Look Back* part 2: the film you wanted to make.
. . .

DAP: What was clear by the end of the first filming [i.e., of the solo tour of 1965 that made up *Dont Look Back*] was that it was a drag for Dylan to go out and support that whole kind of myth—the acoustical concert and doing the talking Bob Dylan concert, which in a sense was Guthrie's, or other people's. He refined it and brought it to an extraordinary level and he didn't want to have to deal with it any more. I understand that. God, I can't think of anything in the world more difficult than having to be perfect every night.

SL: Perfect in what way?
DAP: You gotta be some kind of sacred image and you gotta be perfect in every way. You can't just have a hall full of people, it's got to be overfull: there's got to be turnaways. . . . If the place is full of people and they're all screaming and yelling at you, that's OK, but it's gotta be full of people. So he's got to do that every night and it's all on his head, and musically it's not that interesting.

But when he got the band together and all of them—Garth and Robbie and the whole batch of them—they are playing so fantastically, even Mickey Jones. Nobody understood what Mickey Jones was up to, collecting his Nazi paraphernalia all over the place. He was from the Johnny

Rivers band. I got to really like Mickey. He was the drummer, he filled in for what's his name: Levon Helm. He had, you know, no idea—the rest of those guys were from a different part of the world. . . .

The music was so fantastic and they were all so into it, and Dylan's role in it . . . Dylan was so happy, he was jumping around like a cricket in the middle of the thing. That's when I realized that the only way I could film those concerts, instead of doing them the way we had done the other [solo] ones (which was from a distance, with a long lens watching him as the audience did) was to get down there in the middle of it—be right on top of him with a wide-angle lens, which is hard to do. You gotta be in the concert, you can't hide.

And when I realized that, I knew that this had nothing to do with what he was doing. He didn't care about that. He didn't want to think about that. He was much less interested in how he looked than in what kind of film he could make.

I think he felt in some sense that he was going to be Ingmar Bergman or something, and make some new kind of film. Which was terrific: I didn't want to discourage him from doing that. But what I saw, what really knocked me out, was that it was the first time that I had ever seen him really happy in the middle of music. And the music was incredible. It was a great band. The sound of that band was the best sound I ever heard. People would listen to that stuff and it would just blow the life out of them. I've never heard a concert like that since. Never.

So I knew that that was something extraordinary and in order to film that, you couldn't do it by filming these goofy little scenes in rooms with nutty people . . . what was interesting had nothing to do with that—and I think that they later edited some kind of mystical film to put people off: you know, in a way it was like they were saying no, nothing went on on-stage. My feeling was the opposite. Unlike *Dont Look Back*, which you couldn't center on the stage because what went on on-stage really wasn't that important to his life, *this* film centered on the stage: he came to life in the middle of that stage. That was really the kind of film we started to make, but it wasn't for us to make it; and I didn't feel called on to make a film or die. But I always felt that that film was there and it made me sad that it was never found and never will be found.

SL: Just to clarify the position with the film and the tapes. Where are they now? Do you have any film in your vaults?
DAP: I don't think I've got any of that original film. I think that it all had to be turned over to Howard Alk, because they had to cut that original.

To my knowledge, he took all the original and it all went someplace, probably embalmed it or something. . . . The original film is gone; now we might have some work print kicking around, I don't know. Because we re-duped a lot of material and to keep it from getting confused you keep it separate. As for the tapes, I'm not totally clear . . . we had to have copies of the quarter-inch tapes that Dylan's sound-man Bob Alderman made because of the sync problem. Whether we gave Dylan the originals and the copies, or whether we kept the originals in our vault I simply don't know. [. . .] As for the tapes we made with our separate recorders, we probably have those. But those wouldn't be concert tapes necessarily. There might occasionally be bits of concerts but basically they're non-concert tapes. They were all transferred to 16 Mag, which was given to Dylan, but we'd usually keep the original. So those would be in vaults too.

SL: Are you free to make a movie from any film you do retain?
DAP: No.

SL: You'd have to get Dylan's permission?
DAP: Yes. Sure . . . well, it's complicated. . . . Usually you specify when you make your contract, you say who the outs are going to belong to mechanically. Whether or not that confers license to use them is a different matter. It's just like we could have Dylan singing a song of somebody else's and if we didn't have a release for the music, we still couldn't use the footage. For any creative work that's within your film, you have to have license to use it from whoever owns that work. But we may well own the film and I almost always take the position that I own the material I shoot. But in this case it was a little different. The film itself was clearly Dylan's. We made it for Dylan. I was really doing something for him. He asked me to do it and I was filming—in effect he was going to be paying me to film for him.

I still take the position really that outtakes of that film which didn't involve the production I would own, if only because I hate to see the stuff get strewn around and lost. I would usually take responsibility for seeing that it's archived and protected, and we would never let it go out of here to let anybody use it, or use it ourselves, without Dylan's permission. On that film it was a little grey because it wasn't like most of our films.

On *Dont Look Back* I would take the position that all the outtakes were mine. I still can't use them without his permission. I can't use them without the music clearance. I have no rights to them. But I own them mechanically and I'm responsible for seeing them preserved and kept in a safe place and that they don't get ripped off or destroyed by fire or something else. That's basically what my responsibility is as a filmmaker, and I take that very seriously. [. . .]

We store them [the *Dont Look Back* outs] because film is very vulnerable. People don't tend to store that kind of tape—they throw them out, they put them in a big box and they're stuck someplace and then they move or forget where they are, and since nobody's using them they can get lost. And when they're lost, nobody ever knows what they are, and they just look like rolls of film somewhere. So it's really crucial that some effort be made in the very beginning to make sure that they are protected.

Particularly because most of the films that I've done are about people who, it seems to me, will have some kind of historic interest. So we always make that the criteria, whether it's Dylan or Janis Joplin or whoever. We keep that material for some kind of long-range use, if only for study.

SL: I'm sure Dylan fans will be happy to hear that.
DAP: We've never lost a foot of film, and as far as I know none of the tapes that we have—and we've got a lot of musical tapes of his—none of them have ever hit the streets, unless we set it up to do it with Dylan's concurrence.

SL: And those tapes are in your vaults?
DAP: Yeah. I know Dylan's very paranoid about his material . . . he hates the idea of it floating around. People getting access to it that he doesn't know about; and the fact that he feels that way probably puts a big incentive on people to try to get it. So the thing feeds on its own problem. As far as I know, we never released anything, because from our point of view there's no return to us. We're not a record company—we don't make any money from records. The only way we would ever use sound would be with a film.

SL: There was a rumor a while back that a cable-TV Special was being planned and that Dylan's people were looking for material.
DAP: Yes. They called me and asked me if we had the concert stuff from *Dont Look Back*. I said sure, we have all that. But as for the 1966 stuff, I'm not sure, for the reasons I've explained.

SL: I know a lot of people who would love to listen to it. . . .

DAP: It's very interesting material. Well, I always felt that someday Dylan will have to deal with it. Whether I'm around and involved in it, who knows? I think what happened there on that tour was very essential to where music was. As with Bowie: the Ziggy Stardust tour was central. This is what David and I realized when we decided to re-release *Ziggy Stardust*. That will always be interesting to people. I think that Dylan's stuff is the same way. That tour [1966], musically, was the most interesting that happened anywhere in the world at that period.

SL: And he was at the peak of his career.

DAP: It isn't just that, but that that music was generating all music everywhere. People who didn't even see those concerts were getting something from it indirectly, in many ways. And, ultimately, everybody wants to see what the centers of things are.

We happened to do it a few times in our life—I did it at Monterey. We happened to be at the center of something. So what we filmed [for *Monterey Pop*] became absolutely crucial: people will want to see that forever. A far better film in many ways is *Keep on Rocking*, which is Chuck Berry. But musically nothing was starting there. They were doing the same thing they had done, so everybody knew it was old news. So while that's interesting, it doesn't have anything like the charismatic attraction that the center of the storm will always hold.

So someday Dylan's going to have deal with that material in some other way than *Eat the Document*. . . . And if it's not Dylan, it's going to be his heirs; somebody.

So it's always been my contention that that material should be kept, really as archively as possible. But it's Dylan's responsibility. . . .

SL: Is it your feeling that he has kept that material?

DAP: I hope so. I don't know. I don't know what he does. But I know if we had it, we would have kept it. . . . That material will live forever, as long as people don't lose it.

SL: And it's so frustrating to the fans who never get a chance to see it.

DAP: It is frustrating, but in a way that keeps fans alive. That constant pressure of the myth against the reality—it keeps them all tuned up. I don't think you can set that in motion or build up any kind of appetite, if it isn't really there. All you have to do—you don't have to even try to sell it or get an interest in it; you just have to make sure you're protected: and that's what the business ought to be able to do. . . .

I don't know: I assume Columbia Records protects its music, but I don't know how well. I wouldn't trust Columbia Records. I wouldn't trust any record company because every time they have a turnover in vault workers, you have to assume the old workers took home everything that had any value; so you have to assume in the end that what's left is what nobody ever wanted. So I would assume that that is not a good way to keep valuable material—under large corporate protection. You take a chance with this stuff.

I mean, in the end, some way or other, people like yourself, who really have a strong interest in it, are getting hold of little bits of it and hanging on.

It's amazing how you can find film. We're looking at old footage of Billie Holiday: it's amazing how much stuff was kept. You don't expect to find it, but people just knew, somehow, this stuff is valuable. Even though not much had been filmed, what there was, somehow or other, sooner or later, always surfaces.

Looking Back: D. A. Pennebaker
Interviewed by John Bauldie

John Bauldie / 1986

Interview on July 15, 1986, in New York City. From *Wanted Man: In Search of Bob Dylan* (London: Black Spring Press, 1990). Reprinted with permission of Margaret T. Garner, executrix, the estate of John Bauldie.

John Bauldie: How did *Dont Look Back* all begin for you? What actually started it off?

D. A. Pennebaker: Well I'd been thinking about doing a film on music at the time because music was interesting. I had talked to somebody who knew the Stones—it was a kid who was kinda playing with them, whose mother was a film editor in London, still is, and so I thought of that and went over, but that didn't seem quite right. And then I thought of Baez—she was fairly well known—but that wasn't what seemed to me was interesting. I had a definite idea in my head, you see. But I didn't know about Dylan at all; I'd maybe heard his name, but I had no idea. . . .

So I was thinking about it—had been for about a year and a half—and it got to the fall of 1964. And then Albert Grossman came in one day. I wasn't there, I was out having lunch or something, but Ricky Leacock, my partner, was there. And Albert came in and said, "I represent Bob Dylan. Is anybody here interested in making a film about him?" And Leacock said, "Who's Bob Dylan?" So Albert said, "Maybe I'd better come back again."

He and Dylan had approached us because Sara had worked with us at *Life*. She was working there for about a year and a half, so I knew Sara quite well. Then I came back, and Albert said, "My client's going to England; would you like to make a film about it?" I said, "Sure." And he said "OK, I'll arrange for you to meet him." I don't think at that point that the question of money even came up. He assumed, I think, that we could somehow raise the money for the Dylan film. I figured we could too, so I was kind of astonished when we went to Columbia and said, "You guys interested in putting up any money?" and the guy there said, "Well, we got a couple of records of Dylan's that we're waiting to release—maybe I'll put you in touch with the guy who'll be in charge of that." And he sent me down to some guy, and I said, "Look, I'm not looking to make a lot of money out of this, but if I could get our expenses paid—just getting to England and back—we'll put up all the film and everything, as long as we can get that back ultimately. For five thousand dollars I'll give you half the film." They said, "No."

So I realized it was going to be a tough one to sell! And so I went to some friends of mine who were just beginning to set up 60 *Minutes*, and a guy named Ike Kleineman said, "Well, I'll buy some footage from you— maybe five hundred to six hundred dollars worth of footage—if it's terrific footage." And I said, "Well, that's good." And so I *knew* that it wasn't going to be easy to sell. Then again, none of our films are easy to sell.

JB: So you paid the entire production costs?

DAP: We put up all the money for the film. Albert didn't put up any money. He put up the tickets for Jones and Howard Alk to get over there, that's all, and they were basically friends of his, so I didn't figure that was too administrative—and so in the end we put up all the money for the film. The idea was that we would get reimbursed out of first moneys up to $100,000—that was the deal. It was just written on a piece of paper, the bottom of a menu somewhere, it was a handshake deal. I don't think we ever had a formal contract between us. Dylan and I shook hands and that was it.

Later, I think that when Albert saw that the film was going to have some theatrical run—he hadn't ever envisaged this and anyway I think he had it in his head that Bob was going to make a film with Warners— Bob didn't want to make it, but there was a lot of money at stake—anyway, I remember that Albert had never really thought of my film as a real film, it seemed awfully home-movie-ish to him to have any kind of reality, but when he saw the poster he came in grudgingly and said, "That's a terrific poster. What are you gonna do?" I said, "Well, Albert, we're gonna release it because that's the understanding and we're partners on it. I can't afford to take a wash on it." And he said, "Well, I don't think you should release it. I think you should let me distribute it." And I said, "No, I can't do that." Albert, I think, felt we kinda squished him maybe on *Dont Look Back*.

JB: What do you think Dylan's motivation was?

DAP: I don't know. And I am not sure that it's meaningful to try to second guess. My sense is that the reason that they let us make films—Jane Fonda, Kennedy, all of 'em—was that they figured that they'd find out something interesting by looking at the film. With Dylan there may have been that. He'd seen a couple of films that we'd done, so he knew a little that what we did was peculiar and different. I think that Dylan had a very parochial sense about his operation. He was going to do things totally differently from the way they'd been done; he was gonna revamp network schedules; he was gonna revamp movies; he was gonna make everything in a new way—without being quite sure how he'd do it. In many ways Dylan's very naive, extremely naive about things—amazingly so. In other ways he's an old seer or something—I mean he's not your normal type of person to deal with!

But I think that he thought that this was a way to find out about films and, basically, Dylan always counts a nickel, it was gonna be cheap—it wasn't gonna cost him anything! And I'm sure that Albert explained to him that the deal was for them to pick up some footage they could use for commercials abroad. Everybody—the Beatles, the Stones—they did these TV promo things free; that was standard, that's what you did on English TV at that time to sell a record. In fact, that whole thing with the cards was really done like a TV promo for "Subterranean Homesick Blues." The thing with the cards was Dylan's idea, and we shot three versions while we were in London—one in the park, one on a roof, and one in the back alley right behind the Savoy hotel. I went there recently—they're still working on that goddam alley! It still has the same scaffolding! Anyway, in the one in the park we got arrested in the middle so you can see that the heavy hand of the law comes in just about the time he's doing one of the last cards. . . .

JB: Did you keep the camera running?

DAP: Oh yeah. We've got 'em all some place. Everyone helped in writing out those signs—Joan did some and Donovan did a lot of the signs. You know Donovan's a very good drawer? He turned out to be the artist, so everybody gave him the hard ones to do.

JB: So from the time you were approached in 1964 and you weren't really aware of Dylan, to the time that the trip was set up—let's say in April 1965—presumably you encountered Dylan's music in the meantime?

DAP: Albert sent me a couple of records, yeah.

JB: And what were your feelings about them?

DAP: The songs really hit me. From then on I knew that by total chance I'd fallen right into the place that I should be. That happens maybe 10 per cent of the time in filmmaking. If you're not lucky, you shouldn't do it. You get used to knowing that you're in the right place and not wondering how you got there or why. And that's why you don't look for contracts or anything else, 'cause when you're in the right place, you have a tremendous amount of power—and everybody kind of realizes that.

JB: The High Sheriff's Lady was recently in the newspapers. She still has the harmonica.

DAP: That was hysterical. It's such a funny scene. I love it because it totally takes the curse off Dylan and the Science Student. There was a problem in that scene—it sort of blinks a little as if the lights were blinking. That was because the battery for the camera had run down and I had to wind the take-up reel by hand which pulled the film through the camera, and try to make sure that I did it at the right speed. You could do that with my old camera, but you'd have a hard time doing that with the new rigs. I couldn't believe that that I'd shot it.

JB: I thought that Dylan was being kind to the Science Student.

DAP: I did too. You know, everybody has different feelings about those things—him and the *Time* reporter. I knew who the *Time* reporter was— I have the story he sent back about that meeting and he was not at all vindictive towards Dylan. I thought that Dylan was pretty decent to him too.

JB: He's trying to teach him. . . .

DAP: Yeah, trying to tell him something that this guy had resisted learning his whole life long. I thought that Dylan was very patient with him, and took the curse off it by making the joke at the end. And the final, incredible scene which to me is one of the perfect scenes that you fall on— the moment when you can't make a mistake, and you know you're right in the center and you just shoot everything that moves, and you don't even think about why or how, you just shoot it, it's in your lap—going in the cab to the Albert Hall, when Fred starts talking about his "other" folksinger, Donovan, and Bob says, "How's he doing?" and then Fred does the trashing of Donovan. And Dylan never cracks. He just looks out the window.

Fantastic! It's just fantastic! Just one shot. You didn't have to edit anything; it told you everything. Those to me were really high moments of filmmaking in that kind of film. And they don't come every film—just once in a while.

JB: The scene with Albert dealing with Tito Burns—it's really looking deep into the workings of their operation.
DAP: Neither of them think so! Albert did say that after a while he got tired of little girls coming up to him in clubs, telling him how gross he looked in that scene—he almost wished he hadn't done it; but Tito, he wrote me a letter and he thinks he's a movie star! "I'll be with Albert in about ten minutes"—you couldn't get people to *act* funnier.

JB: In the whole film I can only recall one time when Dylan glances at the camera. . . .
DAP: When they're throwing the hotel guy out of the room?

JB: Yeah. Telling the assistant to go to his fop manager.
DAP: The fop manager! Actually, he does one other; it's when he's playing with Alan Price—when he asks Alan if he's playing with the Animals any more, and he says, "No, it happens," and then Dylan starts to chord in those blues. And then he looked at me like he was kinda pissed that I was filming. But I didn't give a shit. It was one of those things where we were looking right in the eye. And then he looked away. But you can see that mean look he sometimes gives.

JB: The clip of Dylan in Greenwood, Mississippi, in 1963 that you spliced into *Dont Look Back*, did you use that in its entirety?
DAP: Yeah. The guy who sent it to me, Ed Emshwiller, didn't know what to do with it. I guess Albert had told them that they couldn't use it in their film—they did a film on folk called *Streets of Greenwood*, or something like that—it was done by a couple of guys, but Emshwiller was the cameraman. And Ed Emshwiller to this day uses a wind-up Bolex—that's his camera! So he was down there shooting Dylan singing with a wind-up Bolex, and they figured there was no way to sync it up, though they did have a track of it. So they said, "Pennebaker, you might as well have it," 'cause they didn't know what to do with it. So they sent it over to me, and I thought, "God, what am I gonna do with this?" Mississippi was certainly nothing to do with my film. So I stuck it over my editing bench. It sat there, and I put the whole thing out of my mind.

   I wasn't even working on *Dont Look Back*, but there was this friend of

Howard's and Dylan's who was working for me then, briefly, from Chicago. His name was Quinn. And he kept saying, "You're too busy; you're not going to edit that film. Let me edit it." I said, "No, I'll get to it." So it sat there for a long time. And then one day I decided to do it. So I settled down with just a viewer, and I got my first flush of enthusiasm when the guy says, "How did it all begin?" And I stopped. And it started me thinking. And then I saw that thing sitting on the shelf, so I decided I might as well look at it. Now when you use a viewer to edit, you have the viewer and you have a synchronizer sitting here with a reader on the synchronizer, and they're roughly twenty-two frames apart. So you never let anything go out, because once it gets out you gotta thread up—and it's hard to do that. So I had these pieces of film from the last scene still sticking out—"How did it all begin, Bob?"—and I just spliced the Greenwood film on, just to look at it, not as part of the film, 'cause that's the way you look at stuff. And when I looked at it, I thought, "Holy shit!" And I never took it out of the film.

JB: That's one of my favorite parts of the film—not just the cut, but when the guy from the African service comes out with this amazingly demanding question—"How do you see the art of the folk-song in contemporary society?"—and asks for Dylan's approval. And Dylan nods! But of course, we never get to hear an answer to that question.

DAP: Well, he could never answer. He never did answer. You know he's not going to answer that question. I like the idea that he can't answer. He just sits there with that funny look while the guy is going on and on about his friend! I love that.

I had another thing that was funny that I wanted to use but didn't. It was too easy. This guy seemed to be fair game. The guy came in and played Dylan some easy listening music tracks of half a dozen of Dylan's songs—a string orchestra! And Bob had to sit there and listen. He didn't dare catch my eye. And this guy was so excited to be playing this stuff for him, but it was driving Dylan crazy to have to listen to it for five minutes.

JB: The tension that was in the film about expecting Donovan, that was for real?

DAP: Oh yeah. We didn't know who Donovan was. Well, it was kind of a joke that Dylan worked up, because Albert was saying, "We're gonna have the Beatles over—then there's this new folk singer, Donovan!" Anyway, Donovan was gonna come around one night, for supper or something, and so we were waiting—Bob and I and Neuwirth. I said, "I'll shoot it," but Bob said, "No, you can't shoot it." But we all had to put masks on—Hallowe'en masks.

And Donovan knocked on the door, and there were the three of us sitting at the table. And he came in, you know—he was a kid—and there were these three guys, and he didn't know which one was Dylan. And he was laughing. And Dylan kinda broke up a little bit, 'cause he did like him. I used to catch Dylan listening to "Catch the Wind"—there was one little phrase in there that Dylan really got off on—so he liked Donovan before he even saw him. He liked the idea of Donovan. So he laughed and told Donovan to sit down. Well, Donovan was very excited and decided to play something for him. Dylan said he liked "Catch the Wind," but Donovan said, "I've written a new song I wanna play for you." So he played a song called "My Darling Tangerine Eyes." And it was to the tune of "Mr. Tambourine Man"! And Dylan was sitting there with this funny look on his face, listening to "Mr. Tambourine Man" with these really weird words, and about halfway through the second verse, Donovan realizes that Dylan is cracking up—and Neuwirth and I were fighting it back, it was so crazy, trying to keep a straight face. Then Dylan says, "Well . . . you know . . . that *tune!*" Dylan said, "I have to admit that I haven't written *all* the tunes that I'm credited with, but that happens to be one that I *did* write!" And Donovan says, "Oh. I didn't know! I thought it was an old folk tune!" Well, Dylan says, "Go on—keep playing!" and Donovan says, "Oh no, I won't play anymore." I'm sure he never played the song again.

JB: Can I ask you about the Joan Baez relationship at this time? There have been certain statements by Baez herself that she felt very alienated, treated very badly by Dylan at that time, and yet in the film—even for example in the scene where Dylan and Neuwirth are joshing with her about having the see-thru blouse you don't even wanna—there doesn't really seem to be any malice, or . . .

DAP: Well you've got to understand a peculiar situation around royal entourages, palaces, courts in general, politics, and that is that you can be number four or five, but if you're used to being one or two it's a big jolt—and that's kind of what that was about. There were other people in Dylan's life—there was Sara—and Baez kind of knew it. She was having a hard time I think at that moment in her life. I don't know why, but emotionally she was feeling very roughed up by life. To be honest, I don't think that Dylan had invited her to be there, but Albert had said, "Come along," and so she came, knowing that that's not the same thing as being demanded. And I think that that hurt her, y'know, that she was no longer Queen. She was dragging Dylan, who didn't want to be a part of that scene any more, and I think that she knew that; but at the same time she wanted to be there because . . . well, she loved him. And that music was exciting to her—I don't mean what he was doing, but what he was about to do. She could smell it coming. He was breaking away from all the old stuff and she wanted to too; she wanted to do a rock 'n' roll album very badly. I was very sympathetic to her. I really liked her a lot. After that I was going to do a film with her, but there was nobody interested.

JB: I love the scene in the hotel room with Joan Baez when Dylan sings the Hank Williams songs. Can you remember how long he was singing for that night?

DAP: Oh he sang a lot. I have a lot more film of that. They did one marvelous one, Joan and he, that I was going to use, but it was a little too long: "Good news travels slow, but bad news travels like wildfire." Do you know that song? It's a great song, and they sang it together.

JB: You don't happen to have that here do you?

DAP: Probably. Dylan's looked at it, and it's all piled up, but I'd be happy to show it to you if we can get permission. "Brown-Eyed Girl" I kinda liked too.

JB: "Brown-Eyed Girl"? Van Morrison's song?

DAP: I don't think so—I'm not sure. He only sang a bit of it at a mic check. He often sang songs that you never knew about—and never heard again—bits of songs sometimes—that were so fantastic they could make you cry.

JB: You were talking about Albert Grossman before. . . .

DAP: Albert was always a good friend of mine, I always considered him a good friend. I used to talk to him up 'til a few months ago, before he died. So I never had the sense that Albert was in any way an enemy, which I knew had become the situation subsequently with Albert and Bob—that they were really enemies. Which is too bad, because I think Albert was one of the few people that saw Dylan's worth very early on, and played it absolutely without equivocation or any kind of compromise. He refused to let him go on any rinky-dink TV shows, refused to let Columbia do bullshit things with him—which they did with a lot of other people, you know. And Dylan, I think, in his early stages, required that kind of handling—'cause Dylan himself would go off at spurious tangents. One week he'd do one thing and another week he'd do something else—and maybe in the end he would have prevailed. I mean, he came close to not prevailing, we kinda know that, but in the end he pulled himself together and did what very few people in his position have done, which was to really survive. I don't mean just to be hanging around. . . .

And I think that of all the things, that's the most interesting thing about Dylan—that health prevails as well as whatever—genius, talent, whatever else you ascribe to him—the fact that his intelligence made him survive is really interesting. And I think Albert had something to do with that. When Albert died, I wrote Bob a letter and I said a lot of bad things have gone down between them, but I knew that basically Albert was extremely devoted to him and loved him—and I knew that Bob loved Albert; so it was really kind of sad that it had come to that. But . . . these things happen.

JB: Can you say something more about Sara? She's someone who's hardly spoken of or written about at all.
DAP: Well, she was always a very private person. Actually she and Sally Grossman were friends—they roomed together down in the Village. Sara had been a bunny for a while and was about with Victor Lownes—she was Sara Lownds—and Dylan kind of snitched her away from him. She was really a beautiful woman . . . fantastic looking—and she had a very strange personality, a kind that went for health food and mysterious life. It seemed to me at the time a very ersatz philosophy—what mattered and what didn't. She seemed on the surface to have that, but underneath she was clearly a very interesting person. For a long time she worked up at the magazine, for our unit—we were kind of a secret unit working on *Life*. I had a studio downtown and she took charge of the uptown office; so she and I were really managing the whole operation in 1963. Then she quit, she got pregnant, and had a child—although I can't remember whether she was still there when I quit in July 1964. I would have hired her myself, 'cause she wanted to get away from *Life* too, but I really couldn't afford it. And then she went off—went into some sort of mysterious phase in the Village—and I saw her off and on. Then I didn't see her a lot for a long time. But she was one of the first people I showed *Dont Look Back* to. I haven't seen her for a long time.

JB: You said before that Dylan himself was looking at the film you have?

DAP: Yeah, he went through a lot of stuff, and he did make up some kind of a tape—I never saw the thing—recently. He would come in around nine or ten at night and work through 'til maybe three in the morning—he likes to work at night. And he picked out some pieces—one of the things that interested him was one of the songs he sang in 1965, "To Ramona," and we noticed a reference to it in the *Telegraph*! Somebody caught it! That was amazing. I didn't think anybody would notice.

JB: It was shown on the *20/20* show.

DAP: Yeah. It was not from *Dont Look Back*. Well, he did that. He liked that. He came in and he was looking at all the film he could. And he was saying things like, "How do you get that wonderful effect of it all being shot from one point of view?" So I said, "That's easy. You can only afford to hire one camera."

Behind the Public Face of Power: Martha Ansara Interviews Chris Hegedus and D. A. Pennebaker

Martha Ansara / 1994

From *Filmnews* [Australia], February 1994. Reprinted with permission of Martha Ansara.

Americans are obsessed by power: social status, personal power, and above all state power, which they appear to revere even in its most grotesque manifestations. So for Americans there's a very special thrill in seeing the Pennebaker / Hegedus documentary *The War Room*, an inside story of Clinton campaign organizers Senior Strategist James Carville and Communications Director George Stephanopoulos. For Australians, the film's look behind the public face of power offers perhaps more of an ethnographic sort of amazement. Its real-life characters corroborate some of the most exotic aspects of American TV drama, while engaging in the nitty gritty of a campaign which makes Australian politics look like the Golden Age of Athens. In any case, the film is an excellent documentary and it was refreshing to have its makers, Chris Hegedus and her husband, the veteran cinéma vérité practitioner D. A. Pennebaker, as guests of the 1993 Documentary Conference. While some of the most formally and philosophically profound films shown and discussed at the conference were the antithesis of cinéma vérité (e.g., Tran Van Thuy's *The Story of Kindness*), Hegedus and Pennebaker's presence helped to clarify issues facing Australian documentarists who attempt to work in this very demanding form. Some Australian filmmakers, like Robin Anderson / Bob Connolly and Graham Chase, have, I believe, come to grips with the dramatic possibilities of cinéma vérité, but it is a form of filmmaking which has not really made a significant impact upon our documentary community, despite the loud and zealous pronouncements of those who seem to see it as the one true path. Never mind that; I love these films—*The War Room* in particular—and was pleased that conference organizers were able to schedule the following brief interview with Hegedus and Pennebaker.

Chris Hegedus: Documentary filmmakers don't take the art of making films as seriously as those who make dramatic feature films. And that's a real problem. Even films that try to feature themselves as dramatic documentaries, are not really paying enough attention to the art of filmmaking. It's a problem too that documentary is such a broad topic, encompassing everything from short animal films to something in a dramatic feature length. Most people who are making enacted feature films are making a similar product with a similar goal, which is basically entertainment, even though it may inform you or take you through an emotional process or whatever. And for me documentary should be that also, and enlightening and inspiring in some way too.

Martha Ansara: The dramatic impact of your films comes, I feel, in large part from your editing.

CH: Well, the editing process in our type of filmmaking is very much like the shooting process. It's an act of discovery, detective work. You know, in the shooting process you're trying to find your story and stay with your characters, and it's very much the same when you get it back because in the shooting of real life films, you miss [laughing a bit] 90 percent of what you want to get and the other 90 percent is involved in the complicated mess of the technical process of making these films with a tape recorder and a camera and a roll of film that only lasts ten minutes, and trying to get a workable scene in total in picture and sound. So finding what story you've shot that's available to you is a major hurdle to overcome. But I think the rules for me are to follow that character and drama very closely. First in the way it's shot: if it's not shot in a way that's interesting, it's very hard to make it interesting when you're editing.

And if you don't have somebody who's shooting for character development, it's going to be hard for you to make it up in the editing too. So you look for that. And then I guess the second thing is to not be predictable. I mean when you make jumps, it's either to carry your story and characters forward or it's to take you somewhere else in your imagination. And that's what I want films to do for people: to take them somewhere on some kind of experience so that when they walk out of the cinema, they feel it was worth being there. You want to be able to take your story forward, but you don't want to hit people over the head. A problem with a lot of films on real life is that they get so involved in the information that they forget about the art.

MA: I felt that your music background affected the editing as well as the sound track.

D. A. Pennebaker: Music affects everybody you know. If you plant carrots, I assume you plant them in some sort of musical rows. It's hard to dissociate what music does for your life. I do think that a film needs to be assembled, or perceived, in a kind of musical way. Its images are not just visual images, they're sound images simultaneously.

CH: A lot of dramatic films pay much more attention to a kind of pacing within a film that is a very musical concept; we try to pay attention to that too, as much you can within the limitations of real life filming. The musical filming that we've done over the years is brought into these films as a slightly poetic edge that is added to kind of take them somewhere else. For me the most important part of editing the film is the impression I first get when I watch it. And a lot of times it's very depressing to me because I'm expecting things that end up not being there because Penny was, like, focusing and we get in these kind of [ferocious *sotto voce*] "*I can't believe you didn't get that!*" type of things. Or the sound ran out. But in the end, it still is what is dropped on you from that initial feeling you get from watching your footage. And it's different for each film. Basically because we shoot these films in such a very small way—it's usually just Penny and I and half the time we don't even have a camera assistant—so there's so much bumbling that goes on that nothing is ever easy to cut.

His film was thirty-three hours initially; I chopped it down to probably six hours. And then at that point because we didn't have any funding, because unlike Australia there's no commitment in any way to independent filmmaking, we had to raise money. But it's very hard to get an idea of this type of film and what it's about by making just a ten minute reel. So I decided to make a small half hour film of our film to convince English TV that there was human drama and a story there that they would be interested in. That's a horrible thing to do because it takes your initial energy for editing the film away from your end film, and once they committed to giving us money, I had to start again to conceive a whole film.

DAP: But once you have that initial six hours, or whatever, you know a little bit what your story has to encompass. And as you look at that stuff, you start to take to take scenes out and see if you can make them work to-gether—and then you start going back into the other thirty-three hours or whatever—and here and there you pick out stuff to make those little bits work. So you're constantly going back and forth and re-evaluating the whole thing and you try to not be stuck with these things that you do fall into, like "this is the way it's gotta be." And sometimes that gets us so we sort of get into kind of—um—mild—um—altercations—[CH & MA laugh raucously at the word "mild"]. Am I fair in that? I mean no ac-tual bruises are ever detected later; the body is free from physical abuse. But you do have these things. It's like at the end Chris and her editing assistant had come up with this piece of music, "Vote Baby Vote"—dur-ing the headlines. And the first time I heard it, I said, "That's ridiculous. We can't have that kind of shit in this film. Jesus!" And so I just turned it off without thinking about it or looking at it. And later, several weeks later . . .

CH: We had the film cut!

DAP: We had the film all cut and it had to go back in. We didn't have too much choice because . . .

CH: We couldn't get the rights to the music that we'd put in . . .

DAP: So then I looked at it with possibly a more sympathetic eye. Money had been introduced into the equation. But when I looked at it again, I thought, "how could I have not seen that it's the perfect music? You couldn't have better music there." I'd gone 360 degrees around. Often that happens. You're so sure you're right about something and then you see it in a slightly different context and you feel totally the opposite way about it. And I think, well, there probably is no one way to make these films. You're beset by your own uncertainties. I like that aspect of mak-ing a film: that you can reverse your field. There are no rules. You don't have to be right. It's okay to be part of the filmmaking team and be Mr. Wrong.

MS: So there's always discovery, that element of surprise and unpredict-ability. When I read in the press kit that it's a political documentary, I thought, "Oh, of course." But I'd actually seen it as an ethnographic film.

DAP: No, I don't see it as political. Why did we say that?

CH: I don't know. You know those press kit things.

DAP: I see it as *Wayne's World*: it's totally a couple of goofy guys planning the spring prom. And what's funny about it is it hits you from time to time that they're actually planning the president of the United States and it seems inconceivable.

MA: It is extraordinary to see inside this world from the outside. The thing that struck me is how much of a boys' locker room that War Room seemed to be. These particular boys were wonderful people and really did believe in what they were doing—about health and education and so on which was refreshing—but . . .

CH: That was one of the initial things that won me over to Clinton almost instantly. I was very ambivalent when we started. I didn't really know much about him. But then all of a sudden you saw all these energetic, enthusiastic people with all these ideas and hopes and total admiration for this candidate that they had and you went, "What's going on here?" This wasn't the same as the media was portraying it to me. And so it really drew me in to see more. But a lot of people who watch the film want to see the process in a cynical way, because they think it should be like that. They've heard that it is. They've watched films like *Bob Roberts* that show the political process in a totally cynical way, and they're very disappointed, I think, to see our film because it isn't that. That's fiction.

Yes, although those boys in *The War Room* certainly were strong enough for fiction. Given what a film demands from a character and the sort of drive it demands, do you think you could make this type of film following the different way that women sometimes work? Of course, some very modern—powerful—women appear in this film—but I've noticed that cinéma vérité films tend not to look into those quiet kitchen corners. There's the necessity of creating drama and dynamic characters. . . .

DAP: You're locked into the characters and you have to believe that. You don't have the option even that a writer has of kicking the character out of the story if he gets too obnoxious or of shifting or making two of them. You're stuck with what you get and it's got to be character-driven, I think, or it's hard to follow. You have to decide in advance that the character's right; if it's a woman then it's okay if you want to go that way but you gotta think it through. You can't just hope that you'll be able to switch off your main male character and see a few girls hanging around, it won't work.

MA: What I mean is do you have to pick those very strong, dynamic characters?

CH: I don't think they have to be flamboyant to be dynamic. And I don't think there's any exact rule on what makes a person interesting, but if you can find that interesting quality about them and they're doing something that means a lot to them, then I think it'll work as a film. James Schlesinger (in *The Energy War*), was a very quiet person and a very opposite type of person from James Carville, but at the same time he had a sense of power and you knew that if you could get at that quality it was fascinating.

DAP: And George Stephanopoulos too. At the very beginning, he interested me. I felt that power. He was used to having his orders carried out, he didn't worry about it.

MA: When you pick a situation for a film do you generally try to pick one that has an inbuilt dramatic structure? Can you talk about that question of choosing a subject in relation to structure and what you think will emerge?

DAP: Really, you eat the apple that falls off the tree. That's what happens and it usually comes to you pretty much readymade. You don't have a lot of choice. But you decide whether you're going to do it: whether you're going to jump in the river. That's the decision you make. Because once you're in, you're not going to get out easily. It's a big commitment; it's money, time, your children are going to hate you for a while. You know all those things are sitting there ready—they'll fall on you. If you're wrong, you can't get out of it. So the story comes to you—you just get a sniff of something. And if either of us—we're each watching the other like cats on a fence for a few days before the choice has to be made—waiting to see if the other person has the sniff yet. It's like being able to detect water, and you've got divining rods and you're doing prayers and standing on your head and everything else—and is there water there? Do you think there's water? Well . . . it's a little like practicing necromancy. But the fact is that your hunch is your most important tool throughout the film. More important than the camera or the tape recorder or anything else. Because everything else—if necessary you can go out and buy the archival material, which we've had to do—but your hunch on the story line . . .

CH: Because you can have a story that has a built-in ending like the election and it can turn out to be merely a process film. There's more than one element that you have to look for. It's both character and story. When we started this film it was just a process film because we jumped in at the Democratic Convention, and we didn't know who anybody was really except for George, who was our spokesperson about getting in. We didn't know what their jobs were because we didn't work in campaigns, and they all have very official-sounding titles, and so we had to weed our way through all these people and their boring jobs or their boring personalities or whatever to figure out where the heart of the film was. And by the time we got to the fourth day, the end of the convention, the thing was that we kept wanting to film James Carville more. And luckily for us he was heading this strange place that he set up called the War Room in Little Rock. So there was some place to go. But I think if we hadn't met James at the end of that week . . .

DAP: You've got to have somebody that's not just interesting and not just—that the camera loves them. Somebody there to some purpose; there's some treasure at the end of what you're pursuing and the treasure is what you're really after. The other things make it work along the way.

MA: How much filming did you actually do: hanging around, watching, filming?

CH: We did very little filming.

DAP: Three weeks maybe.

CH: We filmed about twenty days total on this film. It was not much at all. Because we didn't have any money. We did the four days at the convention. And then we did these separate trips to Little Rock, during which we could only stay for two days at a time because George was very nervous that we would bother other people in the campaign. A lot of people in the campaign saw absolutely no use for us being there at all, and were very critical of us being there. James and George really stuck their necks out for us to be there because they saw what they were doing in a more historical perspective.

MA: It's not a very long time, especially for this type of film—it's a good thing you could get the archival material.

DAP: In a way it's better. The trick that we often fall into, because it's so interesting for us to do it, is the *Crisis* syndrome. On *Crisis* we actually had four different filmmakers in different places—and therefore in any one instant you could either see Governor Wallace, you could see the students, you could see Nick Katzenbach, you could see the President, you could see Bob Kennedy, you could see any one of these sides—it was like watching the war from both armies and that's fascinating because people don't normally see that. Even TV has a hard time getting that. So you're intrigued by doing that but then you create a monster for yourself, because you can't cut that fast, and when you can't cut it fast it means if you're going to shorten it, you've gotta put narration on to explain what you're doing and where you are, and with that, right away, for me, I lose a very important aspect of the story. The minute you start to engage the other brain pad or whatever it's called, you're starting to put it into people's minds in a certain way and it's no longer like jumping on a surfboard and just going with the wave. Now they gotta think about why they're here, what's this, who's that, and it changes the whole speed with which the story moves. And it stops being a story. It becomes some sort of "educational"—it becomes a "documentary." That's the kind of thing we're wary of. So in a way you're better off if you can shoot it as we did but the problem is: what days? Maybe you could have the wrong twenty days and you'd have no scenes. So in a way you gotta have a lotta luck. But it's really hard for us to sit and figure that out ahead of time.

CH: What makes it expensive is you have to be spontaneous in terms of following the story and what days you shoot or not. Because you go down there and then you figure out what's happening and then you figure out some other time dependent on that you could come back and that has to do with something that you read in the paper: like a week later or three days later, you read that the debate was cancelled or something. You know that they're probably having a crisis over that and you get yourself down there. And there were a lot of areas, outside of the War Room, that George really couldn't commit to us being around—very private areas. Like when we went to the debates. In order to be in that back room in the debates where all of them were watching Clinton on television, he couldn't get us the credentials and Secret Service pins that we needed. So we had to go through an elaborate process of befriending many underlings.

DAP: [laughing] Trading sexual favors for various things to hang around your neck!!!

CH: So we could get these things to get back into these rooms without George having to take it as his responsibility in relation to these very important people who were in that room—and a lot of them were senators—and just all sorts of people that he didn't want to have to front for us for. We had to manipulate the situation to get ourselves there. You spend a lot of time doing this type of thing when you make this kind of film.

MA: You know every film gives us something special. What for you is the important thing about this film—as subject matter, as experience, as lessons from life, about filmmaking, or whatever?

CH: The special thing for me—something special that's common with all of our films—is that we get to meet these amazing people; it's the reason that we do these films and mortgage houses. Whatever you do you meet the most wonderful, amazing people and you've gone through this thing in their lives that is probably the most important thing that will ever happen to them; it's sharing something so very special.

DAP: It's like an affair in Trinidad, you know. But you don't have to tell anybody, 'cause this little film is there for everybody to see, and they know that you've had it.

CH: And I guess the most thrilling thing was that the accomplishment of these people was making the President of the United States. It's thrilling just to see all these people in the White House, and it's so strange because they are so young and they're our generation and I've never had my generation in the White House before.

DAP: Yes, that's good. I have the feeling that it's going to take me a while to look at this film and see something that I don't fully understand now;

I think that we made some kind of a, not a breakthrough, that we pushed the envelope a little in some direction that I don't quite understand. It was a surprise and I think probably, for me, it's important. In terms of filmmaking, it was something for me to learn from how it ended up and I didn't expect it to.

The Burning Question:
D. A. Pennebaker and Chris Hegedus

Kevin Macdonald and Mark Cousins / 1996

From *Imagining Reality* (London: Faber and Faber, 1996). Reprinted with permission of Kevin Macdonald.

We asked a selection of prominent documentarians, old and young, to answer two questions: 1) What in the most general terms do you try to achieve in your documentaries? 2) What is the future of the documentary? [. . .]

A founder of the Direct Cinema movement, D. A. Pennebaker's films include Primary *(1960),* Crisis *(1963), and the Bob Dylan profile* Dont Look Back. *Since the late 1970s Pennebaker has worked in partnership with Chris Hegedus, sharing all aspects of filmmaking, camerawork, and editing. Their films together include the award-winning* The War Room *(1993).*

Why can't we have a true theatre of documentary (non-fiction) filmmaking that entertains and excites rather than explains; why not a dramatic documentary, instead of a promotional one. As big and bright as any narrative fiction film, it would be filmed from reality not scripts, and its protagonists would be the villains and heroes around us that we only come to know through the press, as deceitful a ritual as can be conceived. Instead of pedantic charades on wildlife and government prudence we could, by turning a few filmmakers loose in the world, create a new and different sort of theatre that searches for its plots and characters among the real streets and jungles of our times. Instead of editing testimonials to our more virtuous citizens, we could watch those around us get through or attempt to get through their complicated, normal lives, and leave to newsprint the narration of obituaries, an art form for which it is far better suited. If a new generation of filmmakers is ever going to be interested in a film form called "documentary" for any reason other than present-day career opportunities, it will only be because it can throw off new sparks, not old news. Documentaries could do what the industry dollar guzzlers can't, because that industry doesn't know how, nor would it really serve them to find out. Comparatively speaking there's no money there. These films are the "little impudent verses" about which Ezra Pound sang, that, "jangle the doors of rich people and merchants, do no work and live forever."

And they might also lead us to what Heisenberg once called the "new harmonies."

Documentary Film Pioneer
D. A. Pennebaker Looks Back . . .
and Forward

Marc Savlov / 1998

From the *Austin Chronicle*, April 3, 1998. Reprinted with permission of Marc Savlov.

There are precious few living filmmakers today as influential as documentarian D. A. Pennebaker. Best known for his enormously influential film *Dont Look Back*, which followed a young folksinger by the name of Bob Dylan on his 1965 British tour, Pennebaker has also chronicled Jimi Hendrix and Janis Joplin in *Monterey Pop*, and (with his wife and partner Chris Hegedus) Bill Clinton's 1992 bid for the presidency in *The War Room* (which was nominated for an Academy Award). Pennebaker and Hegedus's new film, *Moon Over Broadway*, has just been released and documents the behind-the-scenes machinations involved in the creation of a recent Broadway play starring comedienne Carol Burnett. Throughout his body of work, Pennebaker has pioneered the so-called "fly-on-the-wall" style of documentary filmmaking, allowing his subjects to speak for themselves without benefit of voiceover narration or other cinematic scaffolding, making him literally one of the most imitated and praised filmmakers working today.

I spoke with him recently while the director was in town for the thirtieth anniversary re-release of *Dont Look Back* at the Dobie.

Austin Chronicle: *Dont Look Back, Monterey Pop, Depeche Mode 101.* . . . You seem to have this affinity for musicians and music and it's a topic you consistently return to. Why is that?

D. A. Pennebaker: Musicians are interesting to me because they're different from normal people and yet they are expected to have the same reactions, and so there's a constant struggle going on there. They want to perform for people, but at the same time they want to get theirs, and the two don't often go together. I think that they lend themselves to performance, and as a filmmaker that's something you look for.

You realize that people who make films like I do don't have a lot of options, you know? We don't write our scripts, we don't have movie stars at our beck and call, we have to go with things which are kind of indigenous to normal life, like aspiring politicians, performances by musicians, maybe dancers.

You can always make a film about your barber or maybe your aunt, but you're going to have a pretty hard time getting a theatre to run that. If you have any serious theatrical ambitions, you have to pay a little attention to the marquee. That doesn't mean you have to make all your films that way, but the ones you want to have work and pay off, part of what you have to do is make those judgments. If people don't think that your work has some bearing on their lives, there's not much reason for them to go and see it. Unless you get your barber at some incredible moment in his life that everybody will instantly see reflects all of our terrible troubles, you're gonna have a hard time. It's a little like trying to figure out who's going to win the lottery. You have a hard time finding subjects that will really work.

AC: Have you found it easier to gain access to musicians than, say, politicians?
DAP: It totally depends on the musician. And it depends on the moment, the timing. Let's take some group that's very big now, let's say Beck: You might have a hard time following him around, his management might say, "How much you gonna pay us?" Usually you have to have something in mind and you have to have some way to do it. Maybe you're going do it on your own nickel, maybe you've got someone who's going to put up money for you . . . that's possible, but you're never going to get a free ride on anybody that's got any kind of clout.

AC: What about Dylan in 1965 in *Dont Look Back*? Wasn't he at the height of his powers back then? Was that difficult for you to get to him?
DAP: Well, when Albert [Grossman, Dylan's manager] came to see me, I don't think he was quite at the height of his powers, that is he didn't seem to me that way. I didn't know him that well, I didn't know that much about him. I only knew that down in the Village he was fairly well known around the Kettle of Fish and those sorts of places because he performed there, but in general, in the music business, I don't think that people took him that seriously.

That was a different situation, though. I don't think that people had an idea that a movie like this—a home movie that somebody would shoot on their own—would have any kind of commercial value, or it was perceived that they were giving anything away of any value.

Albert, I think, had other kinds of reasons for doing it. I think he wanted to have Dylan go through the experience and see how you could make that kind of a film because I think he had in his mind the notion of having Warner Bros. buy Dylan for some kind of heavy feature. He kind of wanted to see if Dylan could handle it.

AC: Did you perceive much difference between documenting the music scene in the late sixties and then doing *Depeche Mode 101* in the late eighties? As a filmmaker, I mean?

DAP: It certainly got bigger, but you know, I wasn't really interested in becoming the king of the concert film, so I really didn't exert myself in that direction too much. In fact I sort of ducked everybody on Woodstock; I didn't really want to film that.

I don't know though, you get in one kind of mood and then you get in another; you follow your instincts on what you're going to do and what you're not going to do and then later you probably can't remember why you did what you did.

Remember, there was no MTV, there was no music video format, there was nothing that you could do with a music film on television except maybe sell it for stock footage. You couldn't do much in the theatre either. I distributed *Dont Look Back* myself and that was really very hard and I think I was very lucky.

AC: When you were making *Dont Look Back*, did you realize what an important film it would be and how much of an impact on popular culture it would have?

DAP: In my mind I had an intimation that it was going to be of some historical value. I did know that and I'm not exactly sure why, except that I saw in Dylan a kind of Byronesque figure who was inventing himself as he went along. It seemed to me that people didn't really understand what he was up to at that time. Even people that liked the music didn't understand why he was so peculiar, why he wasn't like all the other musicians. And it seemed to me that a film about him, that I could do then, would, at some future date, make sense of all that.

AC: Whose idea was the oft-imitated "Subterranean Homesick Blues" opening? Because, you know, that idea's been swiped by everyone from

INXS to Tim Robbins (in *Bob Roberts*) to Kevin Smith for his *Mallrats* Goops video.

DAP: That was Bob's idea. We were talking in a bar and he said, "Do you think this is a good idea for something to do in the film?" and as he described it he would have these cards and the cards would have things written on them and he would hold them up. What he'd do with them after he'd finished—whether he'd throw them away or whatever—we didn't even talk about. I said, "That's a great idea, let's bring a lot of cards with us," which we did. That was shot in the alley behind the Savoy Hotel.

[As for the homages,] we have no cable in our house—as a protection against homework stealing, which cable does—so if it doesn't come in on the rabbit ears, I don't see it. I don't know how I feel about it. They're not sending me checks, so whatever copyright I had on it doesn't seem to be providing much protection. That's the thing about documentaries, though. The very things that copyrights are thought to protect you against aren't covered. I mean, if that was a scripted film and somebody did it, they'd be all over you like a tent. I don't know. I don't feel particularly litigious, so I don't feel like grabbing a lawyer and going after the various people who have done this, but I'm a little bemused.

AC: Tell me about your working relationship with your wife Chris [Hegedus] and your son Frazer. It sounds like a very unique situation you've got going there.

DAP: I even have another son, John Paul, and he's the one who keeps the AVID going, he's the computer whiz. But working with Chris, she's a partner first and foremost, and then everything else after that we do together. She isn't the editor and I'm the cameraman—we both do it all. I like it that we both can do everything, and in the end, no matter how fiercely contested the editing gets to be—and it sometimes does, you can't deny yourself the greed of authorship because it's an overwhelming emotion—we do it together. And I really like that. I like doing it with somebody like that, and having total faith that whatever she does, in the end I'll like it as much as anything I'll do.

AC: Is this husband-and-wife filmmaking partnership something that you had sought out? Was it planned or was it just a lucky coincidence?

DAP: I never set out to have a partner. In fact, I was very wary of partners because it gets hard, especially if you both do the same thing. Chris just came in one day, and I had a couple of films that I had shot but hadn't edited—one of them was *Town Bloody Hall*, which was a film about a feminist meeting in New York with Norman Mailer—but Chris had maybe been there an hour and she saw exactly how to make the film and was really, in fact, instructive. And she did it with material that was so badly shot that I was almost ashamed to have people look at it. And it worked. When I saw what she could do with that, I thought, "I must never let her escape." That's pretty much the way it's been.

AC: Let's talk about *The War Room*, which is your film about then-governor Clinton's '92 presidential campaign. How did you get access granted to you to pursue all these high-ranking candidates around the campaign trail?

DAP: Well, George [Stephanopolous] and James [Carville] to some extent, but George was the one who really had the say. He was the sort of dictator as to who could go into the war room. And basically, the press were never allowed inside. Our being there, we were not perceived as "press" but as visitors. And in a sense we weren't press, because whatever we did wasn't going to come out for at least a year after the election. We were an invasion by the media.

I think that they knew that I had shot stuff with [John F.] Kennedy, and that, as far as George was concerned, put us into a region where they felt they could trust us, and that was important. After a day or two we just became part of the whole operation and nobody paid any attention to us. I don't think they thought about it much.

AC: Were there any particular events from which you were barred?

DAP: Nope. What we could get, we could keep. But they didn't even know what we were getting most of the time because they weren't paying any attention to it. We looked sort of innocuous, too. We weren't really a heavy operation, just really the two of us, Chris was doing sound and I was shooting film.

You're not shooting all the time, only when it's warranted. You're doing a lot of sitting around and listening and being part of a group that was very busy and very proud of itself and really dug what it was doing. It was like we were part of the team.

AC: Having been in that close proximity to President Clinton, did you see any portents of his current troubles back then?

DAP: I would never feel like making any kind of moral judgment on anybody because I don't know all the circumstances and in a sense it seems to me to be a private matter. I certainly am not surprised that he's allowed himself to get shot in the foot, so to speak. From the very beginning, with Gennifer Flowers, it seemed to me that he had somehow . . . something had gone on there. What, I don't know, but that was his business and if she wanted to bring it out in the open that was *her* business, you know? I think George's sense was that [Clinton] would be reminded not to do that again, or at least not to jeopardize what they were doing. That was kind of their bond, although it was never spoken of.

AC: *Depeche Mode 101.* Were you a fan of the band previously to doing the film?
DAP: Never heard of 'em.

AC: So how did the film come about? Apart from being a music-oriented documentary, it seems quite different from much of your other work, not only because it follows a British techno/electronic band, but also in the coverage of the group's many fans.
DAP: These films are all basically the same film, but we try to make them a little bit different so that if you had to see two or three of them at the same time you wouldn't be seeing petrographs, you know?

Some guy called us up and said, "Hey, would you like to make this film?"

AC: Who called you up?
DAP: Some representative of the band here in New York City. They were actually with Sire Records, which is a Warner Bros. deal, and they were very highly regarded, having sold a lot of records for Warners.

I arranged to go out to a concert in Oregon, actually, and I was kind of intrigued by the audience as much as the performance. The performance was hard to evaluate because the songs all sounded exactly the same, to my ear. I wasn't used to them, so I had no sense of the music and all I saw was people standing up on stage whacking away at the keyboards. I couldn't make a musical decision, but I thought it was a very interesting phenomenon to go to a concert where the entire audience appears to never go to any other concerts. The only concert they go to is Depeche Mode. It was intriguing. It had about it a kind of a quality of sort of early pagan English tribal rites. That what was going on here was somehow this prehistoric outgrowth of the music scene.

So we said we'd do it, but we quickly realized that these guys didn't have the hippies' spiritual personas, like Dylan did; they were just working-class kids who had figured out this wonderful way to make a lot of money easily.

We were gonna go with the tour, but we had to concoct a little extravagance which was a busload of kids who were going out to the Rose Bowl to see the band. They turned out to be a really fantastic group of kids, and very interesting to me. As interesting as the band in many ways.

I really liked doing that film because they let us do anything we wanted to do. If we wanted to run around on the stage after them, they didn't say a word. I think they themselves took chances and they liked the fact that we took chances, so we got along very well.

In the end, I really like the film, and you're right, it is different. It's unlike any other film we'd done before and probably ever will again, but it has a quality of "at that moment this was what was happening musically, and will probably never happen again." The whole idea of a group of young Americans who are really interested in music and hip to the clothes and everything, saying Elvis Presley was boring, was really interesting to me. I thought, "God, there's been some kind of turnaround, and we're on it, we're there." And that was a good thing to do.

I think that film will probably survive a long time just because it is a funny moment in American music, just before we got hit with a whole other kind of music. Later, after Nirvana, everything was up for grabs and Depeche Mode has kind of fallen by the wayside, although they still record.

AC: What do you think of this sort of documentary renaissance that we seem to be experiencing right now? It's really getting big.

DAP: I don't know, but yeah, you're right. I think partly it's like in the music: A lot of genius music was spawned in the sixties and out of it came an enormous body of musical possibility that's everywhere today. I think that film also kind of got spawned in the sixties, and I think that when you see the films that have been made in the last twenty-five years or so, young people look at them and say, "I can make that." The fact that they see how to do it—it doesn't matter if they have any reason to do it, or if they should be doing it, whether they have the money to do it, *they just do it*. And that's the wondrous thing about it. It's like poetry, it writes itself. Either you write it or you don't, it's there or it's not.

What's happened in the last five years is that people can take a Hi-8 camera and go out and film something that they see. They can make a film about it, and they *know how* to make a film because there's a lot of them around to look at (and maybe they'll even make up some new ways). They can take it out to Los Angeles, have it blown up to a 35mm print, and release that in theatres. And they do that a lot. Half of the films probably at Sundance are shot in Hi-8 or some kind of video format. In the end, the cheapest and most efficient way to distribute a film is in 35mm—the prints last longer, they look and sound better, and the theatres know what to do with them.

AC: Your celebrated style has been called "fly on the wall" filmmaking, but it's really not, since you're a visible presence in any given situation; you have the camera and the sound gear in people's faces and so forth. Is there any way to get around that; is there any way to get a "pure" documentary recording of a given event?

DAP: No, I don't think so and I wouldn't want to. I never try to pretend that we're not there. That would be *Candid Camera*. I don't care if people know I'm there and most of the time they understand very quickly what we want to film and what we want the film to do. They understand that we want to see what their lives are like, and really see it as it really happens. If they wanted to they could invent something false, but I doubt they could do it for long. In general, if they feel that we're trying to get kind of a picture of what it is they do as truthfully as we can, they can go with that. They know what a camera does as well as I do. They know how it's going to make them look and if they want to be self-conscious or nervous or do anything weird, that's their business. We might not in the end use it because it might seem to us irrelevant to what might be happening in that scene, but I would never try to stop them from doing anything. I let them figure it out.

AC: Your new film [with Chris Hegedus], *Moon Over Broadway*, follows a Broadway show from first rehearsals to opening night, and really exposes the backbiting and rabid hubris of show life that goes on. How did this one come about?

DAP: Both Chris and I have been fascinated with Moss Hart's book, *Acting Life*, which is just one of the great American sagas about play life. We'd been looking for plays for about two or three years, and we wanted to get access to something that was going to come to Broadway and we wanted to see it all the way through. One of our producers on *The War Room*—Wendy Ettinger—told us about this play with Carol Burnett, and that seemed to me a very real possibility for having some drama. And the worst that could happen is that we'd end up with a somewhat off-the-cuff version of *The Carol Burnett Show*.

It had a quality of a person coming in to do something with people who do a different thing, you know? They're not the same kind of creatures, and we liked the idea of seeing that type of drama unfold behind the scenes on top of the thing itself. It ended up being very hard getting everyone to sign off on us so that we could come in and do what we had to do. I think the first two or three weeks we shot, the deal with SAG [Screen Actors Guild] was that at the end of that period, if anybody, *anybody in the crew* felt that this was not what they wanted, we would burn the print. So we went into it with a lot of faith. As it ended up, everybody was terrific, but going in you had no way of knowing that.

AC: What next?

DAP: We're thinking about doing something with golf, with the qualifying round, which is what you have to get on to get anywhere else, and it's a killer. Everybody hates that. They don't get paid anything, they live in their cars, it's hateful. Out of a thousand who go into it, maybe thirty-five will succeed, and then the rest will go back home and try it again next year. I don't play golf, but a friend of ours got us to go down and watch some of this in Florida and it was kind of intriguing. What you see is a lot of human angst leaking out all over the green sod. That and the crocodiles coming to eat you. So we might end up doing that.

I Film While Leaping from My Chair: D. A. Pennebaker on Bob Dylan, John Lennon, Cinéma Vérité, and Mary Poppins

David Dalton / 1999

From *Gadfly*, April 1999. Reprinted with permission of David Dalton and *Gadfly*.

"Almost immediately reality gave in on more than one point. The truth is, it longed to give in."
—Jorge Luis Borges

D. A. Pennebaker has this *bete noire*. It's about the way certain people with cameras have been treating reality over the past hundred years. *Reality! Der ding an sich*. It's no less slippery a concept for him than it was for, say, Heraclitus or Ludwig Wittgenstein, but, if Pennebaker can't tell you exactly what it is, he knows darn well what it *isn't*. The movies. You know, Hollywood, Cinecittà. "The sets are fake and the people are acting. It's not real life," he tells you with droll revulsion. "The camera should be the ally of the *audience*, not of the actors."

I've never quite thought of it quite this way, but once the enormity of the betrayal hits me—hundred years of insults to reality!—I become incensed. Those ruthless charlatans and con artists out in Burbank! It makes me want to round up the last remnants of the Red Guard and burn down all the big studios. Honeypots of illusion and shame! Not that Penny, as he's known to his friends, is actually getting himself worked up about any of this. Not in the least. He's more bemused than exasperated.

"If you consider how many films they make," he says, "very few of them have anything like the substance of Stendhal or Pound. I got drawn into making films through Ricky Leacock as much as anything. He'd been the cameraman on Robert Flaherty's great documentary, *Louisiana Story*. I suddenly thought: here's how you could make a film that isn't a staged thing—because you don't have to have that big piece of glass between you and the film. You can deal directly with the person you're filming, and that for me was some kind of key idea. And from then on that's what I saw myself doing—breaking down the unreality of the stage performance."

When I worked for Penny briefly, crisis seemed to cling to him like a heraldic device. But even during moments of dire peril—like the time Zelma Redding and Otis Junior were about to decapitate us and feed us to their baby shark—Penny remained his unflappable, laid-back self. I figured he must have made some kind of deal with the angel of close scrapes.

About this eel-like business of reality, you want to listen to Pennebaker, because Penny's made two archetypal documentaries of the last forty years: *Dont Look Back* (1967), the classic film of Bob Dylan's 1965 tour of England, and *Monterey Pop* (1968) (with Ricky Leacock), the mother of all rock festival movies. They are so perfect in their own way that filmmakers—not to mention Penny himself—have been trying to remake them ever since. These weren't just great films of their kind, they defined the cultural obsessions of the era: our voyeuristic and quasi-sacramental fascination with our idols and our submersion in the collective rituals of rock.

And this wasn't only a matter of being there at the right time (as Penny somewhat disingenuously insists). He had first to invent the equipment to make these films. It would be as if William Burroughs, in order to write *Naked Lunch*, had to invent the typewriter (and scissors and glue). Before the sixties, movie cameras were unwieldy and heavy, weighing forty pounds or more, precluding the kind of agile filmmaking required for these fly-on-the-wall documentaries.

While working for Drew Associates at Time Life in the early sixties, Penny, along with Ricky Leacock and Albert Maysles, invented a new lightweight, 16-millimeter camera that freed the filmmaker to "float through the world." (Penny is a very resourceful individual—a few years earlier he invented the first computerized ticketing system for American Airlines.) Fortunately Penny had a degree in electrical and mechanical engineering from Yale, and Leacock was a physicist. Their epiphany was to use sound—essentially dialogue—as the organizing principle for documentaries. This way they could dispense with intrusive narrations and let the interaction of the subjects tell the story. In order to do that, they would have to develop an ingenious synch-sound system, which they did. The dialogue in the classic documentaries of Robert Flaherty from the forties, *Louisiana Story* and *Man of Aran*, is so bad because the noisy sound recorders had to be kept far away from the camera.

I went to see Penny at his Upper West Side lair in New York, a cluttered warren of editing rooms and offices and congenial clubhouse where he works with two of his sons, Frazer and Jo Jo, and his partner and wife, Chris Hegedus, with whom he has made some two dozen documentaries over the past twenty-five years, including the acclaimed *Town Bloody Hall* (1979) and *The War Room* (1993). Penny, his affable, voluble self, in fishing sweater and tweed jacket, exudes mischief. We talked about any number of things—an easy thing to do, since he is one of the most beguiling, Homeric talkers you are ever likely to meet. Here, in the words of Laurence Sterne, "Digressions are the sunshine."

On how he decides to make a movie: "Sometimes a strong-minded person appears and says, 'You should make this film.' Followed by somebody else with a bagful of money. Or a promise of money. Usually we'll operate on a promise of money. Stupidly!"

How he and Chris work together: "We go ten rounds," Chris says, "and the last one standing wins. You do tend to need someone, though, 'cause it's a very lonely thing, making these films. At times you're very unloved by the people you're filming! They don't want you around or think they don't want you around or don't know if they want you around. So you're always going through this process of thinking you're a big snoop. Which, actually, you are."

For all his fulminating about the fakery of Hollywood, there's not the slightest whiff of the doctrinaire purist about Penny—if he feels like being theatrical, reality will understand, like that little piece of documentary hanky-panky in *Monterey Pop* where Mama Cass, sitting in the audience, gasps at something she sees on stage. Since in the film this occurs while Janis is singing "Ball and Chain," we assume this is in response to the overwhelming effect of Janis's singing; but this was actually an audience shot filmed without sound, and nobody knows *what* Mama Cass was reacting to. But, it *could have been*. Outside of Hendrix's flaming guitar, what else could cause such an intense reaction? You might say that reality, in the Pennebaker cosmos, is, like the quark, something of a malleable quantity.

Someone Comes into the Room Shouting the Word "Now!"

Since Dylan occupies an almost supernatural place among his most ardent fans, Penny—who worked on two documentaries with him—has become a sort of window into the soul of the Obscure One. He is a refreshing deflator of high-flown theories, Dylanologists being the most relentless seekers after hidden meanings outside of exegetes of the Kabbalah.

Penny has made over a hundred films, worked with Janis Joplin, Norman Mailer, JFK, and David Bowie (to name a few). You'd think he would be exasperated by people still asking him about Dylan after all these years, but he seems as curious as you are about the Enigma of Bob.

In a sense, Penny has made three Bobumentaries. Besides *Dont Look Back*, he shot footage of Dylan's 1966 tours, which Dylan, the filmmaker Howard Alk, and Robbie Robertson of the Band edited into the manic *Eat the Document* (recently shown at the Museum of Broadcasting), and *You Know Something's Happening*, a rough-cut version of that same footage edited by Penny and the *boulevardier philosophe*, Bobby Neuwirth, Dylan's friend and former roadie.

The pretense fostered by cinéma vérité documentaries is that we are seeing the unguarded, unvarnished self, but with a mercurial and multiphrenic personality such as Dylan's, there's always the possibility that what we're seeing is a Dylan-on-Dylan effect. And, in any case, it's the varnish Dylan puts on things that we've come to see. As to whether Dylan's character in these films is a put-on, Penny could care less.

"I don't think it matters at all. It would be like, after a play, if I told you the whole thing was fake. Does it change your opinion of the play? It's assumed that Dylan was *enacting*. But I think, in *Dont Look Back*, that Dylan's enacting his life as he wishes to enact it. Not necessarily as it *is*, and not necessarily as he wishes it *were*, but just as he wants to act it. *Dont Look Back* is a kind of fiction, but it's Dylan's fiction, not mine. He makes it up as he goes along."

As far as his fans are concerned, the "real" Bob Dylan is irrelevant, anyway. It's the Rimbaud of rock, the pentecostal hipster of his songs that we want to see, and that's just what Penny delivers. Part of Penny's success is that, unlike more objective and cynical filmmakers, he shares a reverential view of his subjects: "I think musicians are a strange kind of clergy among us," he says. "They're the closest thing we have to saints."

I was curious about that scene at the beginning of *Dont Look Back* in which Dylan holds up cards while "Subterranean Homesick Blues" is playing on the track. It's become something of an icon of filmmaking, used, among other things, in *Bob Roberts*.

"It was Dylan's idea, actually, and a neat idea. He said, 'Do you think this would be a good idea? We'll draw up these cards and we'll play back the song I've just written and I'll throw the cards up or somethin', I don't know.' So we packed these cards and took them with us for the whole tour, but it wasn't really almost till the last couple of days—when Donovan and Joan Baez came in—that we did anything about it. Donovan drew most of them, he's a good drawer turns out. I did a couple too. Dylan didn't do too many. I'd shot the scene just for fun and it wasn't till after the film had been finished—I originally thought the film was going to begin with him in the dressing room—that I began looking at it for the opening scene. I thought nobody'll even know who he is, so I gotta get him on stage somehow and then I thought about that thing we'd shot and I stuck it in front and never took it off."

Some of the people in *Dont Look Back* come off pretty badly. I wondered how they reacted to seeing themselves behaving loutishly, Dylan's manager, Albert Grossman, in particular.

"Grossman loved it! Nobody ever sees himself as a bad guy, much less as a fool. They might be slightly embarrassed but they think . . . actually, I don't know *what* they think. I'm always amazed.

"It was through Albert that I got involved with *Dont Look Back*. I was working at Drew Associates when he came and asked if I wanted to do something with Dylan.

"Dylan knew about me from my first film, *Daybreak Express* [a five-minute rush set to a Duke Ellington track shot from an elevated train] and Sara Lownds [the future Sara Dylan] was working for us, at the main Time Life office. She had shown Bob a copy of *Daybreak Express*, and he apparently had seen me somewhere by chance at some party. Anyway, they wanted to do a film. I'm not sure what was behind it, whether Albert wanted to get him used to making a film or figured this is the kind of film Bob might sit for as opposed to a Warner Bros. big-budget film. But I think, knowing Albert, he had in mind eventually selling something to Warner Bros.

"I put up basically all the money for *Dont Look Back*. Albert put up some money in order to transport Howard Alk and Jones [Howard's wife], who were friends of Bob's. Jones was the person who did sound for me, 'cause she knew something about handling the Nagra. Otherwise it was just me. Bob Van Dyke recorded all of the concerts.

"Dylan saw that all I did was watch, and he dug that—that I never asked him to do anything. I was part of the group, I hung out with everybody all of the time but I didn't shoot all the time. Often I just sat and listened."

This Wheel's on Fire

Presumably, whatever Dylan thought of *Dont Look Back*, he believed that Penny in some way *could* read his mind, because, the following year, 1966, he asked him to film his tour of Europe. But by now his mental telegrams were becoming harder and harder to decipher. If *Dont Look Back* was in the nature of an objective self-portrait, perhaps what Dylan envisioned for the next film was a self-portrait in a convex mirror, something that would simulate on film the flashing chain of images from his songs. Or, more likely—since the concentration on such a project would essentially have involved changing careers—he wanted to make an anti-documentary.

And, to a certain extent, he got it. Twice. Penny:

"After *Dont Look Back* was finished, Dylan came to me and said, 'You've got your film (which he called *Pennebaker by Dylan*) now I want you to help me make my film, but this time there's gonna be none of this artsy fartsy documentary cinéma vérité shit. This is going to be a *real* movie.' He had some kind of vision of it, but no idea in the world how to get it. He'd occasionally say, 'Shoot that, shoot some of this over here.' That kind of direction. He would occasionally get people to say things or set up situations. For instance, he would get rooms filled with strangers who appeared out of nowhere and get them all into the scene. I don't know what he was smoking, but he was pretty far up in the air a lot of the times!

"It wasn't bereft of ideas. It's just that the ideas in his head . . . what we were going to get on film wouldn't be that! It might have been interesting if he could have figured out how to sit and edit it. I wasn't opposed to the film he was making . . . I just didn't exactly know how to do it. So I started making the same old kind of film—the only film I know how to make, actually! If he had any ideas about how he wanted to make it he never talked to me about it. We just went from thing to thing, did whatever came next. You can see that sometimes he says something but he hardly ever looks in the camera or thinks about the camera. I think he thinks I'm somehow shooting this thing the way he wants it to be shot."

Telepathic direction?

"I don't know. It was not uninteresting. It was a marvelous trip but I was never quite sure what I was meant to be doing. At one point I got so frustrated I quit and went to Cannes. Henri Langlois, who founded the cinémathèque, had asked me to show *Dont Look Back* at the Festival, but when I got there I had such a bad feeling about the place that I just packed up the film and left. I didn't even show it. It wasn't a place to show that film. Audiences have always had to find these films themselves.

"Bobby Neuwirth and I made a first version from the footage. It was all guessing, we didn't figure out what to do with any of these things, we just stuck them together quickly as a kind of a sketch—it's called *You Know Something's Going to Happen*—to jump-start the editing process, because nothing was being done. This was around the time of Dylan's motorcycle accident, so he wasn't working on it. And one day Greil Marcus came in and saw it—he thought it was a finished film; I had a hard time talking him out of it—and wrote a review saying what a great film it was. And Dylan happened to read the review and said: 'What the fuck is this? Whaddayou doing? You're not supposed to be making this film.' And I *wasn't* supposed to be, you know. I just said, 'Hey, it's only a rough cut.'

"Next Albert shows up, saying, 'What are you doing? You're not helping my client.' I said, 'Albert, you know it's hard for two people to make a film. Either one person makes it or another. You want me to make the film, I could make a film, but it's not going to be the film Bob wants. He doesn't want to have *Dont Look Back* again in color! He wants something different and you've got to give him a chance to do that.' Albert planned to do this film for ABC but they eventually disappeared. They gave up on it."

Eat the Document

Jonathan Cott described the bizarre editing of *Eat the Document* in *Rolling Stone* as "quasi-methedrine logic suggesting a self-consciously disintegrating structure." And it is wilfully, infuriatingly disorienting—jump-cutting from twenty seconds of Dylan performing to fifteen seconds of a train steaming through the English countryside to twenty seconds of something else, as if some cinematic sadist is constantly tantalizing you with some amazing scene and then, just as you become involved, yanking you away. Penny shakes his head:

"Howard Alk's concept of editing I found very destructive. I would never let Howard edit a film for me because he really likes the idea of undoing anything—*bump bump bump*—a kind of throwing things against the real time of a scene or a situation. Whatever it is, go against it. So what you get in the end looks to me like somebody just being really smartass. But I suppose by now it looks very current. It looks like MTV.

So maybe everybody assumes I had the vision of . . . Satan or something! Foreseeing what would be going down now.

"What I miss from the version they made are Dylan's profound and amazing performances. They chopped them all up, you don't have any performance continuity. They see it as being an editing effect, when in fact the really incredible thing was Dylan, the way he performed those songs. The title is Al Aronowitz's. He said, 'Documentary? Eat the document!'

"The thing that's upsetting if I thought about it, which I don't let myself do much, is that inside that tumble of laundry there's a fantastic film. And it *is* a kind of follow-up to *Dont Look Back*. A continuation. And if you put that film out, there would be a huge audience for it. But it's not my film; it's never going to be my film. We shook hands on a deal and I'm stuck to it. I can't change it and Dylan doesn't want to.

"Whenever I do discuss it with, say, Jeff Weiss at Dylan's office, he says, 'Well, you know, I was amazed that they let that thing [*Eat the Document*] be shown at the Museum of Broadcasting!' But I realize why. Sony put so much pressure on Dylan because they were trying to sell the album. They were having gastritis about the various permutations of what they could do with the promotion of it.

"Dylan made his film from the outtakes of the rough cut Bobby [Neuwirth] and I had put together. They took these pieces of footage and jammed them together. They were trying to make a point by doing that. It was a sort of put-down of documentaries. It's kind of maddening. But it's also as if Abraham Lincoln had made a film. Whatever it turned out to be, you have to say to yourself, 'Jesus, I didn't know he had that in him.' So it has that peculiar quality, of being substantially something great and strange."

Apocalyptic Bob

What there is of narrative (in either Penny's or Dylan's version) is a series of unrelated scenes told through a frantic eye, a sort of objective correlative of Dylan's flashing chains of images. One amazing scene after another unfolds, alternately manic and sublime.

And, in contrast to the black-and-white cinéma vérité of *Dont Look Back*, the look of *Something's Happening* is positively phantasmagoric. Some of this has to do with the uncoated 7242 reversible film stock used, one of the first fast films that Eastman Kodak brought out. But of course, it's the advantage Penny took of it—intuitively playing on its distortions and technical shortcomings—that makes the film so electric.

It's not quite true, as Penny claims, that in *You Know Something's Happening* he was making the film he always makes. Some of the distortion and abstraction of color from his first film, *Daybreak Express*, has crept in. He admits it turned into something of an expressionistic kind of film.

"None of it," he says, "was cinéma vérité." There is a wonderfully eerie scene of the spectral faces of children in the snow in Denmark. "It was very cold, so the lenses frosted up, giving their faces a haunting, unreal quality."

You Know Something's Happening, in its unfinished, sketchy state, is more intimate and at the same time more artificial than *Dont Look Back*. The avenging angel of hipness from *Dont Look Back* has been replaced by a gawkier, even goofier and more sympathetic Dylan; not so much the seething, amphetamine prophet as a prankish, poetic presence.

Dylan, drawing a filigree mustache and beard on his face with a pen. Dylan, outside a London shop, reading a notice that offers to COLLECT, CLIP, BATHE, AND RETURN YOUR DOG and then, like some inspired monkey grammarian, spinning this unpromising material into epic permutations, the combinations becoming more and more surreal until the words are no more than notes that he can rearrange in any order. It's as if music is his natural mode of communication and the jabberwocky of speech for him is a sort of verbal Bach fugue on which he ecstatically riffs. This is borne out in the film's most moving scenes, when Dylan plays with other musicians. Dylan and Robbie Robertson writing a song together, or Dylan and Johnny Cash sitting at the piano and singing.

While the 10-millimeter wide-angle lens creates the distorted perspective of medieval rooms in paintings of the Annunciation, the quality of the film stock, like the raking light of a sky before a thunderstorm, sheds an eerie radiance on everything. Its instability lends a brooding, flickering flashback effect that can make exterior shots resemble expressionist landscapes and performance footage look like it was shot inside a volcano. Drenched in this luminous penumbra, even the drab, galumphing wallpaper of the interiors takes on the appearance of mutated rain forest foliage.

The opening shot, as the band moves down the highway, is a pulsating sky synced to a Dylan track, the sky involuntarily blinking, as if the day itself is astonished to see such goings on. The performance footage of Dylan singing (an unreleased) "Big Mama" and "Ballad of a Thin Man" is wildly chromatic and strange. Light shatters into spiky arc-welded halos, colors bleed, images break up. There are gravity-defying moments, as when the camera momentarily turns upside down to direct its gaze to the piano keyboard (so that Penny can focus on the black and white keys) and then, like some sort of light-seeking bug, hovers around Dylan, the flaring light turning his head into a celestial sparkler. It's as if some psychic storm had broken out on stage. At times the light itself seems composed of some oscillating phosphorescent substance, and this feeling that reality is melting before your eyes seems the perfect counterpart to Dylan's apocalyptic lyrics.

The John Lennon Bit

Penny says he regrets that he was not there when Byron and Shelley went to Italy that summer. The two "unacknowledged legislators of the world," drinking Corvo, smoking hashish, planning their roles as poet kings and, in a typically sixties fantasy scene, ending up locked in their villa, shooting out the windows at the police. But the scenes he shot of John Lennon and Dylan riffing in the back of a limousine in London come close to being our own equivalent. It's a sight to behold, the two sharpest minds in rock playing with words from which all trace logic has been surgically removed. Even if the parodic sketches they pull out of thin air don't always work, it's amazing to watch them engage in mock patter and surreal quips, running through absurd routines, scrambling up and down fantastic flights of fancy as if they were syntactical staircases, language teetering, like a drunken acrobatic, on the edge of nonsense.

Dylan, though sick (at one point Lennon prescribes an extraterrestrial patent medicine for him), gamely plays his role in this Dadaist repartee. He seems uncharacteristically skittish and jaunty, playing the court jester to a deadpan Lennon, who is in fine "Scarborough-is-a-scarf-that-covers-Yorkshire" fettle.

We see a couple of instances of Dylan directing the film. At one point he insists Penny film something *real* outside the window, and at another point he tells Lennon to go back to the beginning of a piece of nonsense about Barry McGuire, saying, essentially, "take two!"

Sorry, Beatles and Bob lovers, but for legal reasons we can't quote the dialogue. You can find it faithfully transcribed in the November 1993 issue of *Mojo* or on the Internet.

Since we seem to be watching Dylan and Lennon acting out some sort of unfinished play, I asked if Dylan and Lennon were trying to recreate the sort of hyper-rap they engaged in off camera.

"They had a funny relationship to begin with. In this particular scene it was as if they were trying to invent something for me that would be amusing in some way, but at the same time they were doing it for each other. It was not exactly a conversation by any means. Dylan was so beside himself and in such a terrible state that after a while I don't think he knew what he was saying. He hauled him up the stairs of the hotel, and when he got to his room he was really sick."

An Evangelist at Twenty-Four Frames Per Second

Penny's films are an expression of his temperament: quirky, intuitive, laissez-faire, chaotic, and ultimately classic. Although he is a consummate craftsman, his heart is with the brilliant amateurs.

"I've always been interested in getting away from a fixed aesthetic, so I never think about how to frame a shot. It's an attitude I want to put out on the street because I don't want these films to be seen as finished products. I'm more interested that they be seen like the photographs of the French photographer Lartigue—'filmed while jumping off my chair'— so they have that feeling, so you don't see them as works of skilled, aesthetic judgment. The one thing I've figured out about film is that it's of the moment, intuitive. And, in the end, uncontrollable."

Penny's anarchic impulses and idiosyncratic disarray seem infectious (a nurtured chaos being part of the overall plan), often extending to his equipment, cameras at critical moments asserting their own right to be temperamental.

A typical self-deprecating Pennyism goes like this: "I don't know how to direct. I just trust in God or whoever takes care of documentary films." But sometimes his claim that he does nothing more than turn on the camera and point can seem like an inverse form of pride—like a magician's illusion of invisibility, just as his stories about being there at the right time can sound like a man with an Ariflex who just happened to stumble on the Miraculous Draught of Fishes or the Raising of Lazarus.

But how does *Mary Poppins* fit into all this? "That's just a marvelous film," he says, without a trace of irony. "It's so well made. Flawless. I wouldn't know how to make that film!"

D. A. Pennebaker and Chris Hegedus: Engineering Nonfiction Cinema

Liz Stubbs / 2002

From *Documentary Filmmakers Speak* by Liz Stubbs, Allworth Press, 2002. Reprinted with permission of Allworth Press.

D. A. Pennebaker

Pennebaker began in film over forty years ago. With a background in engineering from Yale, MIT, and the Navy, his expertise made him extremely instrumental in developing equipment for recording sound synced to the pictures captured by a film camera. Together with Albert and David Maysles, Richard Leacock, and Robert Drew, Pennebaker developed the first fully portable 16mm synchronized camera-and-sound system, revolutionizing the way films could be shot. Now they didn't have to rely on voiceover narration, but could go in the field and capture life as it happened. With this ability, Pennebaker, Maysles, and the others developed the nonfiction filmmaking style of direct cinema, or cinéma vérité, in the United States. One of the first of this sort of film he worked on, *Primary*, an account of the 1960 Democratic primaries, established Pennebaker as one of the leading documentary filmmakers in the country. His legendary films, such as the 1967 Bob Dylan documentary *Dont Look Back* and the 1968 concert film *Monterey Pop*, are among roughly fifty films in his filmography. With his partner, Chris Hegedus, Pennebaker continues to be prolific—with such films as 1993's Oscar-nominated *The War Room*, a look at Clinton's winning presidential campaign, and 2001's *Down from the Mountain* and *Startup.com*.

Chris Hegedus

Hegedus joined Pennebaker in the mid-seventies and began editing with him on *Town Bloody Hall* (1979), a document of the dialogue on women's liberation between Germaine Greer, Norman Mailer, Diana Trilling, and other feminists. She and Pennebaker have collaborated on countless films including many rock music and music-oriented films. Their recent *Only the Strong Will Survive* follows several legendary rhythm and blues performers such as Isaac Hayes, Wilson Pickett, and Carla Thomas. With Jehane Noujaim, Hegedus codirected 2001's *Startup.com*, a chronicle of an Internet company's meteoric rise and fall during the height of the dot.com mania.

Liz Stubbs: Who are the filmmakers that you most admire?

D. A. Pennebaker: There's a couple of obvious ones. Ross McElwee is a very good one. Fred Wiseman—probably most people think we and him make the same kinds of films, and we think far differently. But we probably do make, in many ways, the same kind of film. Anyway, I know that the kind of work he does on them is really hard and, truly, it's driven by a real understanding of how to do it. But remember, he doesn't use a camera himself—while he does sound on most of his things, he uses a crew if he can, or at least he uses a cameraman so he doesn't see the same movie that Chris and I might see where one of us is behind a camera.

There's others who didn't quite make it until now in terms of high profile—Joel DeMott and Jeff Krienes. They moved down to Alabama because it got really hard for them, and I think Jeff now deals in equipment a lot. But they are two of the best filmmakers of their kind that I know— anywhere in the world. And when certain kinds of things come up we go right straight to them. I'll give you an example. We did a film, *Depeche Mode 101* (1989). Actually, we love the film.

But in the beginning, everybody thought we were gonna make a film like *Dont Look Back* (1967) about these four guys [in Depeche Mode]. Well, they're just not Dylan, and there's no way you could ever make them look like Dylan. We wondered how to do this film for a bit, and then we decided to put together a trip. A bus trip, by a group of fans, and that was gonna happen because the band was going to go out on their tour and end up at the Rose Bowl and put on their final show at the Rose Bowl, and the fans would get to go for free. Somebody would select the seven or eight fans. Well, those two [Jeff and Joel] went along on that trip and made just an absolutely marvelous film, which saved our film in many ways. [Adding the bus journey story to our footage] made it funny and about something; whereas, just about the band it wouldn't have been much. And the band even recognized this early on and said, "Those are the celebrities." There are people like this [Jeff and Joel] who know how to do this, and some of them keep doing it and some of them just get worn out by lack of money and by lack of interest and lack of places to sell it.

LS: Chris, who are the filmmakers you admire?

Chris Hegedus: In some ways I started not thinking of documentary filmmakers as people I admired. I came out of an art background. I was first introduced to European cinema, and my hero definitely was Fellini. I liked Godard. And the whole European movement I was very inspired by. And then, by following the art movement, I liked filmmakers—I remember Maya Deren being very influential to me because she was the first woman filmmaker that I ever came across. It was my first realization that you could do this as a woman. And then, of course, I saw the early work done by Penny [Pennebaker] and Ricky [Richard Leacock] and Al Maysles with Drew Associates and that was extremely influential to me. Especially the film *Jane* (1962) done by Penny, because it seemed almost like a fiction film because you had an actress in it, and the story was very dramatic behind it, very strong characters, and seemed very much to me that you were making a fiction film, but with real people. Those were my early influences.

The movement that Ross [McElwee] was part of up at MIT doing personal cinema—Ed Pincus was a big influence for that whole group up there in Boston doing the diary films. And I've always loved the diary film. I don't have the courage to do the diary film myself as of yet, but I love what Ross does. I love what Joel and Jeff have done, and Pincus was an early influence in that style for me, as well as people like Michael Moore.

DAP: And Nick.

CH: Nick Broomfield. I think they've all added their own personal kooky twist to that style. You know who I love? Barbara Kopple. I think she's been a real role model for women filmmakers and has taken risks with subject matter that other people haven't gone near.

DAP: Yeah, she's fearless.

LS: How do you choose your topics, or are you mostly commissioned? How do you come to your films?

DAP: It's peculiar. They kind of come to us, which isn't to say we stand out in the street and wait 'til an idea hits us or a person runs up with a script. Because they're not scripted, very little initial work can be done on them before you actually even decide to make a film about them. And somebody who sees one of our films . . . people would come to us and say, "This is a terrific film. Why aren't you making this film?" Usually, you say, "Well, we don't have any money and we don't have any access." And if they can provide either or particularly both, you take it seriously and you consider it.

LS: How did *The War Room* come to you?

CH: We'd been interested in making a film about someone running for president, which was really the initial idea for *The War Room*, and Penny had actually tried to do it with Robert Kennedy when he was running for office and, of course, was never able to complete that film. And the election before *The War Room*, we had put out proposals, tried to do that election, follow a man trying to become president.

DAP: We even went to a TV station—WGBH.

CH: We went all over the place. GBH . . .

DAP: . . . offered us $25,000. For a ninety-minute film.

CH: That's it, so in the end we couldn't afford to do it—take that risk at that point, so we didn't do it. So the next election came up with Clinton, and several people came to us that year with different ideas of the same thing—watching the election—and none of them really followed through. Then Wendy Ettinger and R. J. Cutler—two aspiring filmmakers who had been working in theater and radio—walked in the door and said they wanted to do a film about his election. They had actually gone to the Museum of Broadcasting and watched Penny's film *Primary*, and they heard about us from that and they landed on our doorstep. And we basically said, "Yes, we'd love to do a film, but the two things we need are money and access. And why don't you go out and see if you can get that and if you can, come back and see us." So we sent them away.

We all were gonna try in the access—it was gonna be like that thing where everybody's connected in some way, so we were all calling up anybody that we knew who was connected. I think about a week later they came back in and said, "Well, we've done it. We've got money and access." Wendy had gotten $60,000 or something—her own family money she was going to sink into it, and access basically turned out to be . . . the Perot campaign denied they were running; Bush wouldn't let them in. But they got access to the Clinton campaign staff and that was basically it. At that point Clinton was a very unfavorable candidate in New York City. People didn't like him here, especially on the Upper West Side where we lived. So it kind of seemed like you were getting the booby prize. But there was a little money there, which is always enticing for independent filmmakers, so we decided just to jump in and see if we could continue getting into the other campaigns.

Most of the film was James Carville and George Stephanopoulos in the War Room, which was very risky because if they lost, the value of a film about the losing campaign staff wasn't going to be too saleable for us. There is a risk in any story where you're following real life and you don't know what's going to happen.

LS: Tell me about *The Energy War.*

DAP: Ross McElwee worked for us really long ago on a film we made called *The Energy War* (1978). We had three crews, and they all had to maintain poetic silence because we were so afraid the Republicans found out that our people [filming] the Democrats were talking to each other and they might have a fit [if inappropriate information fell into the wrong hands]. So we met in secret enclaves and talked on the phone in dark of night. That was a terrific film to do because we were on it for about two years. We went deep into the heart of darkness with cinéma vérité, believe me, with all those politicians.

CH: It was almost like if we had done *The War Room* part two, where we went to the White House and followed Clinton trying to pass a bill. That's basically what it was, but it was with the Jimmy Carter administration. And we followed this bill where the story line was—you'd think it was a boring subject, like their start-up in government. This was a bill about natural gas, but it ended up being the fiercest battle in Congress ever with the longest filibuster ever—it was fascinating.

LS: Do you find you need to be personally interested in your topic to make a good film, with all the time that you have to put into one?

CH: I think you have to envision that the subject has some kind of dramatic arc to the story, and you have to hope that the characters end up being interesting characters. But sometimes you don't know that right off because quite often you're just meeting them for the first time and you have to go by an initial sense. Certainly, that was the case for me meeting Kaleil [*Startup.com*]. I felt he had a certain sparkle and charisma. I thought he seemed photogenic and definitely, in terms of the subject matter, it seemed like what they were doing was going to be a very big, ambitious idea.

LS: How long were you filming for *Startup.com*?

CH: *Startup.com*, we filmed a year and a half.

DAP: Sometimes you might have an abstract interest and not even know if there is a story or have any idea how to proceed. I've been interested in doing something on physics and I've talked to several physicists. I know something about physics since I was trained, in a way, in physics in college as an engineer. So I had this sense that there is some story, but as yet it hasn't jumped in the window and announced itself. It's just an idea, which may never happen. It might not even make a good film. But it is something that I'm interested in.

A doctor came to me once with a pair of twins and one of them was brain damaged and blind and the other one they weren't sure about. And they didn't even know if they were fraternal twins, and he wanted me to spend time with the two of them and see, if by looking at what I filmed, they could figure out, because they didn't get much chance to study them. And at the beginning, the idea of a brain-damaged child, I thought, was just a terrible idea. I didn't want to do it at all. But I got so intrigued by this child and so engaged that it really was an enormous learning process for me. I never try to prejudice myself in front whether I think it's interesting to me or not, because usually, if you stick with it, you're gonna find out something you didn't know. So it's a peculiar thing.

The process, the filming process, is very much revelatory—it's like a research program in something you didn't think you needed to know about—you end up getting really into it. It itself is a reward beyond whatever the filmmaking is, and I think when that happens you're able to make the film better. It's easier to do the kind of work—because it is hard work—and the concentration and the focus is easier to maintain if the thing gets to interest you, whether it starts out that way or you don't even think it's gonna. If it was totally uninteresting the whole way through, I think it would be a very hard film to make.

LS: Would you do a film you were commissioned for if you weren't initially interested in the subject, trusting that, in the process, you'd get interested?

DAP: Well, you might get interested in the money and the money alone. We've done things like that where we needed the money to do another film—to finish another film, and it was with joy that we greeted that money. And in the end that showers off on the film. We did one in Germany with a rock star there—the film would never emerge from Germany—and we had a great time doing it and we got to like the guy a lot. But it was straight for money. There was no question in our minds. And we tried to put him off three or four times, and he wouldn't be put off. In the end, there's always something about the process that you can take joy from a little bit.

CH: I think there's always something interesting to be learned in every situation if you just go at it like that—and, especially, if you do it with a friend, which is nice about doing it with Penny as a partner. You can make it your own adventure in some ways and it definitely is an adventure that's less painful if you aren't getting paid for it. We usually have done these films with very little budget.

LS: Does funding get any easier?

DAP: I was going to ask you the same thing. Should I get off the bus now? Or is it going to get better? It's like writing long poetry. You just don't do it for money. Like winning the lottery—some people make a film and it goes on to make a lot of money. But you find if you study a detailed following of what happens, the people who initiated the film very seldom realize a lot of money in the end. I think Michael Moore is one of the few I know who actually ended up with some money, and he's busy spending it on other filmmakers to try to get them to make more films. But that was a one-off and a peculiar thing, and don't expect it to happen again. And you don't make any judgments by it because it doesn't hold up for what you're really doing. Every year, you make one or two films and they take all of your resources and energy and sometimes a lot out of your family life, but you kind of are obsessed and you do it.

CH: I always say no one asked me to be a documentary filmmaker. You're doing it for other reasons. But in terms of the funding aspect, there's always something new that's changing in terms of the market for these films because of the technology and the exhibition of it. Digital technology is really changing the whole exhibition of feature films and the making of a feature film, as well as documentary films, because the technology has been put into the hands of so many people now that the prices for these shows has come way down and there's a saturation. It seems like if you're in this field long enough, there's always something like that. I remember there was a really big fear when home video came out that that would take over films being projected in theaters. And then again when cable came out there was all this hope that there would be all this new programming opportunity, which really didn't happen for the documentary filmmakers. But things shake up. There's always something new.

DAP: We have an old film that's in 16mm and it's never going to be a big moneymaker. It's a film called *Town Bloody Hall*—it's Norman Mailer, Germaine Greer, Michelle Johnson. . . . Well, that film, I mean, it's played in Europe in theaters in 16mm, which you try not to think about because it's such a terrible way to show a film. But you think, "I'll just put that aside and when I come back it'll be over." But in this case, we have somebody downtown at Cowboy Releasing, at their screening room, and he wants to run it as a film. Well, we aren't going to do a 35mm blowup of that film for one little running, which is an experimental running, but we can show it in video. We happen to have a PAL video we did because BBC paid us to do a PAL video from the print. Actually, we had to go back to the original film to do it, so it was not inexpensive. We probably lost money on the BBC deal. But we now have at least a PAL video, and this guy is willing—in his theater, he has a setup for video projection—he'll show it in video. That's a big jump for us. That means a lot of our stuff, if we can ever get the money up to get it out of film and into a video format, we can get it theatrically shown without having to go that next step, which is so expensive and so wasteful, to make a 35mm print for projectionists all around the country to wreck at their expediency. So in a way, I already feel the thing changing underneath me, and it gives me hope that a lot of stuff we've been sitting on for years, if we can just get around some of the things like music rights, can be shown theatrically because television has always been pretty much cut off for us. They don't buy from us. They make their own.

CH: We can sell things for television after we make them.

DAP: Yes, after. They buy them as theatrical films. For us to do programming for TV, it doesn't seem to work out that way. Even Europe, where we've always had a market—that's kind of drying up because they have cheaper sources now and they really don't care as long as the stuff is documentary and can be proven to be so. They're not that interested in where it comes from or who did it. So you have to face the idea that it is a market that could dry up on you and then you'd be left with no place to sell them. I think these kinds of films are always going to be someplace that will show them in some fashion. You're not ever going to be cut off—it may get more expensive and you may have to figure out cheaper ways to do it.

LS: *Startup.com* was shot in digital video, yes?

DAP: Yes, and so was *Down from the Mountain*.

LS: So you embrace DV?

DAP: Yes.

LS: How do you think DV will affect documentary filmmaking?

CH: I think it basically puts it into the hands of the masses. Almost every single thing we did as we made any other film, in terms of the digital filmmaking, I mean. The camera's little, but you're not going to make your movie—unless you do narration over it, that type of movie—unless you have professional sound equipment and that equipment remains the same size if you're shooting in film or if you're shooting in video. You have to do that same type of be-on-top-of-your-character and put the mics on, so that part of the process is very similar. You have to carry a lot less and it's certainly a lot less expensive. It gives people the ability to just go out and do it, which is great. It's a liberating thing.

DAP: You're able to do a lot more damage quicker with that new equipment. But I don't think films are made with the equipment anyway. They're made in your head. I think you can give people who make one kind of film, you can give them any kind of equipment you can imagine and they're gonna continue to make their kind of film. It's not gonna change the film. But I think for people who are looking to get closer or maybe even get beyond the edge of what they've always seen as a kind of a wall as far as they could go, I think digital gives you a tremendous leg up. And shooting recently myself, I've seen things I can do with a small camera and it's not just the size. It's the difference between a pistol and a rifle. I would be surprised if I did any film for a while or ever again.

CH: We had to pull him kicking and screaming to video, but now he doesn't want to go back.

LS: With DV you are probably able to shoot more than with film?

DAP: That's one aspect of it, yeah. Not necessarily an advantage, but in some instances it is an advantage. It's something you play off against other aspects, but I think the real work on the film is in your head. And the thing you've got, if you can spend less time loading it with whatever you're shooting with, then I think probably your headwork is more efficient.

LS: What is your shooting ratio, and when you're shooting, are you aware of the big picture of your film, or does it evolve in the editing room?

DAP: You make it in both places. But the editing is when you see better what you've made. When you're shooting you're not sure what you're making but you know when you're getting close. It's like you're warmer or colder. You can sort of tell by the relationship of the people you're shooting.

CH: I always think of it kind of like an investigation in some ways. The process of finding your story while you're making it because you don't really know what it is while you're going along, and there's a lot of that same process of finding the story in the material because when you condense material in the editing process you form character in a way that you really didn't think you had because everything's so stretched out. But when you put the dramatic situations together they reveal the character and start creating the story for you, so both of the processes have a lot of exploration in terms of what the story is.

LS: What do you think your shooting ratio is?

CH: I think we shot somewhere around forty hours for *The War Room*.

DAP: There's sort of a point where you get bored, and it's usually about forty hours. I think the film *Dont Look Back* was forty hours, but some films where they have a little repeat built into them that you didn't expect, like *Moon Over Broadway* (1997), they kept changing the script so we'd have to reshoot all the rehearsals because we'd never see the old ones again. [*Moon Over Broadway* is a film chronicling the opening of the Broadway play, starring Carol Burnett.] So that took a lot more film shooting than we may have thought we would do, so you're always prepared for that . . . always prepared a little to be surprised. And then *The Energy War* took a lot more, because it just went on and on. They couldn't get the goddamn bill through either the House or the Senate, so it went on forever. But some, like *Company: Original Cast Album* (1970), were lovely. [*Company* is a film about the cast recording of Sondheim's musical.] It all happened in one night, except for one more roll. So in that time you can only shoot so much. You shoot as fast as you can load. Certain stories have limitations built into the story.

CH: For *Startup*, we shot an incredible amount of video, mostly because we were bored to just sit around, and it's kind of fun with little cameras so you might as well shoot. This was one tiny aspect of it, but I think we shot around four hundred hours so you can see it's amazingly different, but also because Jehane felt like she just wanted to shoot anything. That was her first film.

DAP: But also I kept telling them she was sort of setting off on a Proustian voyage here, and in the beginning I thought maybe I should discourage her. I'm sure I kept saying, "You just can't shoot that way." And it's true—you don't have time to even edit that much material; you have to wade through it and get rid of material. You don't have that much time to do it. So it's got drawbacks, but, at the same time, it had a peculiar quality of examination that I thought was amazing, and the more I saw it the more I saw what she was doing, or the two of them were doing. I realized that that was the only way to make that film, and that it was a new kind of film for us. And we had to find the physics rules that applied to something with that much material because you don't want to keep going back and making the same old film. They were going off into new ground, which I thought was really fascinating. I think you could make a ten-hour film out of that; that would be interesting to a very limited audience, but limiting nonetheless because it's so, it's like Proust. It's so real and it's so new that I think people would be intrigued to find out what there is to find out there in that world.

LS: With such a low usual shooting ratio aren't you afraid you're going to miss something?

DAP: You're not afraid. You're convinced you've missed something. You edit these things thinking, "This is impossible."

CH: We miss things all the time. It wasn't a matter of courage. We had limited access and George Stephanopoulos did not want us hanging around the War Room all the time because his neck was at stake. We had to continually weasel our way into that situation. We would see discount fares to different cities and, lo and behold, Little Rock was one of them. And we'd fax George and say, "We've got this cheap fare and we're coming down unless we hear from you," and then we knew he wouldn't answer his fax by the time we got there. You kind of befriend secretaries and assistants who feel sorry for you, and you call up and they don't know you're not expected there and they let you in. So you do a lot of tactics like that to get in, but we weren't allowed there that often so we had to judge when something was going on if we could. And then we didn't have any money—we had this $60,000, which doesn't go a long way if you're shooting over a seven-month period or whatever it was, and your airfares and hotel bills, so you have to really limit how you shoot.

DAP: But long ago, when Ricky and I were first trying it on our own, when we left Drew, we would shoot a lot of very short films. There'd be things that we could shoot in a single day and we did a number of them—16mm black and white usually. We got very cheap black-and-white film from Dupont, and you could get it processed fairly cheaply. And you used practically everything that you shot because it was only going to be a ten-minute film and we only shot two or three rolls. And we did this a lot so you get in a habit. . . . I remember in *Dont Look Back* there were a number of scenes in there where I could shoot them in one take, and I liked that idea—a scene that had no edits in it, so it was a real-time scene. When you start shooting and thinking that way you wait as long as you can, you shoot as little as you can, and you wait until the last minute, and you roll in and shoot something that completely exposes whatever you hope to expose, and then go on to the next. That kind of shooting we tend to do because it's easier. And it concentrates some things. Later, when you edit, you always find a way to make it work. I don't know why it is—things that people worry about there, I think they don't have to worry. Because by the time you know what happened and you know how your story should end, you can always get there; you'll find a way to get there.

LS: Do you characterize yourselves as vérité filmmakers?

DAP: Well, I don't.

LS: How would you characterize yourself as filmmakers?

DAP: Movies. That [vérité] was not our phrase—the French made that up—but it's always been applied to American films, which amuses them greatly. Jean Rouch was practically the originator of it. It doesn't seem to me that it's my responsibility to figure out names for these things, because they don't help me much in my work. I want to be able to do a scripted film or a fiction film if somebody brings me something that intrigues me. I don't want to feel that's not my business somehow. So I never think of it in terms of a limiting phrase, but I know that when you talk to people and you say documentary, that means it's got no actors in it. I mean, they know the difference is one's fiction and one's reality, and reality can mean so much to so many different people that I hesitate to even call our films reality films. Cinéma vérité is sort of an elegant French phrase and if people want to use it, fine. And sometimes I'll even use it because it's shorthand. I don't have to explain things. But in the end, I don't think it explains what our films are about because that's what the film is for. It doesn't help me much.

LS: Are there ethical boundaries you don't cross—are interviews verbo-ten; is it okay to become part of the film as a filmmaker?

CH: This is something that has evolved from being something that had much more of a strict censure to it, and I think it not only applies to our kind of filmmaking but also to journalism in general, where there was a journalistic code where you didn't step over this line or that line. And now I think journalism is a bit more blurry. And I think in terms of our filmmaking I don't have any strong rules. At the same time, I am interested in giving people the real experience that I felt in some way. But I know that these films are constructions and works of the imagination, so to say they're like film truths can't be true just from the nature of what we're doing, so I don't like to get pigeonholed into it.

And I think that the whole documentary cinéma vérité style has gotten a lot looser. People are using music. Barbara [Kopple] uses music in a very . . . almost television way, in a very manipulative way in her films, not in a bad way. And we are using music a lot more in our films, too. Things that I think weren't done as much in the sixties. But, in general, I don't need to have strong rules about what we do. I think what we find works with our style is to let a story play out itself and have the audience be able to experience what goes on. We try to use little or no narration if we can, because I think it draws you out of the film in a different way. We tend not to interview people very much while we're making a film—in the beginning I tend not to do it because it makes people think that's what we want from them, because people are used to being interviewed—like, okay, do the interview and go away. And I don't want to establish that as the type of relationship that we want to have with our subjects. We want it to be, "Okay, we're just going to be there hanging out with you as much as we can, following you around." But later on, we interview if we want to because that has been established. But again, when you stick an interview in the middle of a film it sticks out. So you have to use that in a certain way. In certain places, like in a car, it's a very easy way to interview somebody, but make it look like it's part of your movie, so there are certain tricks that you can do to use those methods, but keep the film style.

DAP: I was always very affected by the way Flaherty just used the camera to watch. [Robert Flaherty's *Nanook of the North* (1922) has no conventional plot but tells the story of an Eskimo community through phenomenal black-and-white images of landscape and life.] And I know I heard stories about how he cut the igloo in half to get the light in it. I'm less interested in whatever tricks he may have had to do to give that quality. But just watching somebody do something that he does well or knows how to do, I think that's the highest kind of effort a camera can make. Because you can't argue with it. It's not like a writer telling you what it's like to be in the North Pole. You're getting it secondhand. This way, you're seeing it and you're feeling it even though there was no sound in it. You could just hear that wind and hear that whole feeling of being up there in that kind of condition. I guess I always wanted to use the camera in that way.

You know, it never occurred to me to ask Dylan why he changed his name from Zimmerman, and I'm sure that would be interesting, if you could get him to tell, but I don't think that that's my place. I don't see that as what I was supposed to be trying to do. I think that that extends pretty much to all our films—that it's more interesting—I think in the end you get more.

In *Down from the Mountain*, there's a lot of people in there and that's always a big problem for the documentary filmmaker, especially in a film where there is going to be a concert, or all the people are going to come together. Everybody looks alike in any movie, whether it's fiction or documentary, because you don't know them very well, so you confuse people—people say, "My God, how can you do that? He's blonde and now this guy's dark-haired?" Well, you notice certain things and not other things and you get them confused. People in television land, where they can't stand a moment's confusion, they put the names underneath the picture, so part of the picture is the name. Well, that's not a real picture anymore. That's a sign—like an advertisement of some sort, so I hesitate ever putting names under pictures, even though I know it's frustrating not to know who you're looking at. I sort of feel I'm not going to leave it to chance, I'll give every possible aid I can. I'm gonna take the best portraits of these people and put them in the beginning of the film—try to have it so before I even get on stage, you know the differences and you've got ways of remembering the differences before you're asked to sort it out. And I think a filmmaker can do that work; it's hard and it takes a lot of thinking to do it, but I think when you do it, it's a stronger film if you leave those names off.

I don't feel we have any moral high ground at all. I mean, there are things like where you ask somebody to do something again. I don't think that you've taken a lower folder. It's just that I think you lose; I think you give up something. The only reason for us for any of these rules is that in the beginning we didn't know how else to do it, and the rules were if you asked somebody to do something again, then you lost them. They didn't have time for your movie. They had time for their movie. So if they felt it was going to be their movie from the start, then they did whatever they wanted and you had to follow, and it was your tough luck if you missed it. The minute you start saying, "No, no, it's not my tough luck at all . . . this is an expensive process and I'm going to make you do it right because we need to have the shot," you've lost them and they don't give a damn about your process. They've got their own lives to live. I think most of the rules that came into this all probably came as a result of some sort of objective aspect of the filmmaking.

LS: I'm also exploring the kind of character it takes to make documentaries. It's not an easy road. Funding is difficult to come by. You commit years to a film. What keeps you coming and making documentaries or films?

DAP: Life is not for sissies, as I always say.

CH: It's an amazing adventure to make films, and it's a privilege to live somebody's life with them, especially during a time that's exciting, like watching people elect a president and watching these two kids live through this dream and it ends up being this historic Internet bubble. It's hard work, but it's very rewarding and when you spend a lot of time with people and get to know them, to me it's very rewarding and I always learn something from the people we make films about. I can't think of anything else, really, that I'd want to do.

LS: Do you learn something about yourself in each film you make? Is that part of the appeal?

DAP: It's hard to know when you learn something about yourself— you're so well disguised to yourself. It's like taking a trip where hardly anyone's ever been before. When you come back you're a foot off the ground and you're bejeweled in some way, and that's a great feeling. It disappears rapidly, but just the film itself, playing it before an audience, you feel like you're some sort of minor celebrity. It's that you've brought back some treasure that people didn't even know existed and it's always going to have your stamp on it and everybody is going to know that you were the one who found it. It's a great feeling.

CH: Penny and I like the mom-and-pop grocery store aspect of filmmaking. We do the whole process of the film. We're like a painter—we shoot the film, we edit the film . . .

DAP: . . . we carry them to the lab. We do the laundry afterward; there's nothing we don't do. Nothing's too good for us.

CH: So they become sort of like our children or something.

LS: Do you have favorites?

CH: Definitely, there are films of ours that are more interesting than others at different times.

DAP: We love them all.

CH: Little ones have their jewels, too. There's moments in every film that I love. One of the interesting things, I think, about documentaries is that sometimes they're for a very narrow audience and they mean a lot to a certain audience and other people who are interested in peering into a different world can enjoy them, too. There's that aspect of films that aren't made for major distribution—they're just as interesting, especially to that narrow group, as a film that had a wider appeal.

DAP: And you acquire an entire Baedeker of lines that you can remember your entire life and we throw at each other occasionally. The thing is to remember the film it was from. They're lines you never would have written, you never would have thought up, that somebody said in extremis, and they haunt you for the rest of your life. They're kind of wonderful little bits of poetry that live on in these films.

LS: In order to make the kind of films you and your colleagues made, you needed to devise a portable camera that was quiet and that filmed at a predictable rate. Take me through the invention of the Nagra/sync sound—what was the technological revolution that you were involved in that changed the face of filmmaking?

DAP: [The idea behind sync sound was that cameras needed to film at predictable rates so that] whatever speed it was, you could re-effect that speed later on a projector and whatever sound you recorded with it, if the sound could also be played back at the speed it was taken, they would be in sync together. The effecting of this kind of synchronism [synching sound with picture] took a little doing. [D. A. and his collaborators worked on developing a sync sound system in the late 1950s and early

'60s.] And that was a big job and, luckily, Time-Life had a lot of money to spend on that kind of work because they were hoping to do what the History Channel now does, which is to put a program on every week, or every night or whatever, which is in their field. It would be candid film-making, as they had expanded on candid photography. So they had a big stake in it, they thought, and we also were trying to get a camera that was quiet so you could be in rooms. Normally, cameras are pretty noisy and you can make them less noisy by wrapping blankets and things around them, but that doesn't make an inconspicuous object. So those were the two things.

CH: And the third thing was putting a handle on the camera and sticking it on your shoulder and having it really portable. I think the whole thrust of the invention movement that began cinéma vérité was really to separate the camera from the tape recorder and make them independent.

DAP: That's true, and of course that led to the two-person team. Usually, it was the cameraman and his girlfriend in the independent world. Now that you've got the little video cameras, people are beginning to see that one person can make a movie. The way we were doing it, it really took two. But the two gave the process a certain aspect that was interesting. It gave the basis of two people making judgment calls rather than a single person just doing instantly what he wanted to do. And it led to a little more judgmental aspect in the film shooting and later, if those people worked on the editing, they consorted. It made a different kind of film than a single person would make.

CH: But how did the development of the synchronous camera come about? Which was the first film that used it? *Primary*, right?

DAP: No. First was *Balloon*. I had a camera that I had done some preliminary work on. I made it sort of synchronous—I was using my windup tape recorder that was handmade, but it was very rough and it was crude, and we could only shoot hundred-foot rolls. It had a lot of problems connected with it. When I went to Moscow, we had windup cameras and windup tape recorders if you can believe it. We didn't know how to shoot sync sound, but I knew that if I could take sound at the same time as I shot a windup that when I got back here I could find a way to sync them up. I didn't know how, but I knew we could figure it out. So that's how we were shooting sync sound, but then Ricky arrived with Leonard

Bernstein and they were going to do this concert of this Shostakovich Seventh and it was gonna be a big thing with the New York Philharmonic in Moscow, and they asked us—Al Maysles was with me—to help them shoot because they were using all the big 35mm cameras.

The Russians were going to film the concert but they had no way to film the audience. So we came in with our little windup cameras and a sync-sound rig. It had a tape recorder and a wire for the tape recorder to the camera, and then there was a wire from the camera to a big long microphone that was four feet long, five feet long, with a huge long stick, and that was wired to a big battery that you had to carry. It was about the size of a Volkswagen battery. So it really took three people to carry this mess—and then trying to follow Lenny down the hallways in the Kremlin. . . . Of course, it was impossible, and we're falling all over each other and it got him laughing, so he says, "This is ridiculous. Get that thing outta here." And I could see that no matter how good it was at getting sync sound, it was impossible to carry it. It needed to be portable.

A lot of engineering had to be done on the process before we could follow people down halls and watch them play pianos, and follow them in the desert, follow them anywhere in the world and have one solution to the problem. We didn't want special solutions, one for this, one for that. And that's what I set out to do. That was in '59, and from '59 to about '63, Ricky and I and some other people worked on that problem steadily until I got a camera.

About in '63, when we did *Crisis*, I had kind of a final camera, and later, when I did *Dont Look Back*, I used the same camera, but it was a little further modernized, and that camera was with me 'til the mid-eighties.

CH: But, backing up, the clue to sync was when you saw that Bulova ad or something?

DAP: Yeah, well, we didn't know how to get sync. We didn't know how to do it. And there were several possibilities. One is that in the air in New York—there's so much hum in the air. It's about sixty cycle—everything in New York is sixty cycle. You can put a little antenna up and amplify that hum and use it like a crystal to make a sync signal because it's sixty cycle. The trouble is, if you went to London it's fifty cycles. If you went to the desert, there'd be no cycles, so it's a special way of doing it. Then we started looking around for people that used sixty cycles or some aspect of it. Bulova had just come out with an Accutron watch. And the Accutron watch actually had a little tuning fork in it that produced 360 cycles, which you could use as a signal [a pulse to drive the sync between camera and sound recorder]. And if you mounted [an Accutron] on the camera and mounted one on a tape recorder and you used the one on the camera to drive what they call a flip-flop circuit, which, in a way, became a driver for a synchronous motor, which takes a lot of power, you have to carry a big battery to run it. And since it was the same driving signal—that is, the clock on the camera and the clock on the tape recorder—if they both showed the same time, you knew that whatever you shot on the two of them could be made to match, and that's what we used for a while. And later, they came out with crystals, which were more delicate.

The field expanded because they were doing the same thing for missiles, people getting to Mars and whatnot, so we got caught up in the jet stream of that and were able to get people in high places who had no business even talking to us to try to make stuff for us to experiment, and we did a lot of experimenting. I spent almost ten years trying to get a battery to drive these things, and I must have spent more money on that battery than the government did. In the end, it was impossible because they knew how to make the battery, but nobody knew how to make a charger for it. And they didn't care because they got the thing charged and they sent it up into space and they never saw it again, so they didn't worry about recharging it. But I have this constant problem of recharging these batteries, and that was a big problem for us. We had to be able to carry on our shoulders whatever we were gonna shoot with, which was a camera, three magazines, twenty rolls of film, whatever it was going to be . . . and be able to get in a cab and go to Hong Kong with the guy, if he decided at the last minute he was going to do that, and not question it. We couldn't go back to our hotel, we couldn't have it shipped to us, we had to have it with us, and we never checked it. We just used all our bodies, so anything we could take off that weight, that impedimenta, was a big help. I mean, we were crying. I remember when we were doing *The Chair* in Chicago. Ricky and I each got on the scale somewhere in the airport, and I think I had a hundred pounds of equipment on me. I said, "This has gotta stop." So we went back determined to shave it down even more, and we did over a period of three years.

LS: And now, the DV cameras . . .

DAP: They're wonderful. I like it that you no longer have the curse of the heavy equipment.

CH: It's kind of a blessed thing, now that I'm older and it's harder for me to lug around all the heavy camera stuff, that they made something small for me in my old age.

DAP: There was a tape recorder that was half the size of the Nagra that was called the Stella Vox. I remember when I handed it to Chris . . . the look in her eyes, I will hold forever. It was half the size and half the weight, and it was just as good. In fact, I think it was better than the Nagra; it was also made in Switzerland, but it became subject to the uncertainties of commerce, and the company failed and went down.

LS: DV changed the way films could be made.

DAP: It did. It absolutely did.

CH: The one film that Ricky made before they had this equipment that was just incredible—it's called *Toby and the Tall Corn* (1954). It's kind of an amazing film. It's a very intimate portrait, but he lugged around things like this. . . .

LS: Have you changed the way you approach filmmaking? Do you have more or less serenity or anxiety about the process?

DAP: We don't have such fierce fights anymore. We don't get divorced three times in the editing process like we used to. We get along better.

CH: I think it's the same. You still have those horrible butterflies when you miss things.

DAP: You hate to start. Oh God, that's the hardest thing, to start a film. I'll do anything to put it off. I even clean up my desk. I'll do anything to avoid it. I hate to start a film. It's horrible.

LS: So it is an anxiety-producing process?

DAP: The need to fail. It gets harder and harder to face that.

LS: In terms of the shooting, how do you know when you've finished, when you have the end of your film?

CH: It's different for every film. When you shot the film, or you shot until you ran out of money or got bored.

DAP: Or got tired of loading magazines.

CH: It was one or the other and, usually, it was, run out of money.

DAP: When you're bored by even thinking about it, for me. Boredom is the one thing I have to respect. When I get bored I stop shooting or I stop eating. My mind is telling me, "Don't pursue this anymore. It's not interesting." You always get caught in the coda.

LS: Do you ever think about doing fiction films?

DAP: Sure. I've done a couple. I did some with Norman Mailer. I would do one under certain conditions. I wouldn't try to do what a lot of people can do much better and have already done much better and many times over, but I think you could do a fiction film kind of the way that we did with Godard. I think there's ways of doing a fiction film that would be kind of interesting. I think the Danish would be really interested if we did Dogme films, kind of maintaining the way we shoot and mixing it up with the concepts that would come out of imagined stories and made-up lines. I think that's possible. And I think it'll be done sometime very soon because you can save a lot of money doing it . . . to say nothing of bringing actors that otherwise are bored with acting in general, or the kinds of things they're asked to act; I think you could do that, sure.

CH: Every time we miss some major scene in our film, I always think, that's it, we're going to hire some actors.

DAP: I think there are a lot of surprises in the so-called documentary concept in the next ten years and the lines between documentary and narrative are going to get very unclear. I think that's good. The imagination always gets tired at the obvious.

LS: How do you see the line becoming more blurred?

DAP: I think people will start out with their single little camera and their sound and start talking into it and start making up things into it, and pretty soon it'll be unclear whether it's a biography or a film. It's gonna get mixed.

CH: Also, I think that people start distributing movies in totally different ways because of the Internet and because of the accessibility. I think you can use them almost like letters, and they'll be traded online and sent to each other in whole different ways than we ever imagined.

DAP: I think films will get like letters in some ways. But made for one person, not made for big audiences, and later, they'll get seen by big audiences, like Browning's letters to his wife-to-be. They'll find ways of getting out into the public but, initially, they will not be for audiences of billions. Because that's a boring idea to begin with. Who cares about audiences of billions; how can you ever care about it? You're never gonna meet all those people, hopefully, and what are you gonna tell them? They're not going to respond to your personal life very well. I think there're gonna be many surprises—a lot of which I can only sort of guess at, but it's a great time to be making films because you're in the middle of watching them build the first airplane right in your backyard, so it's kind of interesting.

LS: What are you working on now?

DAP: We're finishing up a tired old duck that's upstairs and it's almost done. It's for Miramax.

CH: We're doing a film on R&B music where we've gone around and found different musicians who are still out there and surviving and doing their thing. Everyone from Wilson Pickett to Isaac Hayes, Mary Wilson from the Supremes, to a whole group of musicians that were part of this famous Stax/Volt recording studio. Anyway, we're in the editing process of that.

LS: Do you do anything other than documentaries right now to make a living?

CH: Well, we make our living by selling footage of dead rock stars. We've been very lucky because—Penny, mostly, but through the years both of us—have been able to keep the rights to many of our films. One of the bad parts of funding these things by yourself is that you're poor when you're making them but afterwards, if you can sell them in a way that you retain the rights, or you can get back the rights, and not be a work for hire, the footage becomes valuable because it's part of history. You know, no one else has that footage of Janis Joplin or Jimi Hendrix, so you end up having these things to keep you alive. Basically, we do that. We haven't done many commercials. We never seem to be able to get the job to do the commercials. We have done music videos. We've been lucky to do a lot of long-form music films to make a living from. Like Penny was saying about this Westernhagen film, which was probably the largest concert we ever filmed—it was for this rock star in Germany that was done for Warner Bros.—it was a big deal, but you know it'll never be seen here because it's all in German. But this guy is basically the Mick Jagger of Germany. So, you know, we get hired to do strange things like that.

LS: Are there any special challenges because you're a woman documentary filmmaker?

CH: When I first started film, there weren't very many women filmmakers and it was hard to find role models. Now there are women everywhere in filmmaking and that's very gratifying to see. I think women's stories are very suited to the filmmaking process, whether it's fiction or documentary, and it brings a certain sensitivity to it. It's wonderful that it's now appreciated and accepted. Recently, because I just worked with a woman, basically Penny functioned as a producer for *Startup*. Jehane and I shot together, and that was pretty interesting, for two women going into a situation where we were following all guys around. I think it worked to our advantage, actually, because we were not threatening to them. There were a lot of guys who were very alpha, very ambitious, so we were very unthreatening. I think it helped us get into a lot of the meetings and things that we did because we didn't look very threatening. We looked like two girls with a movie camera, so it worked to our advantage. So, if you can make it work to your advantage, more power to you.

D. A. Pennebaker:
At Eighty, Looking Back and Ahead

David D'Arcy / 2005

From *Greencine*, August 19, 2005. Reprinted with permission of David D'Arcy.

"The idea was that I could do it all by myself."
—D. A. Pennebaker

In *Dont Look Back* (1967), the images that seem to stay with you are of Bob Dylan on stage during a British tour, standing alone, spot-lit, singing with a guitar and a harmonica strapped around his neck, in front of sell-out crowd after sell-out crowd, with a composure that you find only with the most self-assured performers. It was 1965, and Dylan, all of twenty-four, looked a lot younger.

Here we see Dylan, a self-invented Dylan, reinvent himself day by day in the glow of youthful creativity. As he stumbles through the tour—unscripted is the understatement here—Dylan's self-invention is indeed a crude process, but no less watchable for its roughness as D. A. Pennebaker films it step by step, song by song.

But there's another scene that a lot of us who think we know *Dont Look Back* probably won't remember. Dylan's manager (and one of the film's enablers), Albert Grossman, is plotting with a British booking agent to wring an extra hundred pounds out of a few already booked appearances. Pennebaker records enough of the finagling to show the show business behind the Bob Dylan who seems pure onstage.

Of course, we all know that the entertainment business lives off agents who can scratch out an extra 10 percent. But do agents and their clients really want us to see how folk music sausage is made? Pennebaker makes sure that we don't miss it.

Yet everyone being watched by Pennebaker's camera in *Dont Look Back* seems unfazed by the lens that's watching the whole time—it's not just because the tour was fueled in part by hashish. And here you can see what makes D. A. Pennebaker unique. He has the confidence, the trust of his subjects, which gets him the free access which few entertainers and even fewer public figures will grant these days. The result is that the subject tells a story or, more precisely, is the story, whether it's Dylan, or James Carville in *The War Room* (1993) or Norman Mailer in *Town Bloody Hall* (1979) or Carol Burnett in *Moon over Broadway* (1997).

Pennebaker is often called, almost automatically, a "fly on the wall" filmmaker, because he's so present that you stop noticing him. Like most clichés, this one misses the point. This "fly on the wall" could just as easily be called the "fly in the soup," except this fly is there by mutual agreement, not by accident. He just makes sure that you don't see him in the final product, but you see what he sees.

Any documentary is far more complex than the advantage of unimpeded access that Pennebaker demands as a prerequisite. But that access always gives Pennebaker and his team (led by wife/partner Chris Hegedus) a head start. It also gives Pennebaker's films that special feel of the real story told from inside, or from behind the scenes of a performance or a political event. Note that in Pennebaker's case, behind the scenes never involves hidden cameras or ambushes.

I'll let others argue whether Pennebaker's uncanny skill at getting inside his subjects is at the core of this filmmaker's legacy, or whether that legacy is the unscripted vérité style that Pennebaker pioneered. Bear in mind that this is not the later vérité style of Fred Wiseman's great marathons. Watch a Pennebaker film now, and you'll see that the work is as much in the editing as it is in the observing.

And any young filmmaker would do well to watch Pennebaker's documentaries, if only to understand how you can reach dramatic effects not just by artful editing but also by just letting the camera roll. In *Monterey Pop* (1968), which Pennebaker shot with a team of peers behind the camera, your eye stays with Jimi Hendrix on shots that go on for what seems like an eternity. Here's one performer who doesn't need much editing, and a filmmaker who knows how to shoot in service of a performance.

Thanks to *Monterey Pop*, Pennebaker's influence is everywhere, whether today's music video slapdash directors know that or not. Nor should his role as an archivist or preservationist be neglected. Our memories of the young Bob Dylan are vivid, largely thanks to *Dont Look Back*. And the same can be said of Jimi Hendrix, thanks to *Monterey Pop*.

John Hartford, the songwriter and performer, never had the broad stardom of Dylan or Hendrix and probably never will. But we'll remember him as his own era's Will Rogers in *Down from the Mountain*, Pennebaker's 2001 doc of the Nashville concert performed by musicians who recorded the soundtrack of the Coen Brothers' Mississippi odyssey, *O Brother, Where Art Thou?* Hartford's irresistible warmth is all the warmer here since he's fighting cancer while he's telling all the jokes that are making you laugh. He died just as the film was released, and we're richer because Pennebaker put so much of him in front of us.

Another thing you learn from that film is that you don't need to really like country music to admire the people who make it in *Down from the Mountain*, although it's hard to come out of that film not loving the music you just heard.

With *Moon over Broadway*—Pennebaker's chronicle of the making (and the near-unmaking) of the farce *Moon over Buffalo*—which returned Carol Burnett to Broadway in 1996 after thirty years, the backstage story will win over even the skeptics who think that theater's been lifeless for the last fifty years. Burnett enters tentatively, losing battle after battle with a director who resists improving the many flawed jokes in the book. She forgets her lines, sometimes even in mid-performance when the play is previewing in Boston. But when a winch fails during those previews and Burnett improvises—live—with a restless audience until the machinery is fixed, we see the magic: a natural entertainer's triumph over the kind of challenge that every performer in our scripted world dreads. (Of course, moments like this one are just what documentary filmmakers live for.)

I spoke to a spry and voluble D. A. Pennebaker, who has just turned eighty, in Manhattan, where he lives. He talked about films, the future, and the evolution of documentaries during the six decades that he has been making them.

David D'Arcy: What's it like to turn eighty?
D. A. Pennebaker: If you put it that way, it sounds like a pumpkin rotting, or turning green in the corner.

DD: What was the first movie you saw?
DAP: Something with cowboys falling off their horses, but I have such a vague memory of it, I wouldn't know what it was called. The first movie that made me jump up and down was either the Buñuel *Robinson Crusoe* or it was Michael Powell's *I Know Where I'm Going*, which had such a documentary quality to it. It made me suddenly want to do that. He'd witnessed documentary, and he was holed up with Robert Flaherty for a

year or so, in an editing room in England. He kept trashing Flaherty, who was doing *Man of Aran* (1934). He was taking two years to get the right storm, and Powell said, "That's bullshit. I could make five films during the time you take to do that."

DD: When did you first hold a movie camera?
DAP: I got a little rental camera with some film and I shot one of my children when it got christened down in Florida.

DD: Eight millimeter?
DAP: No, sixteen. The first time I ever held a camera with the intent of doing some real damage was on *Daybreak Express* (1953). I don't know if you're familiar with John Sloan's paintings of New York, of the elevated train on 6th Avenue. He did one, a view of New York, from a big high building, and you can see what for a while was the Waverly Theater—it's now become the IFC Theater—it was a church then. If you look down into the street, where the elevated turns up 6th Avenue, it's the most lovely picture. Somebody had it in a loft and they were selling it back then. It was only forty-five hundred dollars—even thinking of it now makes me sick. I knew I was going to make a movie about that when I saw that picture.

There's also another picture, a picture from the ground, looking up at the Elevated as it came out of 3rd Street and zoomed up 6th Avenue. I just thought it was the most magic thing, with people running under it and crossing, all those Irish girls that he loved. You can see the edge of the church in that picture. I set out to do *Daybreak* because I heard they were tearing down the 3rd Avenue El, and that upset me quite a bit, and I set out to do a documentary of that, all of five minutes long. I made it as a silent film, with Duke Ellington's music.

DD: Did you ever want to make dramatic features?
DAP: I didn't understand how they were made. It was like, did I ever want to build an automobile? Sure I did, but it has no meaning for me. When I saw Francis Thompson's film, *N.Y., N.Y.* (1957), which he made by himself with a hand-wound city special, I said, "Shit, I can do that." I'm a graduate engineer from Yale University, for Chrissakes, I've got to be able to do that. That set me off doing it, because the idea was that I could do it all by myself. I knew I couldn't do features by myself because you had to have it written, you had to have actors, and I was a loner, so those things were not part of my life at all.

DD: Was television a place where documentaries showed in the 1950s?

DAP: Television wasn't interested in anything independents did. They were all showing top comedians and quiz shows.

DD: I suppose it didn't help that politics became one of your recurring subjects and that you avoided the omniscient correspondent voiceover.

DAP: I worked on *Primary* [about the U.S. Democratic presidential primary of 1960] and there we had a little problem, because Robert Drew [my partner on the project] wanted to tell the story by way of narration. He wanted that authoritative background to hold it together. That was the thing that I felt very nervous about. I didn't think that authority in these films really helped you. It took away the whole adventure of it. It made it seem like it was a geography lesson or something. In television those days, you always had someone telling you what he knew.

DD: Often it wasn't a hell of a lot.

DAP: And you never saw the action take place.

DD: Was there any continuity between *Primary* and *The War Room*, which you shot in 1992, more than thirty years later?

DAP: Not really. *Primary* was about a person, and in the end, what really came to life was Kennedy. The sections that Ricky Leacock shot of Kennedy gave it the feeling that we were in a special place, which is what really makes those things work.

In *The War Room*, we didn't have to get with Clinton. Clinton was going to turn you off all the time. He was going to give you front porch parlor talk. He was never going to say "shit." We needed to be in a special place with people who would say "shit," who were interesting, and who would talk to each other. It didn't matter whether they talked to us because we weren't going to interview them. We never wanted to do an interview show out of that. From the beginning, it was definitely not what we had in mind.

DD: Your films seem to depend on the willingness of the subject to be recorded, to be observed.

DAP: Yup. To live their lives for us. It wasn't just that they were going to allow us to indulge in their wisdom. It was like race car drivers. They were going to actually race while we were filming, so we could see the best they could do.

DD: So would you say that if a person isn't going to allow that, there's no point in making the film?

DAP: No—you just go home.

DD: Why did Bob Dylan agree to be filmed in 1965 for *Dont Look Back*?

DAP: Dylan had seen a copy of *Daybreak Express* and he really liked the idea of the Duke Ellington music on it. He really loved the music in it. I don't know what he thought about the film. He wanted to find out about what making a film was like, because I think Warners was after him. Warners wanted to do the first big Dylan film. So Dylan and his manager decided that I could come along and shoot during the tour and then they'd figure out what they'd do as a next step. I don't think they had any idea that I was going to make a movie, especially after they saw that little homemade camera. I was all alone, really. I had one guy recording all the concerts on the tour and one person doing sound.

DD: He seemed comfortable with the camera there, to the point where, in contrast, Joan Baez is ill at ease with a still photographer from a newspaper who comes to take her picture—but she's comfortable enough to show all her discomfort in front of the movie camera. It makes you wonder which camera is more intrusive.

DAP: Yeah, it's funny. I don't think Dylan took it all that seriously.

DD: What's the key to shooting a performance? These days music video directors seem to be editing with a Cuisinart, the more the better. Yet *Monterey Pop* is full of lingering long shots of musicians as they're playing. Is your assumption that the musician might know more about his performance than the filmmaker?

DAP: In *Monterey Pop*, I worked with a few cameramen who I knew would listen to the music. I wasn't so concerned about how good they were as cameramen, because the cameras, you just turned them on and turned them off. It was simple. I never thought to direct anybody as to what to do. I assumed that if you turned them loose and said, "Just get the best pictures you can of Hendrix or Janis or whoever's on there," somebody would get a good picture, and they all got good pictures. I realized that not directing is the strongest thing you can do for performance, as long as your people aren't klutzes. Letting people go was the strongest thing that I did there, and I learned a lot from that.

DD: Did *Dont Look Back* do well in theaters?
DAP: It went worldwide, but it never made much money because the theaters would never pay us. It ran in England for years, but I don't think we ever took a dollar out of England. They probably thought they'd never see another film by us, and it looked so ratty that they didn't think they ought to pay for it. But then *Monterey* came around and that changed everything.

DD: Did the studios come after you to do anything after *Dont Look Back*?
DAP: No. It just looked too ratty. I remember the letters. There was one from an executive at Seven Arts who said he went to the film and didn't understand it, but his daughter really liked it. You could see that they looked at it and it just didn't have the production quality that they thought was mandatory for a film. It probably wouldn't have gotten into a theater except that it was seen by the Art Theater Guild, who were distributing porno on the West Coast. The guy who ran it said, "That's just what I'm looking for. It looks like a porno film, but it's not." We were booked in a falling down porn house and there were lines around the block.

DD: When did you get a sense that the younger generation was moving in?
DAP: Not for a long time. Over the years, I've seen films that people have done here and abroad that have really charmed me, but I never got a sense of what I thought would happen after Monterey. I thought that people would come in and just start wrecking the place, because anybody can do it, and the stuff is out there waiting to be found. And they didn't, for a long time. Wiseman was turning films out—I think he began with a camera we gave him.

DD: Did you ever think of doing a film on Ronald Reagan?
DAP: No, but I did want to do a film about Nixon, Thanksgiving dinner with Nixon. I wanted to see him human, while he's serving up the Thanksgiving dinner. He had almost become a kind of Donald Duck figure. That always bothered me, when people lose their humanness.

DD: Has anyone approached you about making a film about Iraq?
DAP: No, and I'm not interested in going to Iraq. I don't want to make films about things that don't work, and Iraq doesn't work.

DD: With this profusion of documentaries, has it gotten any easier for you to make films?

DAP: No. It has to do with this new era of documentary that began with 9/11, in which it was proven absolutely that what I call the Zapruder Concept [named for the home movie that recorded the Kennedy assassination in 1963] was going to hold the field for the foreseeable future. People with tripods and trucks full of equipment are not going to get the picture of 9/11. They weren't going to be there. The guy with a cheap camera in his hand saw the plane go into the building. That's the thing that no one will ever replicate. It was so extraordinary, that he got it in such a perfectly clean, clear way, just like watching Kennedy's head blow apart. You couldn't have imagined having a camera there to do that. And there was no other camera.

People now figure they're not going to go around with trucks in tripods. They're going to go around with a camera in their pocket. It means that the films that win, the films that get distributed, are like people that win the lottery. You don't set out to try to win the lottery, nor do you try to figure out what the secret is of winning the lottery. It seems like an act of God. These films come around, and they're like the one about the dancing, or they're like *Spellbound*, they're all one-offs. They're always going to be one-offs. They may shoot some more, they may get lots of offers, because their film wins prizes and everybody loves it, but it's doubtful that it will happen to them again.

It's like Zapruder going out and becoming a filmmaker. There's no point in it. So what you've got is a situation where a preconceived concept is very hard. You've got so many people out there with cameras that anything that happens that's at all peculiar or out of the ordinary, someone is pointing a camera at it. And that wasn't happening twenty-five years ago.

DD: What are you working on now?

DAP: A few things. We're shooting a project about drugs for HBO. We're filming people in drug situations. They've got a number of filmmakers out doing it, of which Chris [Hegedus] and I are just one team. It's not sure what the final film will be. A few weeks ago, we went up to Maine to meet a couple that was using drugs, and they agreed to let us film them while they were still using. And then we watched them go into a hospital that's using a new drug that somehow gets at the part of your brain that is exposed to the drugs and makes the whole thing work for your body; this treatment is not being generally used for various peculiar reasons.

We watched the effect on this couple over two or three days. We also got kind of an insight into the degree to which drugs have taken over America. People have no idea about it.

D. A. Pennebaker Looks Back

Carol Caffin / 2007

From *BandBites* 1, no. 7 (May 15, 2007). Reprinted with permission of Carol Caffin.

"Legendary" is one of the most hackneyed adjectives in the English language. Every once in a while, though, the description not only is apt, but also, somehow, necessary. In the world of documentary films—particularly those in the often unscripted, usually no-frills "direct cinema" style, of which he is considered by many not only a pioneer but a master—few names are as legendary as that of D. A. Pennebaker.

It was through the lens of Pennebaker's hand-held camera that the general public got, if not its first glimpse, certainly its most real, most lasting, and, ultimately, most iconic, filmed images of Bob Dylan. Those unforgettable black-and-white scenes of pre-electric Dylan on and off stage, in hotel rooms, in cars in London, and flipping hand-drawn cards to "Subterranean Homesick Blues"—and the still images of the shadowy figure who seemed to follow him, camera on his shoulder and whimsical stovepipe hat on his head—are permanently etched in the psyches of Baby Boomers everywhere.

Of course, D. A. Pennebaker, who will be eighty-two in July, and Bob Dylan are indelibly linked. And, by extension, "Penny" is linked to the Band as well. After all, it was Pennebaker who shot the footage of Dylan's 1966 electric tour with the Hawks/Band that would become one of the music world's most celebrated film fiascos, the much-bootlegged but never officially released *Eat the Document*. It's no wonder, then, that although the award-winning filmmaker's body of non-music-related films is large and impressive, to many, he will always be the pioneer of the modern rock doc.

It was truly an honor to speak to Mr. Pennebaker, who happily shared his memories of Dylan, the Band—and the ten-plus hours of footage sitting in his vaults of Rick Danko, Jonas Fjeld, and Eric Andersen.

Carol Caffin: How did you first get involved with Dylan and the project that became *Dont Look Back*? Did Albert Grossman call you?

D. A. Pennebaker: Well he came to visit actually. He came to see us.

CC: When you say "us" . . .

DAP: I had a little studio down on 43rd Street. And Ricky [director Richard Leacock] and I had a little company called Leacock Pennebaker. We had two or three people working with us—it was not a big company or anything; it was just a small . . . we were on the top floor of a building that was later torn down. We were doing different films. Ricky had done a film on the quintuplets in North Dakota [1963's *Happy Mother's Day*], and I had done a film with Lester Pearson [*Mr. Pearson*, 1962] who was then the Prime Minister of Canada. So, we'd been doing some films, and we had done a lot of short films. And when he [Grossman] arrived, he asked me if I would be interested in going to England with them on that tour they were gonna do.

CC: Grossman had seen your films and had been familiar with your work then?

DAP: I don't know what he had seen. Dylan, I know, had seen the little *Daybreak* film, the short film [Pennebaker's five-minute documentary, *Daybreak Express*, set to the music of the Duke Ellington song of the same name], because Sara, who later married him, Sara worked for us and she had given him a copy. And I think he had also seen some stuff that we may have done that was shown on TV, stuff that I had shot—Rick and I had gone to Hungary with Casals, you know, the cello player. And we had done a film for CBS, and I think he [Dylan] had seen that somewhere. I didn't know that until years later. That's all I know that he saw. Other than that, I have no idea why he called me.

CC: So Sara, when she was Sara Lownds, worked for your company?

DAP: She worked for Time Life. We had an office at Time Life and were connected to Time Life at the time. We had done, oh, two or three films—actually, it was more than that, it was about six or seven films—for Time Life, and then I had quit and started my own company. [Sara and Bob] did not get married until after '65. But anyway, she knew me and she certainly knew Dylan.

CC: Do you know what she did there at Time Life?

DAP: Yes. She ran an office that was set up in the Time Life Building in 49th Street, or wherever it was, and we had an office down on 43rd Street. She kind of acted to connect the two. The one uptown was tied to the Time Life Bureau and the whole works, and we were just in a production studio downtown, which I had run, and we produced the films for Time Life down there. She sort of ran that office briefly—not forever, but during the time I was there. I think she got out of there afterward.

CC: That was around '64 or '65?
DAP: Yeah . . . well, a little earlier than that, maybe '62, '63.

CC: Who was it that you dealt with on *Dont Look Back*? Was it Grossman or was it Dylan? And did they tell you "this is the type of film we want" or did they leave it up to you?
DAP: They didn't tell me anything. They just said "Would you like to come along?" I mean, I guess they assumed I'd bring a camera. But in a sense, I did a film and I paid for it. I think that they put up some money for Jones and Howard Alk to come along. Supposedly, they were gonna have this other old girlfriend of Dylan's come. But then she didn't come along.

CC: Do you know who that was?
DAP: Yeah, it's the one that . . . oh . . . [pauses]

CC: Suze? Suze Rotolo?
DAP: Yeah, yeah. They told me about her [but] I never did meet her. She was supposed to come but they had broken up by the time he had left, so she didn't come along. There was kind of no hierarchy involved, but there never was with Albert and Dylan. They would talk together, I guess, and figure things out. In fact, there was nobody there who was my boss. I kind of did whatever I needed to do.

CC: So it wasn't "Come along to make a film," it was just "Come along."
DAP: I don't think they understood how to hire anybody to make a film. I mean, they'd never done it before. Howard Alk was gonna be a cameraman, so I brought another camera for him. Jones [Alk] knew something about doing sound, so she was gonna tape sound for me. So, it was really just me, and these two people who were friends of Albert's and Dylan's too, I guess. And I brought along Bob Van Dyke, who was gonna do the concert sound; we were gonna record every concert on tape, although we weren't gonna make any kind of a music film.

CC: Mr. Pennebaker, for a person my age—this music and your images were part of the background of my childhood—this is quite an honor. So I hope you don't mind, but I have to ask you one "fan-y" question. It's about "Subterranean Homesick Blues." The cue cards: where are they?

DAP: Where are they now?

CC: Yes!

DAP: You know, I know a lot of them got blown away . . . they were showering over London somewhere. We lost quite a few of them that afternoon because we were up on the roof of the hotel filming the last [version]. I don't know if you've seen that [version]. . . .

CC: Of course. There were two versions of that, right?

DAP: There were three, actually. There was one original one that they started with in the park back behind the hotel. And we—that was kind of rough, because a policeman was sort of grabbing at me from behind while I was shooting it, so I couldn't do it.

CC: Yeah, that could hinder things.

DAP: We finally went into the alleyway so we could have some peace. So what happened to the cards that remained—we just may have left them there. I didn't want to bring them back, although I probably should have. I just have no idea what happened to them. They disappeared.

CC: Well, in 1965, they probably meant nothing, but now, like the film, they've become almost iconic.

DAP: Oh yeah, you could get a lot of money for them on eBay! [laughs] Or make some new ones and sell them on eBay—who knows?

CC: So did you and Dylan just sit there with markers making up these cards?

DAP: Joan [Baez] did some of them and Donovan did some—Donovan was really good. I remember doing some, but I can't remember for the life of me which ones now. It just sort of happened. They appeared.

CC: Well, thanks for clearing at least part of it up. In the film, in addition to Dylan, there's [Allen] Ginsberg and Bob Neuwirth and somebody else.

DAP: Yes. And there's the guy who was Dylan's producer—you know on the record with Captain Ahab ["Bob Dylan's 115th Dream" from *Bringing It All Back Home*]? His name is Tom Wilson.

CC: I didn't realize that was Tom Wilson.
DAP: I liked him quite a bit. He was a terrific guy, I thought.

CC: One more question about that tour, and then we can go to '66. Do you know what the dynamic was between Dylan and Joan Baez, why she left that tour?
DAP: There was probably lots more going on under the table that I wouldn't know about. [From] what I've gleaned over the years—I'd known Joan slightly, I don't know how, but I knew her through somebody—she had been on a tour with Dylan just before this tour, around the States. It had been much more kind of *her* tour and Bob was invited along. It had that quality to it. And I think she came along thinking that he'd reciprocate, you know, and that he'd invite her up on stage to sing with him. He didn't want to do that at all and it was clear from the beginning that he didn't. But she was also there because she had started this school near Monterey [the Institute for the Study of Nonviolence], and she wanted it in England. There's this very famous school, Summerhill, and she wanted to go see how that was run. So, one of the reasons she left us was to go see that school. She spent some time there. When we came back [from the tour], I actually went to her school and we talked a little about Summerhill.

CC: Well, some people think—and it could appear—that Dylan was taunting her a bit.
DAP: I think he just didn't want—he wanted to go through that thing by himself. He didn't want to make it a joint concert thing. He had some new songs that he was gonna sing for the first time and he didn't want her onstage. And when she realized that, she split. There may have been some bad feelings; I don't know. I'm sure she was upset in a way. But I know later, she came back when they did the Rolling Thunder [Revue] and she was involved with that.

CC: Okay, that was for the Dylan fans. Now for the Band people. Can you tell me about *Eat the Document*? Tell me about your first meeting or first awareness of the Band, of who these guys were.
DAP: It was in Los Angeles, and they were on their way to Australia. That was the first time I really met them.

CC: Were they with Dylan?
DAP: They were with Dylan. He was recording there and then they were

gonna go out to Australia. And I went out because he wanted to talk to me about making another film. I'd finished *Dont Look Back* but I hadn't released it. I don't think I'd even shown it to him. I'm not sure. Then he said he wanted to make this film and he didn't want to make it like *Dont Look Back*. He wasn't sure what he wanted to do, but he wanted to direct it and he wanted me to film it for him. He would figure out how to edit it and everything. So it was gonna be his film, and all I would do is be the cameraman, and I agreed to do that. Then off he went to Australia, and I didn't see him for a while. The next time I saw him, I was flying off to Sweden with Howard and Jones again, and I met him in Sweden, and it sort of began there. And we filmed.

CC: And that was in '66?
DAP: Yeah.

CC: And when was it that he was going to Australia? Also '66?
DAP: You know, I think he'd gone up to Newport—I'm not sure about the dates. The years all run together for me. But that was the first time that I'd met the Band. Although he did do a concert at Carnegie Hall, but I don't remember if he had any of the Band there.

CC: What are your memories about those guys, individually and collectively? And what was the dynamic on that tour?
DAP: You mean before they went to Australia or in England?

CC: When you actually went on tour with them.
DAP: Well, we got on very well with the organ player.

CC: Garth?
DAP: Garth. He was a very good friend right away. I don't remember why, but we hit it right off. Then, Robbie sort of hung out with Dylan a lot, so I filmed the two of them a lot, you know, at night playing music or whatever. Then—I'm trying to remember—there were some other people involved. They were just guys. I didn't really think about their differences because I was so busy trying to think about what to film. It was a lot different than filming a single person on stage, you know. So we had two cameras and Howard wanted to interview people in the audience and stuff, and I wasn't sure I wanted to do that. It was a little complicated.

CC: You guys all travelled together though, right? Did you hang out with Dylan and the Band?

DAP: Yeah, we were at the same hotels. We hung out, yeah, very tight. And Mickey Jones was there, who was the drummer in place of Levon, because Levon was not with them. He had played with Johnny Rivers, so I kind of knew who he was. Lou Adler was a big fan of Johnny Rivers, so I knew about Johnny Rivers. They [the Band] were just people. I don't have a strong memory of them as individuals except for Garth.

CC: I interviewed Mickey recently and he mentioned that everyone called Robbie "Barnacle Man" because he was always attached to Dylan.

DAP: [Laughs] Yeah.

CC: Was there that kind of sense on the tour?

DAP: Very much so. But see, I didn't get in on any of that attitude. But I knew that Robbie was definitely with Dylan—a lot. I mean, he did sort of hang onto him [laughs].

CC: Whatever happened to that footage for *Eat the Document*? Dylan owns that?

DAP: That was not like *Dont Look Back*. There was a definite difference between them. *Dont Look Back* was mine and later—it's really a shared thing because we're partners in the film. So we let him have copies of a lot of the *Dont Look Back* stuff. But the problem with the film [*Eat the Document*] was it was supposed to be an ABC program; that was the plan. But ABC was getting very nervous. It was gonna be a one-hour program, but nobody knew who was doing it or what was being done. It almost got to be a mystery. And Albert said to Dylan and me, "I want you two guys to put something together so we can show ABC." And I'd say "It's not my responsibility; I'm just the cameraman." [ABC said] "We're looking for a film out of it" and I said "Well, you'll have to talk to Grossman." And then Albert would call me and say "What are we gonna do here? We gotta have something ready for them" or whatever. So Dylan and I put together . . . it was really kind of a sketch of a film. But it certainly was not what Dylan wanted to do, for sure. But I kind of did it the only way I knew to do it. And we never really did anything with that; and then Dylan decided to get to work on it. You see, he had his motorcycle accident somewhere in there.

CC: That was summer of '66, right?
DAP: Yeah.

CC: Do you think that motorcycle accident did happen?
DAP: Well, something happened, because when I went up to see him he was strapped in a chair of sorts. But, I mean, I don't know. I heard all sorts of stories. But from what I knew, he was definitely recovering from something. And then we set up an editing machine, and [got] an assistant editor, and they worked up there for a few months.

CC: In Woodstock?
DAP: Yeah. Well, in Bearsville.

CC: Bob Neuwirth—he's somebody who—I never understood quite what his role was besides being Dylan's buddy.
DAP: Yeah, he was mostly that. Well, he was actually on *Dont Look Back*. He was a musician. He was also a painter, which is interesting. He spent a lot of time up in Cambridge. He sort of . . . Dylan likes to have somebody around that he can talk to. It's a funny thing, and Neuwirth knew exactly how to do that. When I saw him early on while I was filming, I realized that he understood exactly what I was doing with the film. So I knew that he was somehow gonna make it happen, which he did. Neuwirth was a very important part of *Dont Look Back*, and it's hard for me to describe exactly why, but we both knew.

CC: It seemed that way to me, too—sort of an intuitive relationship.
DAP: Yeah, absolutely. The problem that Dylan would have with people in general was that, if they saw him as kind of a minor celebrity or whatever they took him to be, but they didn't know where he'd come from or what he was doing or anything else, they'd be wondering why he changed his name, things like that—he couldn't stand that. That drove him nuts. He needed a person that really understood everything about him from almost the moment they met him. That's what Neuwirth could do. That made him very comfortable with Neuwirth. The problem was—and I guess this has happened with other people with Dylan—that after a while, he [Dylan] sort of changes and becomes a different person, and that person is no longer necessary so he sort of shoves them off. But I don't think he's ever really shoved Neuwirth off. But, it was something that I didn't need to know, so therefore I didn't bother to. What I saw was what I saw.

CC: Okay, there was *Eat the Document*, but also *Something Is Happening*. What was that about?

DAP: Well, that's the film that we made for Albert to quiet down ABC, and it never got shown to anybody—well I think a couple of people saw it. But I didn't want to get into a film competition with Dylan at all, so I just kept it under wraps here.

CC: What happened to that footage?

DAP: That's still around. It's just a work print that's never been released.

CC: And that's yours or Dylan's?

DAP: Well, it's my doing. I put it together, but it's really Dylan's footage.

CC: Do you think either of those will ever see the light of day? I mean I know *Eat the Document*'s been around. . . .

DAP: Yeah, and I think he's no longer too happy with it. Well, who knows? I always think anything sooner or later will see the light of day, but it's not going to in the immediate future, no.

CC: Which brings us to "the trio"—Danko Fjeld Andersen. Well, let me backtrack for a second. Did you have any contact with any of the guys in the Band after the '66 tour?

DAP: A little bit with Rick. And I also saw . . . [pauses] the hippie-type guy. Not in the Band, but in the trio.

CC: Eric?

DAP: Yes, Eric Andersen. I know he lived in Norway, but I'd seen him and talked to him for some reason, some place or another.

CC: How did you get involved in filming Danko Fjeld Andersen in 1991?

DAP: I think Eric came to me. He said that they were gonna do a tour, and he brought me the record. We heard the record and we really liked it. And it came up that there was gonna be this little tour up in New York State. And we had a little time, so we said we'd go along and film it, which we did. It was as simple as that. It wasn't put out as a big film we were gonna do or anything. And the problem, we knew, was gonna be getting rights to the music, which would always be difficult. It had a limited kind of possibility for it.

CC: How many hours of footage were there?

DAP: Oh, about ten hours. I know at the time, Rick thought that maybe we could get money from [the label in] Norway to make a music video to go with the record, but it wasn't forthcoming. Nothing ever came of it, so we just finally put it away and figured someday it would emerge, when it was time. . . .

Interview with D. A. Pennebaker and Chris Hegedus

John Berra / 2008

From *Electric Sheep Magazine*, December 1, 2008. Reprinted with permission of John Berra and *Electric Sheep Magazine*.

The Return of the War Room is the companion piece to *The War Room*, the groundbreaking 1993 documentary by D. A. Pennebaker and Chris Hegedus that went behind the scenes of Democrat Party candidate Bill Clinton's successful 1992 presidential election campaign to focus on the tireless staffers who pioneered the political concept of "rapid response." The new film, which was financed by the Sundance Channel, catches up with Team Clinton sixteen years later, allowing those involved to reflect on their victory and the unconventional approach that was adopted to take the Governor of Arkansas to the White House. Pennebaker was one of the founders of the Direct Cinema/cinéma vérité movement of the 1950s, and he has since aligned his interests of music and politics with documentaries such as the legendary *Dont Look Back* (1967), which followed Bob Dylan on his first British tour in 1965. He later partnered both professionally and personally with Chris Hegedus, and the couple formed a company to specialize in documentaries that sidestep traditional voiceover narration and interviews in favor of capturing interesting individuals in real-life situations. Recent projects have included the concert film *Down from the Mountain* (2001), which contributed to the commercial breakthrough of bluegrass music, and *Startup.com* (2001), which chronicled the short-lived Internet business boom of the new millennium.

John Berra met with Pennebaker and Hegedus at the Sheffield Doc/Fest to discuss the evolution of campaign strategy, the similarities between musicians and politicians, and why their documentaries are, in fact, plays.

John Berra: *The Return of the War Room* comes sixteen years after *The War Room*. Was this an opportunity to comment on how the political landscape has changed with regards to campaigning since 1992?

Chris Hegedus: Definitely, we are interested in the ways campaigns evolve and they changed while we were making the film. Every day there was some aspect of technology that would not only be groundbreaking but change campaign strategy. They had some Internet fundraising, and it all of a sudden took off, and then it was people making movies with their phones and putting them on the Internet and catching the politician saying something he didn't want to be seen saying. It became obvious that a candidate did not have one moment of his public life when he could be unaware.

JB: *The War Room* was a new concept that influenced the campaign strategy of the Labour Party in 1997. What was the reaction to the events depicted in the first film in 1992?

D. A. Pennebaker: The film was received in different ways in different countries. In France it was successful, but in Germany, to see a politician who was younger than eighty years old was shocking. They didn't know what to make of it!

JB: The original film was supposed to be a study of the Democrat Party candidate Bill Clinton, but he did not want a camera crew following him around. How did you feel about adjusting your focus to the staff of his War Room?

DAP: I thought we were lucky because my experience with the candidates of the major parties is that you don't really get anything that surprises you, but we were with people who were wonderful characters who really said what was on their minds, and it made it a better movie. I had started a film with Bobby Kennedy because I knew he was going to run, and I had said, "I would like to make a film about you, and the end of the film will be you walking into the White House." But it was too expensive and I couldn't raise the money to do it. Kennedy would have been good because I knew him, and he would have talked, but trying to dissect the person who is looking to be the perfect candidate, who wants to share every religion, is not realistic; he becomes a cartoon figure.

CH: We were just so lucky that we stumbled across James Carville and George Stephanopoulos. James Carville was brilliant, he was so eccentric, like someone's drunken uncle at a party, and then you would have this opposite, this brilliant Rhodes scholar, so you would have this buddy thing going on, and on top of that, James's girlfriend [Republican Party strategist Mary Matalin] was running the Bush campaign. It was absurd.

JB: That relationship plays an important role in both films. Were you aware that James and Mary were romantically involved before you started filming?

DAP: We don't really edit that way. We're trying to make a piece of theatre, which means we're thinking about people sitting in the fifth row and what is going to keep their attention. Carville was behind things like "the economy, stupid." He's a guy who manages to take these realities and squeeze them down to an epigram and everybody understands it right away, so when he was talking to George we would keep an eye on him. But you don't make them think that you're looking to make them be something that they aren't. They have to feel that the film you're making is really representative of what they do because they dig what they do and they want people to know what they do.

JB: You have made celebrated documentaries about both music and politics. Is the circus that surrounds artists similar to the one that surrounds politicians?

DAP: They're not too different. They both have a career based on a talent that they happen to possess, and how they came to decide to exercise it, you don't know. Musicians are people who, when they go to the party and there is no instrument to play, slip out of the window. They don't know what to do with themselves.

CH: What they both have is the character to provoke something, they are both taking risks with their careers, and the good ones feel authentically for what they are trying to do. It makes them very similar, and it makes for a very sympathetic character.

JB: *Startup.com* is probably your most downbeat film in that the subjects suffer the failure of the dot com boom. Is it difficult to remain professionally detached when the people you are documenting experience such bad fortune?

CH: It's very hard because you become their friends. Even though these guys were really young, they were part of this very exciting moment and within three months they raised $60 million. Their website wasn't a goofy website. It was actually a very useful government website which had some really good ideas and a lot of altruistic ambition, so it was very sad. You kind of wanted to say something and intervene, but you don't know the whole story as a filmmaker.

JB: Don, you were a pioneer of the Direct Cinema movement in the 1950s, and yet you have often described your documentaries as "plays." Is that because you look for a narrative and emotional arc within the subject?

DAP: I used to read a lot of plays, and I think that the idea of dialogue driving a situation is what plays are. But in the early days of movies, documentaries were silent; you hired a religious zealot to play organ music over the film because you didn't have cameras that could shoot synchsound, so you couldn't get what happens in a real situation. I think that the theatrical experience is very important to people. I know it's not real, and I know those people are just actors, but the minute it starts, all that recedes, and all I see is the situation, and I want to know where it's going to go, and I can follow that through the dialogue.

CH: We do look for situations that have some theatrical arc to them, especially when you make the kind of films where you're following someone's life. *Return of the War Room* was a challenge for us because it was our first interview film, which proved to be a strange new experience. We started out trying to shoot people in their real lives, but that didn't work out because George Stephanopoulos ended up being owned by ABC Television, and they would only allow us to film him for forty-five minutes sitting in a chair. We thought it would be weird to have all this real-life stuff with everybody else, and then George sitting in a chair, but what people were saying was so interesting, that all that other stuff just fell away.

JB: *Return of the War Room* features footage of Barack Obama, but only passing reference is made to his campaign. Did you not want to compare Obama-mania with the Clinton campaign of 1992?

CH: There were already two filmmakers who were making a film about him, and they were very protective of their access, and we shot this at the end of the spring when the Hillary-Obama dynamic was going on, so we never had a moment. Like our other films, whatever the people talked about was where the film went and that directed us.

DAP: There is no long-term plan. Making one of these films is like wandering into one of those gardens you have here in England, a maze, and you go in knowing it's going to be a maze but there is a movie there; every turn is a surprise, and that's interesting because you have to take that turn into consideration.

Ninety Years of Cinematic Confections: An Interview with Chris Hegedus and D. A. Pennebaker

Dan Lybarger / 2010

From *KC Active* (www.kcactive.com), October 8, 2010. Reprinted with permission of Dan Lybarger and kcactive.com.

Documentary filmmakers Chris Hegedus and D. A. Pennebaker may not be household names, but their films have captured Bob Dylan, Janis Joplin, Jimi Hendrix, John F. Kennedy, Bill Clinton, and future senator Al Franken as their stars were rising. Because the two have been making movies together and apart since 1954, there's a pretty good chance you've seen some of their footage without even knowing it.

Donn Alan "Penny" Pennebaker was born in 1925 and has been making films since 1953. He edited the 1960 breakthrough documentary *Primary*, which captured the Wisconsin Democratic primary where Kennedy took on Hubert Humphrey. His 1967 documentary *Dont Look Back* featured Bob Dylan touring England and giving reporters who hadn't done their homework a much-needed scolding, while *Monterey Pop* had star-making performances by Joplin, Hendrix, and the Who.

Pennebaker started working with Hegedus in the late 1970s and has been married to her ever since. The two have collaborated on *The War Room*, which chronicled Bill Clinton's successful pursuit of the White House in 1992 and *Moon over Broadway*, which features Carol Burnett attempting a stage comeback. She also co-directed *Startup.com*, which unknowingly followed the demise of the dot.com bubble and *Al Franken: God Spoke*, which features the comedian becoming a forceful pundit.

Together the two have ninety years' experience of making movies and have received an Oscar nomination for *The War Room*. They've also created thousands of indelible moments such as Dylan flipping signs to

"Subterranean Homesick Blues" in *Dont Look Back* and George Stephanopoulos calmly dressing down a Ross Perot operative in *The War Room* or David Bowie giving his last "Ziggy" concert in *Ziggy Stardust and the Spiders from Mars*.

Their latest film *Kings of Pastry* proves that even cooking can be oddly engrossing even if you can't try the dishes on screen. The two follow sixteen chefs as they compete in the challenging Meilleurs Ouvriers de France (or Best Craftsmen in France) bake off. The event is held every four years, and only admits the best of the best as participants. The MOF is so prestigious that French President Nicolas Sarkozy is on hand to help reward the winners with a coveted red, white, and blue collar. If you see a chef wearing one of those, your mouth may never recover from the joy of what you're about to eat.

These chefs don't make mere cakes. These are often delicately crafted sculptures that take an astonishingly amount of practice and precision.

If time has dulled Hegedus and Pennebaker's skills, the wear and tear aren't on screen. As of this writing, *Kings of Pastry* has an 82 percent approval rating on RottenTomatoes.com, and it opens at the Screenland Crown Center this Friday. Contacted by phone from their home in New York, Hegedus and Pennebaker have a fascinating past to recall, but it's remarkable how easily both seem prepared to face the present and the future.

Dan Lybarger: In the audio commentary tracks for *Ziggy Stardust* and *Dont Look Back*, you said that you really don't direct your films even though you have that credit on your films.

D. A. Pennebaker: We don't direct. If you have somebody who's interesting, who knows something, you're not really paying attention if you're directing them. What you really want is what they know.

Chris Hegedus: Since we film real-life stories, you're not going to be directing real life, what you're going to do is hook on to your subject and hold on and try to follow it. And that's hard because a lot of times they're not telling you exactly what's going on. You have to figure it out, and I think that's part of the gamble in making these films. You miss the playing field between you and the person you're filming.

DAP: You're sort of solving the case. You're like a detective, and you're looking for clues because basically people who do know something or who are really smart generally don't throw it out on the street. They kind of keep it to themselves because that's their jewel that they trust. So you have to kind of be watchful and find ways of doing things they're interested in and find ways of filming them so that you can see that.

DL: That's what you're doing with *Kings of Pastry* because the chefs go to great lengths to make sure their creations don't taste like anybody else's.

DAP: They produce material that is perceived as almost perfect. That's the test of a good pastry cook. If you had somebody turning out the kind of things that I would turn out on a Sunday morning, they would not be an art form.

DL: Interesting. What do you turn out on a Sunday morning?

DAP: I make toast, usually. I'm known for my waffles with all my children because there are quite a few of them.

CH: And those are pretty good.

DAP: They're OK. I have to admit; I get them right out of what's-her-name's cookbook. I add a few frills, but nothing serious. It's not on the same level as watching [Jacquy] Pfeiffer making a round cake. That's like somebody painting the Madonna. It's heavy duty.

DL: These folks are both visual and culinary artists.

DAP: They're artists in whatever kind of way you perceive artists. It's interesting because you would never for your birthday have somebody make you a six-foot cake out of sugar.

CH: The skills to make those type of things, especially the sugar sculptures, they're much more than cooking. They're more kind of chemistry and especially engineering and physics, really. Those things just don't stay in the balanced way you see some of the sculptures you see in the competition without knowing that type of information.

DAP: It's a kind of theater: The theater of the kitchen, which you need because one kitchen is always competing with another kitchen for your breakfast money. They have to do more than just fill a bowl with some oatmeal. You have to put things on a table that you can choose. You've never had anything as good as that. That's what they want to do.

DL: From watching the film, it seems that food isn't the most stable of construction materials. A sculpture that stands properly one day is fragile the next.

DAP: Humidity is the great villain in sugar cooking.

CH: There are so many different variables. They have variables in them that we don't even know. A lot of the measuring is so precise. When we made this film, we couldn't use radio mics because they would throw off their scales because they measured so minutely with these ingredients.

DAP: Milligrams.

DL: In addition to the mics, the hallways looked really narrow. Was it tricky negotiating them?

CH: It was very funny, especially the doorway out. I just loved the shot I was getting of these chefs carrying these five-foot sugar sculptures, and they couldn't get them under the doorway. So they'd be crouched down trying to carry them. It was pretty phenomenal.

DAP: And they were running because they were short of time.

DL: One competitor came within five seconds of failing. [To Pennebaker] Isn't it true you used to be a linebacker?

DAP: Actually, I was a quarterback, but then when I went into the Navy and later went to Iowa, the coach said I'm going to put you at linebacker. After first, they put me in as a guard, which I really didn't want to do. I could be destroyed at that, and I wasn't very heavy.

CH: He didn't have a serious sports career.

DL: I mentioned it because from the photos I've seen of you, you appear to be a pretty big guy. Is it tough to be a fly on the wall when you stand out in a crowd?

CH: He got a little bigger eating all that pastry [laughs].

DAP: It's all attitude. Attitude makes you big or small.

DL: Now with you, Chris, I heard in an interview on *Fresh Air* that you said that being women helped you and Jehane Noujaim blend in more easily.

CH: I don't think it was blending in. What we said there was that we were filming pretty much a male world also at that point, which was the beginning of the startup entrepreneurs, where a lot of them were very alpha males—both on the entrepreneurial side and on the investment side. So being two women with cameras, it kind of gave us access in a way that was interesting. I think more than anything you have to establish a relationship with your subjects. And a lot of that is based on trust and respect.

I think if they think you take what they're doing seriously, they'll take you into their lives.

DL: The MOF is such a cultural institution in France. Was it tough for them to trust a couple of Americans?

CH: I think that was very much the case. They didn't know who we were, and as a matter of fact, I don't even think a lot of the films that people here might know of ours or Penny's on Bob Dylan [*Dont Look Back*] or Janis Joplin [*Monterey Pop*] or Clinton [*The War Room*]. They didn't mean that much to the chefs. I think what they went on was the opinion of Sebastien Canonne, one of our characters in the film and a partner and coach for Jacquy Pfeiffer.

DAP: He was our linebacker.

CH: He was part of this chefs' brotherhood, and he vouched for us.

DL: Even though you have uncertainty hanging over your heads, your movies have tons of dramatic moments, like the one where George Stephanopoulos chews out that Ross Perot operative or when one chef's delicately crafted creation falls apart.

DAP: Well, it's chance, you know. Making these films is a game of chance, and the harder and more you do it, the luckier you get.

DL: I've only seen *Startup.com* once, but the scene where dot.com entrepreneur Kaleil Tuzman refuses to get off the phone so that he and his girlfriend can start their vacation has haunted me to this day.

CH: I know. He was obsessed. I think that's a common denominator in a lot of our films is that these people are totally obsessed and passionate about what they're doing, and that's what makes it so riveting. And I think that what makes us be able to film in the way that we do is because they are so totally focused on what they're doing that after a while, they just can't worry about you filming.

DAP: And also you're holding up a mirror to them, and they are interested in kind of seeing how well they're pulling it off.

DL: From watching Bob Dylan, David Bowie, James Carville, Kaleil Tuzman, and Jacquy Pfeiffer, it's obvious they've got the same obsessiveness, but they apply it to different fields.

DAP: Well, they have to be. It requires that kind of concentration, but all hard and good work does. Writers have to take parts of their life and just abdicate them in order to be able to face the page or a machine or however they're doing it.

CH: It's people going for the best and pushing themselves to the limit. They have to have that kind of personality where they really, really want to win and really have the outcome that they're trying to do, whether it's electing a president or creating a multimillion-dollar company. It's a lot of work, and unless you work hard with that type of focus, I don't think it's going to happen.

DAP: Just imagine making a cake over and over again. The guy [Pfeiffer] said there were like twenty different tastes. Imagine you had twenty different tastes, and you had to decide which one was the best. I can hardly tell the difference, so it did seem like the work of a genius to me.

DL: I can see that in your musical films because to the untrained ear, one Wilson Pickett performance sounds like the next.

DAP: Well, sort of. It depends how much you listen to, I guess.

But you're right. With musicians, you don't really have to make a judgment about which is their best anything. They've done that in their time on the stage. They've persuaded people that they know something that no other musician can quite get out. That's what you're recording on the film. Musicians are a little different from this, but there is an aspect of genius that you're looking for.

DL: You two have been pioneers at handling sound and picture at the same time. I can still see in my head that image of you hidden behind Dylan while he's at the piano. We take it for granted today, but what was so tricky about handling the image and the sound in a documentary?

DAP: Well, it took two people because the sound was recorded on a recording machine, usually a Nagra [a Swiss-made battery powered tape recorder, that used to be the industry standard] or a tape recorder. And the film was run on a camera. And they were usually run by two different people.

Our problem for a long time was to get them to sync up. The cameras that were around when we started didn't do that. And that took a couple of years to sort out, so that when you were out somewhere in the desert filming somebody talking, that the soundtrack from the tape recorder would match the film that you were shooting.

CH: Basically, you had to line up the audio and the picture to kind of run them together to make them sync sound. And both of the different machines would be running at slightly different speeds. So part of the challenge was to make some kind of common denominator so you could have them meshed in the end.

One of the challenges in following real life things is that when you're not able to tell people to stop and do it over again, is that shooting on 16mm film only lasted ten minutes for a reel. And then you had to step under a little black bag or do something and change the reel on your camera, which was a big interruption.

Luckily, the sound went a little bit longer, so you could keep recording sound, and the picture would come back in. The challenge was to shoot cutaways, do it other ways, find other stylistic means to continue your story. And we did that right through *Moon over Broadway*.

Startup.com was really the first film that we shot in digital. It was when digital cameras first came out and an acceptably sophisticated medium not only to record [film picture and] sound but also to be able to reproduce them on 35mm film so that you could save them on what was a stable medium.

DAP: And put them in a theater.

DL: Getting back to *Kings of Pastry*. Ms. Hegedus, you say that you've come from a long family of cooks is that correct?

CH: Yeah, I do. In some part of my family, part of it is quite distant where it's my great-grandfather and my grandfather, both of whom were chefs. One of them went along a path that was quite similar to most of the chefs in *Kings of Pastry* where at fifteen you were an apprentice to a baker in Europe. And then he moved to the United States, and then he opened two confectionaries and chocolate stores in New York City.

My real influence was my grandmother I think on my other side of the family. And she wasn't a professional chef. She was my Hungarian grandmother. She was a fabulous chef. I grew up with just incredibly complicated baking and food.

DL: Your approach is just about the opposite of what I see on a typical Food Network show, where you have this almost Machiavellian competition.

DAP: Well, they're going for a different thing. Remember, in the MOF competition, you get no money, you just get this piece of ribbon to put around your neck for the rest of your life. I can see the producers on the TV show trying to persuade a big time chef that this wasn't enough.

CH: Not only do you not get any money but you practically mortgage your house and wreck your family life because you've been so obsessed at practicing this thing for so many years. The competition is just so incredibly grueling. That's what you've seen in our competition. They had to do the same thing for two days in order to be chosen for the three-day competition that you see in *Kings of Pastry*. It's just an enormous expense for chefs. And that's a huge difference.

And then it's something that's real for their lives. It's an award that has cultural and historical value. It's known throughout France. If you see a shop that has the tri-color sign outside saying that this chef has won this competition, people really go to that chef. They know that those people are the best.

I think we were also interested in who these people are, more than the cooking shows, and in seeing their lives and their families a bit and in seeing what the stakes really are for them.

DL: It looks like the competition has taken quite a toll on Rachel, Jacquy's girlfriend.

CH: She should get a prize as well [laughs]. Definitely. It's horrible. They live those moments with them. One of the reasons we decided to do this film was when we went to lunch with Jacquy, and he told the story about Rachel waking him up every night and telling him that the competition has been cancelled so that he didn't have these horrible nightmares about it.

It was kind of incredible because it was like, "Wow! This is so important to this person." This means that much that he's just having these fearful, terrifying nightmares.

DL: Unlike your some of your previous movies, you actually have the subjects talk to the camera about what they're doing. I don't think this competition would be understandable to outsiders without them.

CH: It's a different culture, and people don't know about it. And also there was a big language barrier for me and Penny because we don't speak French, so to speak, enough to really make the film in a way that was . . .

DAP: That you could just watch.

CH: Or that we knew answered some of the things we were trying to get at.

DAP: The thing is it isn't like we've avoided doing interviews. The fact is in all our films the people who want to talk to us were perfectly happy to listen to them and talk back. And in many of the other films, you'll find, for instance, in *The War Room*, James talks to us sometimes. It's just that we're part of the process itself. We don't always mean to be, but we are because they take it into that. We're part of their group. And exchanges with them are perfectly reasonable to us. That's part of the filmmaking.

CH: In our type of films, you have to work with the challenges and use them as excuses but use them to think of solutions. And stylistically we had a lot of them. In the competition, we weren't allowed to have lights or boom microphones [large overhead microphones] or anything, so we had to find a way to tell the story using these challenges to our advantage.

DL: How much sampling did you do of these pastries?

DAP: From time-to-time you'd take a bite, but you're so focused on the process of being sure you're getting whatever it is that's important at that moment, that eating is kind of not a big deal.

CH: I didn't eat anything during the three-day competition, which was a little bit difficult [laughs] after days of watching these delicious things being created. But during the practicing aspect we sampled what a lot of these chefs were doing, particularly our main characters, and their pastries are really amazing.

I think our favorite is that wedding cake that Jacquy made. It was so complex and delicious. Every bite had a different texture. I almost learned how to taste pastry in a way that you would learn to taste wine.

DAP: It's not a cake you generally see because I don't think it's cost-effective. You can't sell it with anything like the amount it costs to make it.

DL: You two have been really good about recording commentary track for the DVDs for your films, even with the older ones. Your comments sometimes help younger viewers better understand some of what we're watching.

CH: That's nice. I'm glad you think that. A lot of that has to go to the skills of a lot of the people who are putting out our DVDs. And one of them is this woman, Kim Hendrickson, who's worked at New Video and Criterion, and she's just fabulous. And both of those companies, they love film, and they love the history behind film and especially at Criterion who are going to put out *The War Room* again for us. They just do things at such a high level of expertise and competence and archival restoration. They're really a gift to the cinema world.

DL: I discovered that I had seen more of your films than I thought I had because I'm a huge Dylan fan.

DAP: It's amazing how he's persisted, and nobody knows why. Dylan doesn't know why. The one thing that he's determined to do is that he's a singer. He's like some medieval creature that goes around putting out lights in all the towns or something. That's what he does, and he'll do it till he dies. And it doesn't matter if he gets one hundred people in a gym somewhere or the biggest stadium you can find. It's the same thing.

DL: Speaking of Dylan, your footage of him flipping the signs to "Subterranean Homesick Blues" has recently been used in a commercial for Google. How did you feel about that?

DAP: We were paid for the ad . . . so any way that filmmakers can get paid for their films is to be sought after eagerly. Where are you calling us from?

DL: I'm afraid to say Kansas City. One of our local critics blasted *Dont Look Back* when it first opened. Dennis Stack, the *Kansas City Star*'s second-string critic at the time, called it "the worst movie I've ever seen." [Both laugh]

DAP: Kansas City is the home of a lot of my favorite jazz musicians from the thirties and forties. Everybody was working their way up to Chicago because that's where all the crooks used to live and spent a lot of money in the clubs.

About the music, and what I remembered of the people who started and played it: It was a big name for me, Kansas City. Most of the musicians I associate with Kansas City really originated elsewhere in Missouri, but since the big clubs were in Kansas City, I always assumed that was where they lived, at least during the music part of their lives.

I know that Benny Moten was Kansas City and Basie, stuck there in a band layover, took root with him and as well Walter Page, Lester Young, and even, I believe, Coleman Hawkins. And some of my favorites, though lesser known, Red McKenzie, Pee Wee Russell, Teschemacher, and of course Joe Turner, Mighty Joe Turner, the voice that replaced Rushing with Basie wailing "Shake Rattle and Roll."

I'm sure that there were many others I don't remember or didn't know, but Kansas City was always the beginning of a certain kind of driving big band sound that led to Fletcher Henderson and the great swing music of the thirties. I know because I still have some of the old 78s to prove it.

DL: Except for *Dont Look Back* and *Ziggy Stardust*, most of your films have been domestic. Is that correct?

CH: No. The largest concert we ever filmed was for a German rock star named Marius Müller-Westernhagen [*Keine Zeit*]. And he loved Dylan also and had seen our films, and asked if we could do a film of his concert tour. We did it in the mid-nineties. He played at stadiums that I think were the largest that we filmed because he was the German competition to say, the Rolling Stones if they came on tour in Germany. He was just as big as they were. It was incredible. It's an interesting film, but it's all in German so nobody sees it.

DL: Would it be fair to say that a lot of your stuff is commissioned?

CH: Well, no it's not necessarily that it's commissioned. Music stuff is often commissioned because you can get a record company involved in it. For example, when we did Depeche Mode, we had Warner Bros. involved with us, but for a film like *Kings of Pastry*, we're still trying to raise money [laughs].

We get a lot of our support from European broadcasters. They tend to understand some of our films better. There's very few slots for independent one-off documentaries on American television. In the U.S. there are some slots for individual documentaries, but they tend to be very political or somewhat sensational, so our films tend to fall somewhere in-between like *Kings of Pastry* or the kind of, you know, "delightful" film category. I don't know where you'd put it.

DL: Even though you shy away from sensationalism, the ending to *Kings of Pastry* is pretty dramatic and moving.

CH: I know. There are a lot of twists and turns in the story. You don't know when you start making these films, but I think they're very moving for people because they reflect more people's real life experiences because not everybody wins. Maybe your dream doesn't get fulfilled in that way, but life steps in in some other way and fulfills it in some way that's better than you could ever imagine.

It was interesting for me when I was editing this film because when you watch life kind of go by past a second time, you can see where things went wrong for people, and I probably understand what went wrong or right for some of these competitors more than they do.

DAP: The fact is we're making history by little chunks. It's not the history that maybe your father was teaching, but in the long run, maybe years from now, it may be the history that people want to read. It's a little like Herodotus [the Ancient Greek historian who lived from 484 B.C. to 430 or 420 B.C.]. He's one of the most interesting writers I've ever read. He took history just by tiny chunks. And when you read the whole thing, what you get is such a fantastic idea of what it was like to live back two thousand years ago, that it's like going there. It's an amazing effect that taking tiny chunks ends up as something much bigger than you would expect. You can't undertake to do the whole thing in one sweep.

Sometimes when people get a camera and decide "I've got to make a big film." And first of all they think of the films that come out of Hollywood, in which a lot of money has gone into the conception and the writing. And of course, they don't have that.

They think, "I'd better pick out an important subject, say orphans in Cambodia. That would be a good idea. That'll be important." The problem isn't that they haven't picked a good subject. They just don't know enough about it. Therefore, there are films made by people who don't know a lot, and you don't want to spend time watching them because you'd rather read a book by somebody who knows something.

That isn't always going to be the case. The talent is always drawn to money. As more and more documentaries get some kind of status and more and more get their costs back, smarter and smarter people are going to make them. And it's going to be a different sort of voice than entertainment films, not just necessarily a more intelligent voice, a more wide-ranging voice. The furthest the Hollywood film has been able to range is cartoons. And that only holds you for a little bit, you can't watch cartoons endlessly. So I think there's a big future for this kind of filmmaking. It just hasn't quite happened yet.

D. A. Pennebaker: Interview

Sam Adams / 2011

From the *A.V. Club*, May 4, 2011. Reprinted with permission of the *A.V. Club* (www .avclub.com).

There aren't many filmmakers who can claim to have changed the face of their art form, but D. A. Pennebaker could make a strong case twice over. As a sound recordist on Robert Drew's 1960 documentary *Primary*, he helped invent what would become known as cinéma vérité, as well as the tools that were critical in its establishment. And with *Dont Look Back*, which has just been reissued on Blu-ray, he effectively gave birth to the modern concert film, shadowing Bob Dylan on a European tour just as the literate folk singer was reinventing himself as a plugged-in poet. Thanks to *Dont Look Back*, *Monterey Pop*, and films on Jimi Hendrix, John Lennon, David Bowie, and Jerry Lee Lewis, Pennebaker is best known for his music documentaries, but he's made landmark films in many other areas, many co-directed by his wife, Chris Hegedus: *The War Room*, which documented the rapid-response strategy of Bill Clinton's first presidential campaign; *Company: Original Cast Album*, a fascinating look inside the recording of Steven Sondheim's *Company*; and *Town Bloody Hall*, a confrontation between Norman Mailer and the leading lights of seventies feminism. In the process of reflecting on *Dont Look Back*, Pennebaker talked to the *A.V. Club* about Dylan, Depeche Mode, Jean-Luc Godard, and his many films that have disappeared from the public eye.

A.V. Club: What sort of context was there for *Dont Look Back*? Had you seen *Lonely Boy*, the portrait of Paul Anka?

D. A. Pennebaker: *Lonely Boy*, I think, was done before, but I didn't see it until later. We went up at the [National] Film Board [of Canada] and they showed it. I kind of felt a little uneasy at first, because when he was doing his song, they were narrating over it. Whether I like his music or not, that sort of seemed like a poor thing to do. That depressed me a little bit. I had done a film—we just saw it last night, oddly enough—with Jane Fonda, called *Jane*. That was done when I was with [Robert] Drew at Time-Life. For years, since it was about a play she was in on Broadway, which folded the next day, it's always been sort of a sore point for her. But she's finally decided she rather likes it, and we're going to release it. It was a precursor to *Dont Look Back* in that when I did it, it was only going to be half an hour, and it was supposed to part of a bunch of shows we were hoping to get on television. It didn't have quite the, I don't know, whatever you call it, the angst that I thought was there, that we could have gotten. When I did *Dont Look Back*, I no longer had Time-Life looking over my shoulder, so I could kind of do it as I wanted, and it was like I was really correcting *Jane*.

AVC: When you and cinematographer Ricky Leacock decided to split off from Robert Drew and Time-Life, was editorial independence the crux of it?

DAP: Well, I could see that we weren't a big hit at Time-Life anymore. I think that what had been going on in the heads of those far above us was that maybe they were going to buy ABC, or get a network, or something where they could join TV the way they had magazines. I think they were looking for something that would play on TV that would have that same sort of behind-the-scenes quality that their candid photography had. They welcomed us in at the beginning because they needed to train people and do it. I think their expectations were a little beyond us. They were looking for a film a month, and we were lucky if we could do one in a year. It wasn't very well thought through, but I don't think anybody, even us, understood what would happen when we got the equipment, which was what we were able to do at Time-Life, when we were able to develop the equipment. When we got equipment in hand, what was possible was so much more incredible than we had ever imagined. I think Drew thought that we were going to be making documentaries, which is to say, we would be interviewing people about things going on and it would be kind of a journalism thing. I had no such intentions, but I didn't quite know what else to do. There was nobody else in town, there was no place you could sell a film. Well, *The Quiet One* I think got into theaters, but it was a written film, it was acted and written. The idea of a documentary, whatever, that was anathema. Nobody quite knew what it was or quite how to handle it when you got one.

AVC: Speaking of technological developments, one of your major contributions to *Primary* was to put the sound back in sync with the picture after the fact, right? That could easily have ruined the whole film.

DAP: Well, Ricky too. Ricky was a physics major at Harvard, and I was an engineer at Yale, in electronics. So I had some idea, but really we were dependent on outside engineers and people who had gone much further with camera development than we could. We just knew what we needed. We knew what the parameters should be, that it should be light, it should be quiet, and it should be sync [sound]. At that point, there was nothing, so we had to make a camera, and the making of a camera got us into working out things that if we had just gone to a camera designer and said, "Make a camera," we would never have gotten. So in a way, it formulated us, and it formulated the thinking of the films. Because the problem was, how do you keep a camera steady when you're walking around with it? It took us a while to sort of understand that it should be against your eye socket, your forehead, and probably on your shoulder. But getting it on your shoulder, that had to be figured out. It had to come to us that we needed a handle on the front that you could to hold onto and turn it on. We were making what we now have as a video camera, but at the time, we didn't really know that that's what we needed.

AVC: So it was trial and error, mechanical problem solving?

DAP: It's like going into a hardware store and seeing what you want for Christmas. It was weird.

AVC: With *Dont Look Back*, how much did you envision beforehand?

DAP: Nothing. I didn't really know much about Dylan. I had heard one of his songs on the radio, and I had read in *Time* magazine that he was not a very good folk singer, which interested me a little bit because I didn't think that their recognition of folk singers was going to be world-renowned. I didn't really know what to expect. I had made a film with [jazz singer] Dave Lambert, he was a friend of Bob Van Dyke's who was doing sound for us. He had put a new group together. And I knew him because I had the earlier record that he'd done for Columbia. I also knew that he'd been an arranger for Gene Krupa, when Krupa had his orchestra. He'd been arranging for two or three trumpets, which was astonishing. So I was always intrigued by him. When I met him, it turned out he was also a carpenter, and he helped us build our studio. So we got to be very good friends with him. He brought his little group in that he'd been putting together, and had written three or four new songs for. He was going to go to RCA to do a tryout to make a record. We were doing films then; anything we should shoot in a day we would try to do, because the film was cheap; we were shooting black and white. We were trying out the cameras, which by then I had made three or four of them, and we were renting them out to the film board, in fact, in some cases. And we were walking in place, as it were, with no idea what we were doing. That is, we no longer had a job. Ricky and I were sitting there staring at each other. There was no place to sell these films. They were little ten- to twelve-minute films. TV didn't buy films from us. You couldn't show them in movie houses. They just were something that we did. So this film [*Lambert & Co.*], when we got through with it, it was kind of a nice little film, but I didn't know what to do with it. I didn't even edit it. I just put it up on the shelf in our little editing place on 43rd Street.

Some weeks later, Dave got killed in an automobile accident on the Merritt Parkway, and Art DeLuca was going to do a little thing for him, some sort of a memorial, and a guy came over—I think he was from Europe some place—and he said, "I understand you have a film. Could we show it at the memorial?" I said, "Well, we haven't edited it or anything." So [we] stayed up all night editing all this material into a ten-minute film, and the next day we got it to a lab, and then we got it down to them. I didn't even go to the memorial, I had to do something else, but months later the guy came back and said could he take a print back to Europe, 'cause Dave was very well-known in Europe. I gave him the only print we had, and I didn't think about it again until we started getting letters from people saying, "Where can we buy the record?" Of course, there was no record, because RCA decided not to make it, and so this whole thing was like a ghost presence, and I loved the songs, but they were never going to be released because nobody was ever going to sing them except David's little group. So I said in my head that maybe my reason for existing was to make films of people that nobody else was going to make films of because I like the music or I like them or whatever.

So when Albert [Grossman] came in and said, "Would you like to make a film with my client, Bob Dylan?" I said, "Sure." It seemed like a reasonable thing for me to do. It wasn't like he was saying, "We'll pay you a lot of money to do it." It was, from the very start, apparent that I was going to pay for it. But that seemed all right, too. I felt that that's the way it's going to be. The rest of my life I'll be shoveling out to make all these films of these musicians, because I had a huge record collection and had grown up in Chicago amongst this whole exploding music scene that was going on there. I had to buy the records to hear them; you couldn't hear them on the radio. No black performers were allowed to be on radio. They only existed as names. I had no idea what Fats Waller looked like. But they were our heroes. So the whole idea of being able to now film these people seemed to me very appropriate, very historic, so I fell into that without even thinking. So the whole thing with Dylan just emerged as some psychosis of my own. And then when I met him, he was really interesting. The way he talked, he would change words around in a funny way. It was very original, and I noticed it right away. And I thought, "Well, he's some kind of poet." Everybody kept saying, "Oh no no, he's not a poet, no, he's just a folk singer. That's not poetry." But I kept hearing poetry in things he would say or words in his songs, so I thought, "Well, this is more than a music thing, this is a person of interest." So I was intrigued by the whole trip.

AVC: You've done so many films of musicians, whether documentary or concert films, and so many different kinds of musicians. Is liking the music a prerequisite? Do you end up liking the National or Depeche Mode as much as Jimi Hendrix or David Bowie?

DAP: We don't sit there with our yellow pads in hand cogitating who would make a good film or what we could do that could make a lot of money and pay our rent for the next year. It isn't like that, because I don't know how to do that, and I've never been partners with anybody else who did. We sit here and, on the basis of a film we've made or somebody's heard we wanted to make, people come to us and say, "I have an idea for a film. Would you be interested?" And we have to be interested because, unlike when I was at Time-Life, we have people from all of the world throwing ideas at us to do and all you had to do was say, "Okay, we'll do this one," or somebody there in charge would say, "Do this one." And then you went off and did it. In our case, we have to commit to what is going to be maybe a year of our lives to a film. But in general, if it appeals to us and we can get it going and somehow we can raise the money for it, these films come to us to be made. We don't initiate them very much.

When Depeche Mode came in, we didn't know who they were or anything about them. I went out to listen to a concert in California or Oregon or some place, and I came back and said, "The audience for this band, I don't think they go to any other music concerts except Depeche Mode. I don't think they have any other life except for Depeche Mode." They have mystic signs they make with their hands. It's like some sort of a Celtic assemblage, and it's so interesting that we would be crazy not to get with them and make a film. So we did. It was just out of that, because the music made no sense to us at all in the beginning—we couldn't even hear it—but by the end of it, of course, we loved it. When you live with something you get to like it.

AVC: You did a film about Jennifer Lopez that was meant to be released with her album *Rebirth*. What happened with that?
DAP: I really liked her husband. I thought he was pretty nice. But she wanted to sell jewelry or something. She was not looking to get into the film world at all other than as an actress. She wanted to be a movie star. We weren't who you hired to become a movie star. It doesn't work that way. I think she was curious to see what we might do. I rather liked her, but there was no story there. We were just doing a kind of a music promo.

AVC: And it ended up just not being what they wanted?
DAP: I don't know who did what, but I never saw it. It may have been used somewhere, and I think somebody else came in and did something. I don't even know what happened, because after we spent all that time with her we just went on and did something else. It got lost in the fog.

AVC: *Town Bloody Hall* is one of your great films, an onstage debate between Norman Mailer and the leaders of the feminist movement, including Germaine Greer, in front of a very vocal and engaged audience. It's an amazing piece of history as well as drama. How did you come to make it?
DAP: *Town Bloody Hall* was something that Norman persuaded me to do. It was at the Town Hall on 43rd Street, or 45th, maybe it was 44th Street. It was a place that did not want us to be filming, so the manager was chasing us around, turning the lights out, making it as hard as he could for us to shoot, and there were only three of us shooting. We had three cameras. I could only find two people to go with me there that night. I had to get onstage because that was the one place the manager didn't dare go to chase me. So I was filming from the stage. It was such an interesting thing to see Norman in that assemblage, because I think a lot of the people there in the beginning assumed he was the enemy. By the end, I think maybe half of them changed their minds. Norman, he was at the height of his powers. I just loved him that night.

I was thinking last night, because we had the screening [of *Jane*], Jane Fonda came and we showed the film at the Paley Center. This was a fundraiser for a women's group that she's head of or involved with. I kept thinking, in ten or twenty years, almost all the history of what's happened will all be in documentary films. And they won't be proper films. They'll just be people who've saved the tapes and they've been put somewhere and they are now history. I think the films we see, the Hollywood films, which are basically entertainment, will still be there, but they'll be in a totally different category. People won't take them seriously. They'll kind of end up the way comic books have. A side view of things.

AVC: With each passing day, it becomes easier for people to capture something visually; anyone with a smartphone is walking around with a video camera in their pocket.

DAP: And they don't have to have any authorization, they don't need much money, they just do it because they kind of want to do it. The best documentaries, the ones that get prizes and things are, for me, what television should be doing but doesn't, because their main interest is in selling cheese and paying mortgages for people. It does a lot of work that everybody needs done, probably, but it doesn't commit history. Even if they saved it, nobody would want a history of the nine o'clock news, because it would be boring in ten years. But they do want to see what happened to Marilyn Monroe or whatever, and if somebody had made a film of that, that's what people would be charmed by.

The whole way in which the candid still photography had taken over—I mean, it's hard to remember now, but every week everybody got *Life* magazine. It just didn't fail. And the best things in it were not—the writing was usually somewhat fallible. It needed Hemingway or Norman to do something, but generally it was just circumstantial. What was interesting was that the photographs came without any intention of instructing you. You just saw them. Of course, they always had to have underneath them what they were about, but you could almost not even bother with that. They were just such amazing pictures. I think from the very beginning, I felt it wasn't our business with this incredible device, which cannot lie. If you point it at something, it's what you see. We would just watch. We wouldn't instruct, we wouldn't confirm, we wouldn't say anything, we would just watch what was happening in front of us, and if we could get into places where that was interesting, that would be the movie. That's pretty much the way we do it now. That's hasn't changed much.

AVC: Once you get in the door, the battle's half over.

DAP: You're like a cat looking out the window. You don't have to even know what you're watching, but you're watching it, and you're watching it very accurately.

AVC: How did what became *1 P.M.*, your film with Jean-Luc Godard, come to be? Has anyone tried to put it out on DVD?

DAP: Believe me, it's not legally anybody's except ours, but that has never stopped anybody. I know that most of our stuff is on YouTube. So, you know, what can you do about it? Hire lawyers, and nothing changes? What happened was, I had met Godard through [Henri] Langlois at the Cinémathèque [Français] at one of our various things in Europe, festivals or whatever. We had sort of talked about doing a film in which he would go to a small town in France somewhere, and he would arrange everything—bodies would appear, and then fingerprints, and then guns and whatever—and Ricky and I would come in and we would film what we found and see if we could get the story that they had planted without our knowing. It was one of those intriguing cocktail conversations that never goes anywhere, but he remembered it a little bit, so . . . We had a guy who'd come to work with us from Goldman Sachs, and his intention was to make a lot of money for us, which, of course, never did happen. But at the time he took Godard very seriously, because he could see Godard could be a moneymaker if you just promoted him correctly.

He arranged somehow that the incipient PBS, which was PBL then but it became PBS, would pay us. I think he even signed a contract in which Godard would come over and make a film with us, and it would be called *1 A.M. One American Movie.* And he would have Ricky and I be the cameras and he would be the director and tell us what to do. And since we were going to be paid something too, this seemed like a good idea. Not something to be struggled against. He appeared, and his plan was that we would load up, because he knew the cameras worked, he used a cameraman, a 35 cameraman, who was really good. We'd have these four-hundred-foot magazines, which would be ten minutes of film. We would shoot them continuously; we wouldn't stop. We would figure out a scene that we were going to cover and we would shoot four hundred feet in one continuous roll, and we would never edit it. We'd just put it with another four-hundred-foot roll similarly shot in some other scene. That was the plan.

AVC: Kind of the *Rope* of documentary film.

DAP: Sort of. Yes. It didn't really matter because Godard was there with Anne Wiazemsky, who was delightful, and in the beginning he had her over at the hotel right behind us. What is it? The place with the round table.

AVC: The Algonquin.

DAP: The Algonquin. She was supposed to sit up there and listen to her records. Well, she didn't want to sit up there, she came right over to the office and hung out with everybody, and she herself, she had a camera and was taking stills of things. So she was terrific. We kept her around. I think Godard was a little miffed at this; he kind of didn't like to be outgunned by anybody, but I loved him. He's one of my favorite filmmakers because he never did the obvious, you know? He always surprised you. And in the course of the filming, we shot the film and he was in a big hurry because he thought that revolution was going to envelop his country. It might have looked that way from Europe, because they'd gone through one themselves, but we kept saying, "I don't think it's going to happen, Jean-Luc. I wouldn't wait around for it if I were you." In the course of it we shot the thing, we got some people to tell us whatever was going on in California, which was always very ripe, and then he went away. He met the guy that he did *Wind from the East* with.

AVC: Jean-Pierre Gorin.

DAP: They got bored, I think, with doing it. And I was left with a contract, or I was told a contract, and a lot of footage, with four-hundred-foot rolls of footage. I was told I had to deliver on the contract, so I just decided to put it together, and when I did, I found that the idea of the four-hundred-foot rolls was really very boring. I mean, after a while you just cried out in pain. So I made a film, which we called *1 P.M.* [*One Pennebaker Movie*]. That film was kind of interesting. Just because Godard was involved, it kind of caught an urgency that was going on in this country in terms of filmmaking. It got shown a few times. It got shown out in California at some theater where the police were throwing tear gas down the ducts of the air conditioner because everybody assumed what was going on was illegal.

AVC: We've been talking a lot about movies that aren't out on commercial DVD. Are there people working on that?

DAP: Well, we're a family operation. There's not many of us. My son runs it. Chris and I work. We have a couple people who come from time to time who work with us. Two of my sons are themselves filmmakers, and we can't afford them nor they us. They work in the real world and earn money and are pretty good at it. One of our problems is that we've set ourselves up as having this archive, which a lot of the material we shoot is sort of bound to go to if it doesn't go to YouTube only, and the problem with that is that it's film, and it has to be turned into video, and every few years the video has to be turned into a new kind of video, so it's way beyond us in terms of the funding necessary to keep this thing in the real world where people can come and look at things. Because it's not just the films, it's also all the outtakes. So this is a thing we've now sort of taken on as our next problem, which is to say, we're going to have to raise a couple million dollars to do this. I cleaned up one of Ricky's films, a thing he did with Stravinsky—we both actually worked on it. I edited, but it was mostly his shooting with Stravinsky over a period of six months or so, and it's just the most wonderful film. It's one of the best films he ever did, and certainly the only film of Stravinsky in which Stravinsky is a real human being. We took it out—somebody wanted it in Washington, to show it—and it was so dirty that they said, "We can't show this film." In the old days, when you showed film, it was like the scratches on 78 records; you didn't notice it, 'cause you're used to it and you looked around it. Now, video has no such things on it; it's just pure, perfect picture. So if you're going to reuse this with video, it's got to either be cleaned up, or I don't know what you do with it. It's hard to interface it. So cleaning it up is a frame-by-frame procedure, which is very expensive. I spent maybe $15,000 cleaning up this Stravinsky film in order that it can be shown at this Washington showing. So I can see that all of our films—*Dont Look Back*, all of them—are going to have to be dealt with in this way. And that's not something we can just do as we go along. We're going to have to really do that in a very serious fashion, I think.

AVC: It would be great to see some of them out there. We were talking, a few years ago I think, about Criterion doing *The War Room*?
DAP: Yes, and they are doing *The War Room*. They're doing that, but they can't take on all of them. We have maybe a hundred films here. So Criterion is only going to save one or two of them, even as Steve Savage did with *Dont Look Back*.

AVC: Watching *The War Room* now, you seem to have been there at just the right moment. With the way information gets out now, there's no chance anyone would allow a camera inside the strategy meetings of a political campaign.
DAP: When they did the Obama film, they came to us and asked if we

had any suggestions on how they could prevail, and the problem that I saw, and I saw it very quickly . . . I had started a film with Bobby Kennedy, which I had to break off because I was in way over my head, the cost of doing it full-time was way beyond me and I couldn't raise any money for it. This was going to be watching somebody become president, we were just going to do the same thing with Clinton and try to raise money to do it. And I could see right away that you couldn't actually occupy space with a person who intended to become president in a very interesting way. They were constrained to act; as soon as the camera appeared, they had to pretend to be something else. That was never very entertaining. But with somebody like [James] Carville or [George] Stephanopoulos, they didn't give a shit, you know? They didn't see us as the press because we weren't the six o'clock news. We actually hung out in the war room, in which no press was supposedly allowed.

AVC: And they knew that it the film wasn't going to be out until after the election.

DAP: We were recording what happened that year, and I think it allowed us to get access to real events that normally you're cut off from. People could say "shit" if they felt like it. To set out to make the film of the guy running for president, I think is maybe a mistake. I could have done it with Kennedy because he was so arrogant he didn't care what anybody thought. I mean I sat in the car and watched him swear with the prime minister from Canada, and afterwards the PM said, "I can't believe that Kennedy would talk that way seeing you filming him," and I said, "You have to understand, he knows that I can never use that material." So it isn't a problem for him if you think about it. But you're right. It's like *Crisis*. Nobody would let us do *Crisis* again. Bobby, he helped us sneak into the White House. He took us over there through the back door because they wouldn't let us in the front door. So we had people on our side who saw more than just news footage, they saw it as some sort of history. That was crucial.

D. A. Pennebaker

Harvey Kubernik / 2012

A shortened version of this interview appeared as "Treats Q&A: D. A. Pennebaker" in *Treats! Magazine*, November 14, 2012. This extended and unedited version is printed with the kind permission of Harvey Kubernik.

"An audio visual Walt Whitman of our musical heritage."
—Andrew Loog Oldham

On December 1, 2012, D. A. Pennebaker received a Lifetime Achievement Oscar for his six decades of nonfiction filmmaking from the Motion Picture Academy. He is the first documentary filmmaker to be given such an award.

Harvey Kubernik: What are your feelings about being given an Oscar? You told Annette Hinkle of *The Sag Harbor Express*, "It's a surprise. What I do—and now what a large number of people do—is make independent films; independent of whether they should or not. It's like home painting—you just do it. You're always surprised when you're included in Hollywood."

D. A. Pennebaker: It's a little complicated. It's like being given the champion pilot's award when you don't fly. I mean, I never thought the Oscars were a waste of time or anything. They helped a lot of industry and people who are actors, and probably helped get a lot of films get seen that otherwise might have gone awry. Although the process of distributing films is so huge—it's like aspirins or something. There must be thousands of theaters waiting to hear what Paramount has this week to give them.

HK: You never moved to Hollywood, and for over fifty years you didn't make the predictable move into huge budget feature films. Now you are honored by Hollywood.

DAP: I never had the temptation. It was like I was an architect and somebody was saying, "We have a lot of need for watercolor pictures," and I'm saying, "But I build houses and I don't need work." I saw it as a totally difference of dimension for me.

HK: The Oscar people—and the public in large—missed your 1955–1965 life as a documentarian.

DAP: The first documentary after I quit [Time] Life was a harsh moment. Because that was my salary. And I had a child by then, but I had to figure out that it wasn't gonna work for me and I had to leave. So for the next two or three years Ricky [Leacock] and I made films that we couldn't distribute, but they were some of the most wonderful films.

HK: Here you are in the late 1950s and television really started to look like a potential option for your work.

DAP: Ricky thought that television would be our marketplace. And the fact is, they didn't even want to answer the phone. They were busy creating their own kingdom. They didn't need outsiders. People who didn't walk the halls in the morning weren't part of them.

HK: It seems you always knew it was about removal of ego as a filmmaker.

DAP: You know where I think it arose? I grew up in Chicago. And when I was there, Chicago was changing in a musical way that nobody understood. That is, a lot of musicians from New Orleans, Kansas City, St. Louis were coming to Chicago because the money was there. The criminals owned all the clubs and so they had the money. And talent always goes for the money. Sometimes they pretend they don't, but in the end they have to—they don't have any long-range assistance. All they have is as long as people want to hear them, and then they're gone.

HK: You subsequently made many music films and documentaries. Why has music informed a lot of your work over the last half century?

DAP: The fact is I learned about jazz from records—78 rpms—not hearing anybody play it. I never saw anything live in Chicago in my whole life. But the record was interesting. It did a couple of things. It created a time limit. No matter how great your ideas were they had to be contained. And containing ideas musically with artistic talent meant you had to shape it in some way that people would follow it. You started slow or fast but you moved in an orbit and then you ended it. And some worked better than others. But when they worked . . . You might have had some music written for people, but basically jazz musicians never paid much attention to it. So what happened was you began something that you knew kind of where you wanted to get to—a quality, a ring, or a tune—and everybody worked on that and figured it out while you were playing. The thing happened while it was being played. When you heard the record, you witnessed how that thing came out. And that was kind of exciting, the improvisational aspect.

HK: An example of this is *The War Room*—we discover the real star of that film was not Clinton, but George Stephanopoulos and James Carville, the two masterminds behind the campaign. And the film was nominated for an Academy Award.
DAP: When we went to do *The War Room* with James and George, we didn't explain how documentaries were supposed to look. We told them nothing. They had to figure it out. We just watched. And they figured it out very fast. They didn't have a lot of time for it. What they figured out was to see for themselves what would happen. So they were perfectly happy to have us go along and witness what nobody had planned. I think that gives it life. And that's the thing I miss in the carefully figured-out documentaries where a lot of yellow pads are involved. It takes the life out of it because nothing happens unexpectedly.

Clinton was number four in New York at the time. We went to the convention, looked around for people to film, but most of them were pretty boring.

HK: Can you talk a bit about and James Carville and George Stephanopoulos.
DAP: Well, one is the master, and one is the junior.

HK: And you didn't have the access in *The War Room* that you had years earlier with *Dont Look Back* to your subjects?
DAP: It didn't seem like it to me because I always felt I had to stay kind of in the background, but not always. With Carville, I hear myself all the time talking to him around the camera. I could see that I had a much more participatory role than I planned to, or than I should have maybe. But Carville invited that. I found my best friend was James Carville and I had never even met him before. We got on in a way that you don't often get along with people you're gonna make a film about.

HK: It appears you found yourself as the true artist around the *Dont Look Back* experience.

DAP: I learned to trust myself. Before then I wasn't sure I could make movies, and it wasn't until *Jane* [1962] that I knew I could do it. Then I felt like I just shot five fifty-cent pieces. . . .

It's like the tennis player Chris Everett Lloyd. I adore her and I want to make a film of her. I love that she's in the zone. She was the first person I ever heard use the term, "in the zone." I understood exactly. When you're in the zone you can't make a mistake. You can jump out the window and land soft.

I was in the zone for *Dont Look Back*. Maybe Dylan was also in the zone. I knew that once I got started, I just had to roll and not plan anything. I didn't try and be smart about anything. I never asked him a question. I didn't want to know anything. I just wanted to get inside that camera and not come out. For me, that's in the zone, and I felt like Chris Everett Lloyd. The feeling that you are God.

In 1965 I would look through my lenses and the words would drop on the music. I was just amazed at how anybody could produce that kind of electricity. To me that was what art was about.

HK: Travel was a big thing in *Dont Look Back*. Taxis, cars, trains—movement in general.

DAP: Yes. That's what we did. I had shot transportation and car shots before. I think it's like when people are driving cars, they become more absolute in some ways. They become realer. I like the information they give in those situations. So it's a good place to get people, especially if you want them reflective. They feel in charge of something and they don't mind letting you in.

HK: What about Dylan as a camera subject?

DAP: He is what he is. He's different in the afternoons than he is in the mornings. So you're never sure who you are getting. He's the twins. I think he's a person who understood theater very well. It amazed me where he got his kind of primal information because it was always right on the nose. It didn't seem like he'd been through a lot of education. He seemed to have got it from the streets.

HK: *Dont Look Back* has been viewed on the silver screen, a TV screen, and most recently, a computer screen. You even released a laser disc version. Did you initially welcome the home video format for *Dont Look*

Back knowing there would be a small-screen reduction, at least in the visual aspects of the presentation?

DAP: I think it's kind of a Zen thing. How big is the moon? Your mind is able to deal with it on any size. Big is nice—especially if you have bad eyesight. Big is terrific in a theater. And we've made a 35mm blow up of that film. I love seeing it in 35mm, and we've shown it at some festivals and it looked great. But the fact is that I think people who are used to video look at a video and see the same movie. The laserdisc had good quality because it's not compressed, but people don't care much about that. Only the guys in the studio worry about compression.

HK: When you view *Dont Look Back* now, what strikes you?

DAP: I think when I see it now what kind of surprises me is that it's going into a noisy situation; I mean noisy in a sense that there's a lot of strong wills involved that are often in contention within the group. I'm surprised going into it how calmly I could film. I had Jones Alk doing sound, but basically I put the Nagra in the middle of the floor and turn it on. It would be like going into the middle of a forest fire and finding a place where there was no heat. They all could sit. That's always been the way for us since. We found the place where we could sit unmolested and just shoot what you wanted, and film what you wanted. You didn't have anybody pushing you to do something or not do something. You were totally on your own. And that was a marvelous feeling for me.

Up to that point, all the story films I had made—some of them are good. *David* [1961] was about Synanon, and was a terrific film. And the one about Jane Fonda's Broadway debut is terrific. But we had to come back [to the Time Life offices], and somebody would write a narration, and we'd have to hide the film so they couldn't find it. You were always dealing with people who had other notions about what you should have done. And I loved the idea that narration was not there. That was really why I left [Time] Life. That was what I was looking for. And when I found that it was so simple I thought, "You know, it's amazing that other people don't do this."

HK: After working in 1965 with Bob Dylan on *Dont Look Back*, in 1966 you worked with Dylan again on a color music movie that was commissioned for ABC-TV, *Stage '67*, that initially you titled *But You Know Something Is Happening*. Later Dylan edited that movie footage as *Eat the Document*. And a few years ago half an hour of that footage was sequenced into Martin Scorsese's *No Direction Home*.

DAP: After *Dont Look Back* Dylan said, "I want you to shoot a film and I'm going to direct it, and it will be my film. You have your film and this will be mine." That was the kind of handshake arrangement. We didn't have anything signed, no papers about it. So we went off.

I only knew how to film one way. I didn't change the way I filmed. And Dylan really didn't know how to direct, and nor did I. It kind of stumbled along. We were moving around a lot—Sweden, France, England. It just wasn't a tour of English music halls.

I think that Dylan got really intrigued by the kind of locales he was in and how they responded to him. And then John Lennon came in and we sort of got involved with John. At no time did I think "I'm gonna capture this movie and do it myself." Although I could sort of see how to do it, because it was different than *Dont Look Back*. Dylan was playing on stage with four or five musicians and having a great time doing it—I mean, it was so much more interesting than what he had been doing all by himself. He kind of took to it. And I could see that shooting the stage performances were really an important part of it. At one point I actually got out on stage with the band and he didn't know I was gonna be there, and when he saw me he really cracked up, because it was such a funny idea that I was just like the band.

There was no difference in shooting Dylan in color than in black and white. By then I was sort of interested in shooting color, and I liked the fact you could make the contrast between one scene and another much stronger, whereas in black and white it went from black and white to black and white. But with color you could make sky blue turn into blue velvet. And that was sort of interesting, but it didn't affect the storyline.

HK: Then this footage sort of morphed later into *Eat the Document*?
DAP: Well, you see, Dylan had the motorcycle accident. The thing was done for ABC-TV, and Albert [Grossman] came and said, "We gotta give them something. Can you guys cook up something?" So Bob Neuwirth and I cooked up the beginning of *But You Know Something Is Happening*. Then Dylan said he wanted to edit *Eat the Document*, and then he and Robbie [Robertson] kind of had a competition about doing that, which always soured Dylan on the film. And so that film got made, but ABC didn't want any part of it. That film just sat in limbo. And my film was kind of in limbo.

I wasn't trying to compete with Dylan at all. I showed it to the critic in San Francisco, and he wrote a review of it, which was unexpected, and Albert took not kindly to it because Dylan thought we were playing games with him. But I never had any intention of releasing that film, and I haven't. But still I have it, because I think we were on to something that was really interesting, and I don't think anybody else knew it and did anything with it at the time. I hated to see the film go down the toilet.

HK: However, portions of what you shot were utilized in *No Direction Home*.
DAP: Yes. I turned it all over to Marty [Scorsese]. That was the only way it was gonna get released. Someday my version will get released, but it doesn't really matter because all the work was done on the first film, *Dont Look Back*. And that's what people remember. And the rest is just kind of—you know—throwing pictures on the sides of the pages of the book.

HK: What was the biggest change you noticed in Bob Dylan as an artist and songwriter when you filmed the 1966 European tour that became *Eat the Document?*
DAP: Well, I felt that he was really writing music sort of with Robbie [Robertson] and for Robbie. He was trying to show Robbie how to write music. There was something going on that drove him so that he would stay up all night. I filmed him endlessly where he'd write many songs during the night and Robbie would play along. Robbie somehow made him do it. And on the first tour there was nobody doing that. Neuwirth never made him do that. He never felt competitive with Dylan.

HK: Jim Morrison spoke to you about doing a documentary. You saw a 1969 Doors set in Toronto where they shared the show with John Lennon and the Plastic Ono Band, but you didn't film the Doors.
DAP: Morrison had come to me a couple of times and he obviously was interested. He and Neuwirth came and showed me Jim's film, his student film. I was not impressed, but that didn't mean anything—I was interested in anybody who was a poet and wanted to make films. That was interesting to me. I didn't look down like he was an amateur. But the fact is that he was a boozer. And, you know, that's a hard thing to make a film about. My father was a boozer. You can't count on getting their real lives. You get something else. They put on a kind of a show. And that was a problem.

And I had the same problem with Janis [Joplin]—the drugs. I had nothing against drugs, because I didn't know enough about them yet. I loved Janis and thought she was a fantastic person, and I always thought there was a film there. I shot a lot with her, but what was she was doing was so hard for her it was hard for me to film her.

Morrison was funded—he had some kind of money—but I had some concerns how he would look at it in twenty years. When the Doors got to Toronto, they were all very puffy. They looked like chefs in a big restaurant.

I would have shot them, but we couldn't afford to stay for the two days. But I heard them and we couldn't afford the tracking. We paid for the track for Yoko and John and gave it to them to release as a record.

HK: John and Yoko Ono performing in Toronto blew your mind as you rolled the camera.

DAP: It's an amazing thing. Coming at the end of that whole concert, it was the end of the Beatles. They understood it, and at the end they fell silent. And John looked out and it was kind of scary, like nobody was there. It was a funny moment. They all left the stage, and I remember a piece of paper blowing across the stage, and slowly the audience came to life. I thought, "My God. This is a fantastic wake."

Yoko was so crazy, but still, there was something so fascinating about what she did. You could see she did it with absolute conviction. What she was bringing to me was a kind of funeral cry for something that was lost. At the time I wasn't sure how I felt about it, but I did welcome it.

It was the same with [Jimi] Hendrix when I first heard him at the 1967 Monterey International Pop Festival. I thought he was chewing gum on stage but it was actually his flat pick. I thought, "This is not blues. This is bullshit." But, you know, about the third song I saw that I didn't really understand, and I began to dig it. And that was an amazing moment. That's why we shot every song that he did. Because it kept growing in a way that we hadn't expected.

HK: And this was done with concerns about having enough film to shoot Jimi as well as all the other artists at the festival?

DAP: It burns a little hole in you, but at the same time what was so marvelous, and just sitting on the stage with our legs hanging over with Janis, saying "What do you think will happen to you next?" And trying to see ahead into the future. And this woman has got such a future if she doesn't blow it, that I just want to be part of it.

Otis Redding was stunning. Dylan in 1966 had taken me to hear Otis at the Whisky a Go Go in Hollywood. When I heard Otis was going to be at Monterey, I got really excited. We shot everything he did. It's a great film, almost a perfect film. He had a pretty good band, I was editing—or re-editing—the section of his for *Monterey Pop* in late '67, and changed the film a little bit when he went into the lake. I remember that's when I got into all that stuff of doing things with the lights, and I know at the time I felt, "Gee. What am I doing? This is crazy." But I left it that way, because I felt so bad that he died on us, and that made me sad. So the only thing I could do to mark that was to edit it that way.

In editing *Monterey Pop* I had my first Steenbeck [editor].

HK: It's the forty-fifth anniversary of the Monterey International Pop Festival. What did you learn from the process of doing *Dont Look Back* that you applied to doing *Monterey Pop*? I know for *Monterey Pop* you shied away from the use of interview footage.

DAP: Bob Rafelson [director of the Monkees TV series] called me up and he said, "Would you like to do a film of a concert in California?" And I thought about it, and I had just seen Bruce Brown's *The Endless Summer*, which is not about surfing at all, but all about California.

Interviews didn't interest me, I didn't want to take the time—I wanted everybody to concentrate on music. Well remember, the guys I had filming for me there—except for Ricky [Leacock], he was the other camera—they were all beginners. And I put them in pivotal positions 'cause they could be with the music. They served the music, and that was the thing. I didn't want them to think about anything except getting film to match the music.

I think of these films like *Monterey* much more as if they were plays on a stage. And every play has to build to some sort of climax, something it was all worth sitting there for. That's how you decide what comes next. There was no dialogue.

What you want to do is get so that when you're shooting, you don't have to think. You don't have to think about, "Should I be closer?" As soon as you think those things, the film disappears. You want your feet to take you where you should be. You want the camera to film what you want to film. You don't *want* anything to happen, so you won't have to think about it. And then it can happen in some part of your brain that's non-word-oriented, or something . . . I don't know. But I get in that camera and I don't want to come out.

HK: When you view *Ziggy Stardust*, what strikes you now, more than ever, when you see Bowie and this character on screen?

DAP: Well, we had no idea of what we were going to find there. We got there the day before the concert. We just saw his next-to-last concert, and we could get an idea of the lighting in the theater and what we were gonna run into. I saw him perform, and we were only going to film a half an hour for RCA, and there were just three of us: Nick [Doob], Jim [Desmond], and I. And I said, "This is a movie here. Do you think we can do it? Do we have enough film?" We sort of figured out what we needed. RCA had supplied a real good 24-track machine, so we had good sound. It was just a question of getting in there. We have very few shots of anyone else in the band, other than his pal [guitarist] Mick Ronson.

Bowie surprised us at every turn. And, boy, that was exciting to film. Because you had no idea what was coming next. I had put signs around the lobby, "Bring your camera with light bulbs and shoot all the film that you want." What he had was the whole theater as a backup for him—they all sang backup for him. That was amazing. I had never heard that before. So I wanted that place to just be alive. You know, the girls singing along on "Moonage Daydream."

The dressing room was where you see him just sitting there. In the beginning you use a long lens, and you can stand far away and the sound person can be close, and you can really get on stage physically, so people know that he looks different from somebody else. If you take these faces right, you do portraits.

But then as the movie goes forward, somewhere down the line there comes a point where you don't need to do that anymore so you go to wide angle. And usually with wide angle you start getting what is happening rather than picture to music. From then on everybody is going to recognize who's who and you don't have to worry about it. That's the way the films go, most of them.

There was a lot of kinetic energy around Bowie. He was like an orchestra leader. I was a fan of the *Ziggy* album and we used to play it all the time when I was mixing that film. I had actually set up a real Dolby system and we showed it in this little room where the sound was fantastic, and that was the sexiest film you ever saw.

HK: Earlier this century, Miramax Films released *Only the Strong Survive*, a music documentary that you and Chris Hegedus directed that chronicles live performances and interviews filmed in 1999 and 2000 with twelve R&B artists.

DAP: It's people like Sam Moore, Isaac Hayes, Mary Wilson, Wilson Pickett, Carla and Rufus Thomas, and Ann Peebles. These guys actually perform all the time—they are doing songs from twenty-five years ago, and they're just as good. Somebody like Ann Peebles will make you cry, she's so wonderful. When she does "I Can't Stand the Rain," it just knocks me crazy. All this stuff is there, but you know that it's outside the mainstream.

And there's a sadness about it all, because basically it comes out of a religious conviction—it isn't like jazz. Well, they're all church and they're family. When they get together and they have a birthday, they're all in there and love each other, you know. They're not competing for the only dollar in the house. There's something about it that is different from the jazz that I grew up in, and it's different than rock 'n' roll. It's something really wonderful.

If we had all the money in the world we could have arranged a big show at the Apollo Theater for them to do it, and we'd get the musicians and the whole thing, but we didn't want to do that. We wanted it to be *their* gigs that they set up, with *their* musicians, and we sort of wanted to be there just like the audience. In the end it seemed righter than trying to set it all up and do it like television. We tried to find people who were coming into the New York area, and found groups that represented different aspects of soul music—a Detroit, Chicago, Philadelphia, Stax. . . .

We had heard about this Luther Ingram benefit in Memphis, and a lot of the Stax musicians came for that event. We filmed Mary Wilson during her fortieth anniversary tour of the Supremes.

The U.S. film release [of the film] also coincided with the reopening of the long-closed Stax Record studio in Memphis. It does have an arc, but it's much more operatic. Seeing Carla and Rufus come together has such an operatic quality, and to see Carla really belt that song out so beautifully, it's like suddenly you realize what she was all about. You know she knows music upside down and backwards.

Rufus . . . what a face. He has such a marvelous way of dealing with the instant, you know. Everything is as funny as it is in that instant. It's amazing. He's like a twelve-year-old. I love that. I'd seen a picture of him before we did the film, and I thought, "that's a great face to film!" And when we went to visit him at the radio station, there he was—I couldn't take my camera off him. He was so wonderful just to look at. We had two cameras, which normally we don't—Nick Doob and I. But we started shooting Rufus on air the way we would shoot a narrative film, so we could cut quick dialogue, and it gave it a whole kind of style that I thought was radio-like.

HK: What has happened in the last decade or two with the increase in film festivals and more film schools?

DAP: I think it's like the rise of the electric train. I think nobody at the beginning of the century had any thought that a child would want an electric train. When Lionel or whoever invented it, when they came out with something that resembled the real world and in a very artistic way, it was really well done. The trains were not realistic exactly, but they were kind of beautifully crafted, with all the scenery. So a person could create a whole kind of thing just because they existed, and everybody got one for Christmas.

Well I think that the making of films by yourself, as opposed to going to a movie theater and seeing what somebody else has done—the idea of making your own is a contagious notion. It isn't just a home movie. You're getting an audience of people, who in a way pay to see how good you are. It's a shootout.

It's like when people went to Revolver, Arkansas, in the heyday of the cowboy to shoot it out with the local sheriff to see how good they were. You ended up throwing silver dollars in the air and hitting them if you were any good. By shooting from the hip. In other words, it became a whole thing—a process that had its artistic and its spiritual aspects that people hadn't planned on. But there they were.

So I notice when I go to festivals, every show is sold out. Why is this? Why are people so fascinated to see documentaries? Well, at first I thought they were getting a kind of news that they didn't get from theatrical films, and that they certainly didn't get from television. But now I'm not so sure. I think it's become the electric train. And they want to see it; they want to see it run. And it's different from the other movies they pay to see, and the craftsmanship on Hollywood films.

I think it's more than just the news, but a lot of documentaries address the news, and the problem I have with most of them is the theater is lost. These films have that quality, a kind of news event that you're gonna find out about. But the theater is missing. And I must say, when I'm doing them I always think of my films as plays. Because the playwright had the same problem we do—he had to get a lot of people on stage that had never been seen before. From the very beginning he had to give you an insight into what was going to happen, what the play was about, why you were there, what was important about it. That was done in different ways. [George Bernard] Shaw was good at it.

Now the problem with the films is that they find some situation that needs redressing, and so they go and interview people about what happened, and they tell the story—but they *tell* it, and what you hear is what *had happened.*

HK: At film festivals and question and answer events around your career and body of work, what are some of the almost-routine things film students and fans ask you. Are they careerists?

DAP: I think a lot of students—because nobody knows what to teach— they don't know where to start. Well, I think that in the film world, students gather and want to hear some kind of wisdom, and they are considering their own careers and how to begin them. They start off with questions taken from the various wisdom from Hollywood—things like, "Don't cross the line," whatever that means. And they're not sure whether there are any rules. And I tell them there are no written rules that I know of. I don't have any myself, you know. I wait and see what happens in the lens of the camera, and then I kind of go with it if I can. And that leaves them wondering why they are in school. They can learn this at the drug store. So it's a funny thing.

I start with *Daybreak Express* [1953], a silent film with Duke Ellington's music. Then I show them something with dialogue. It took us two or three years to get cameras so that we could do this, but when we could get dialogue in a film, the story is driven in what people say to each other.

That's where you are going ahead of the fiction film, which has to start with somebody making up a story and then everybody ironing it out, and it can't change because money is involved, and it doesn't open up a field of something that they can enter into and be proud of in which their parents can applaud. So you have a problem convincing people.

But then you show them these [documentary] films, and they then wonder what will happen, and that's life. That's very vivid. The fact is that when you can produce something in front of you that kind of resembles life, like even as Picasso could in painting, it's something people really want. They need it in some way. It's like I needed those jazz records, my 78s. I need to hear some of that music because it was people jumping off a high board and not sure where they were gonna go.

HK: Your company shot a well-received portrait on actress Elaine Stritch.

DAP: I kind of loved her. She was like a sister to me. We're the same age. She shows me no humility. She swears at me when she thinks I've done something wrong. I loved that sisterly affect. And I trust it. She's not gonna give me anything. I've got to earn it.

HK: Your early films were done with Ricky Leacock. Then you did your own thing. And for the last thirty-five years you've teamed with Chris Hegedus.

DAP: I've changed, but you're never aware of your own changes too much. With Ricky, he was kind of a father figure, but he was also more than that. I knew that he had done these films, and I just felt very lucky to ride along with him. And I learned things from him, but they are things I would have learned along the way—I don't think it was a total teaching situation. But we differed a lot in a kind of spiritual way. Ricky was always ready to accept defeat.

The thing about Chris, who I've been partnering with for over thirty-five years, is that the moment she walked into my office looking for a job—this is gonna sound very unlikely, but this is a fact—we talked in a room across from my desk, and within fifteen minutes I said, "This is what I've been looking for all of my life. Never let her leave this office."

We were almost in bankruptcy at that point, and almost about to have an auction there. We didn't have any jobs, and the woman who was working with me told her we didn't have any jobs. But I called Chris the next day, "Actually, we do have a job." We didn't, but she came in and started working right away on *Town Bloody Hall*. And I knew that she and I are actually spiritually on the same course.

What she did on *Kings of Pastry*—the way she did it showed that she understood exactly what the film element was. And I thought, "That was what I always knew she knew." It was in her. Everything she ever did with me and the people that we filmed understood that too.

Additional Resources

Beattie, Keith. *D. A. Pennebaker*. Urbana: University of Illinois Press, 2011.

Couchman, Jeffrey. "The Freewheelin' Bob Dylan." *American Cinematographer*, December 2002.

Cunningham, Megan. "D. A. Pennebaker and Chris Hegedus." In *The Art of Documentary: Ten Conversations with Leading Directors, Cinematographers, Editors, and Producers*. Berkeley: New Riders, 2005.

Darling, Cary. "'101' Director Makes Fans the Center of the Concert Tour." *Orange County Register*, May 5, 1989.

Galupo, Scott. "*Only the Strong Survive*: Pennebaker Has Soul of a Musician." *Washington Times*, May 10, 2003.

Good, Hermione. "Look Out Kids! D. A. Pennebaker and Chris Hegedus." *Variant*, Winter 2001.

Grove, Lloyd. "'War' Is Hell . . . Until It Makes You a Star: 'The War Room's Peek at Carville and Stephanopoulos May Give New Meaning to 'Brat Pack.'" *Washington Post*, November 7, 1993.

Harrington, Richard. "A Deserving Look at Dylan." *Washington Post*, February 23, 2007.

Hirschberg, Lynn. "Shooting for Pop History." *New York Times Magazine*, May 4, 2003.

Hodara, Susan. "Documentary Maker Starts by Focusing on a Person." *New York Times*, March 18, 2007.

Karlin, Susan. "Filming inside Clinton's Camp." *New York Times*, January 31, 1993.

MacInnis, Craig. "Film and Loathing on the Campaign Trail: Cinéma Vérité Pioneer D. A. Pennebaker Turns His Lens on Clinton Camp." *Toronto Star*, December 20, 1993.

Macnab, Geoffrey. "Looking Back . . ." *Sight and Sound*, April 1997.

Maslin, Janet. "Visionaries with Their Eyes on the Truth." *New York Times*, May 2, 1999.

Mitchell, John Cameron. "Loving the Alien: D. A. Pennebaker's Stardust Memories." *Village Voice*, July 10–16, 2002.

Paphides, Pete. "It's All Right, Bob (I'm Only Filming)." *Times* [UK], September 26, 2005.

Pennebaker, D. A. "My Favourite Movies: Documentary Film-Maker D. A. Pennebaker." *Sunday Telegraph* [UK], June 25, 2006.

Pidgeon, John. *"Keep on Rockin':* Interview with Film Director D. A. Pennebaker." *New Musical Express* [UK], September 30, 1972.

Pizzello, Stephen. "Waging a Film in *The War Room.*" *American Cinematographer*, January 1994.

Silvestri, Melissa. "Interview with *Kings of Pastry* Directors D. A. Pennebaker and Chris Hegedus." *Filmmaker Magazine*, September 15, 2010.

Simmons, Michael. "Lights. Camera. Dylan!" *Mojo*, April 2013.

Southern, Nile. "D. A. Pennebaker Looks Back." *Stop Smiling Magazine*, March 22, 2006 (part 1), March 27, 2006 (part 2).

Stelter, Brian. "Back to 1992: Revisiting the Clinton 'War Room.'" *New York Times*, October 12, 2008.

Swift, Lauren Lowenthal. "D. A. Pennebaker Makes 'Em Dance." *Film Comment*, November–December 1988.

Williamson, Nigel. "D. A. Pennebaker." *Uncut*, December 2001.

Willis, Holly. "D. A. Pennebaker Gets into the War Room." *Filmmaker Magazine*, Fall 1993.

Index

Printed in the United States
by Baker & Taylor Publisher Services